D1565588

PIONEERING WOMEN

WITHDRAWN

PIONEERING WOMEN

Short Stories by Canadian Women

Beginnings to 1880

CANADIAN
SHORT
STORY
LIBRARY
No. 17

Lorraine McMullen
and Sandra Campbell

University of Ottawa Press

Canadian Short Story Library, Series 2
John Moss, General Editor

© University of Ottawa Press, 1993
Printed and bound in Canada
ISBN 0-7766-0385-X

Canadian Cataloguing in Publication Data
Main entry under title:
Pioneering Women: Short Stories by Canadian
Women, Beginnings to 1880

(Canadian short story library; 17)
Includes bibliographical references.
ISBN 0-7766-0385-X

1. Short stories, Canadian (English)—Women
authors. 2. Canadian fiction (English)—Women
authors. 3. Canadian fiction (English)—19th century.
I. McMullen, Lorraine, 1926–   . II. Campbell,
Sandra. III. Series.

PS8325.P46 1993   C813'.01089287   C93-090564-4
PR9197.32.P46 1993

Series design concept: Miriam Bloom
Book design: Marie Tappin
Cover photo courtesy of British Columbia Archives and
Records Service (95970 G-2567)

For our foremothers—
the Canadian women writers
of the nineteenth century

CONTENTS

ACKNOWLEDGMENTS

The editors are grateful to the following for their advice and assistance: Suzanne Bossé, Phebe Chartrand, Gwen Davies, Carole Gerson, George Henderson, Carrie MacMillan, Duncan McDowall, Leslie Monkman, Jeremy Palin, Stewart Renfrew, Shirley Spragge, David Staines, Frank Tierney, Tom Vincent, and Elizabeth Waterston. For their efficient and cheerful assistance on more practical matters, we thank Joanne Kloeble, Julie Sévigny-Roy and Marie Tremblay-Chenier. We also wish to thank Mrs. C. E. Humphrey, grandniece of Isabella Valancy Crawford, for her kind cooperation in the publication of "A Rose in His Grace," and Queen's University Archives, repository of the manuscript.

Research for *Pioneering Women* was made possible by a grant from the Faculty of Arts, University of Ottawa. We wish to express our gratitude to Marcel Hamelin, Rector and former Dean of Arts; Carlos Bazan, Dean of Arts; and Jean-Louis Major, Associate Dean of Arts. Lorraine McMullen's research on Canadian women's fiction is also supported by the Social Sciences and Humanities Research Council of Canada.

INTRODUCTION

ioneering Women, the earliest in time span of three consecutive anthologies of short stories by Canadian women, presents a selection of stories written before 1880. Its two companion anthologies, *Aspiring Women* and *New Women*, cover the periods 1880 to 1900 and 1900 to 1920, respectively. While it is a truism that much of women's writing needs to be recovered and made more accessible, this is particularly true of the early period of Canadian literary history covered by *Pioneering Women*. Canadian women were sometimes writing in primitive conditions, and often were published in obscure and/or short-lived periodicals not always widely available today. In fact, one story, "A Rose In His Grace," by Isabella Valancy Crawford, that apparently was never published, has been recovered in manuscript for inclusion in this collection.

The stories in *Pioneering Women* were written at a period when the short story form was beginning to emerge. In Canada, various periodical forms hospitable to short fiction—newspapers, gift books, magazines and story papers—struggled for viability, longevity and profitability. In the early nineteenth century, it was difficult and expensive for writers to place material with the more lucrative story papers in the United States or Great Britain. Both Susanna Moodie and Crawford complained early in their careers about the cost of foreign postage. Nevertheless, writers published as widely as they could, and some women writers enjoyed remarkable success. New Brunswick native May Agnes Fleming published her first story in the widely circulated *New York Mercury* when she was fifteen, and a story of hers appeared on the first page of her hometown newspaper, the *Western Recorder and Carleton Advertiser* (Saint John), when she was sixteen. Her short fiction as well as her sentimental and Gothic novels reached American readers in the 1860s and 1870s in popular story papers such as *Saturday Night* (Philadelphia) and the *New York Weekly*.

Large circulation and handsome remuneration for contributors were not found in the fledgling Canadian periodicals. British North America's best-known and longest-lived literary periodical in the pre-Confederation period, the *Literary Garland* (1838–1851), published by John Lovell of Montreal, was the first in Canada to pay its contributors, but it eventually expired because of circulation inadequate to support its costs.[1]

Many of the women in this anthology were staple contributors to the *Garland*, including Catharine Parr Traill, Moodie, Rosanna Leprohon, and Mary Anne Sadlier; and Eliza Lanesford Cushing edited the *Garland* in its last year of publication. As well, in an era when women were more restricted to the domestic sphere, the degree of activity of many of these women in editorial and publishing work is remarkable. Five of the authors in *Pioneering Women* were involved in some way in literary publishing. Cushing not only edited the *Garland* (much of whose audience was female), but she and her sister Harriet Cheney founded and edited *The Snow Drop* (1847–1852), the first Canadian magazine for children. Moodie and her husband founded, edited, and wrote much of the material for *Victoria Magazine* (1841–1842) out of Belleville.[2] Sadlier was very much involved in D. and J. Sadlier, the family publishing firm which, from the 1840s, catered to the interests of the Irish Catholic community in Montreal as well as New York. Mary Eliza Herbert founded the short-lived periodical, *The Mayflower*, in Halifax in 1851, as a women's magazine, providing opportunities for Nova Scotian women both to publish their own writing and to read local material.[3]

In the preface to an 1845 novel, Sadlier told her readers with what diffidence a member of the female sex ventured into the "arena of Literature" at all: "It is foreign to a woman's nature ... 'to move in the uncongenial glare of public fame'—hers are, or should be, the quiet shades of retirement, and woe to her who steps beyond their boundary, with the hope—of finding happiness."[4] As the plot of Herbert's story "Light in the Darkness" (1865) outlines—

and as its subtitle "A Sketch from Life" suggests—authorship and editorship for women was unusual and could be reconciled only by the material necessities of a family. Sadlier was frank: initially only family necessity had prompted her to become that anomalous Victorian figure, a woman in the public eye. As editors and publishers, the women writers of *Pioneering Women* were pioneers indeed.

Women in early nineteenth-century Canada who ventured outside the domestic sphere were mostly impelled to do so in the name of good works. The narrator in Cheney's "The Emigrants" (1850) exhorts women to such acts of Christian benevolence as establishment of homes for indigent women. While such exhortation to acts of organized charity outside the domestic sphere may be considered a forerunner of the maternal feminism of later Canadian women writers such as Nellie McClung and Jessie Georgina Sime, for example, the pre-1880 expectation for women was confinement to the domestic sphere. Although women's rights was a topic of discussion in Canada before 1880, wider aspirations by Canadian women met with much censure. In 1853, the *Anglo-American Magazine* bluntly editorialized:

> ...because women are sometimes abused, they [feel they] must hold "Women's Rights Conventions," and assert for themselves the duties and perogatives of men, unsexing themselves, openly defying the commands of God and exposing both sexes to barbaric degeneration....
>
> The woman's true social position is that summary of human happiness—HOME.[5]

A decade later, the *Canadian Illustrated News* (Hamilton) made a joke of the matter, listing one of woman's "sadly overlooked" rights as the "right to stay at home" to humour and care for her husband submissively at all costs.[6] Given such social endorsement of restriction of the possibilities for women, it is not surprising that many of the stories in *Pioneering Women* have as subtext patriarchal power and its effect on women. Moodie's "The Walk to Dummer," Ellen

Vavasour Noel's "The House-Keeper at Lorme Hall," and Crawford's "A Rose in His Grace" all include tyrannical male figures, and in Leprohon's "Alice Sydenham's First Ball," only a rich uncle can provide financial redemption for a mother and daughter. Cheney's "The Emigrants," like the Herbert story, shows the vulnerability of a family without a male breadwinner. Cushing's "Grace Morley" valorizes female restraint and maternal feeling—qualities that are rewarded, since they are shown to be the basis upon which the male suitor chooses a wife.

For the most part, women in Canada remained in the domestic sphere throughout the years preceding 1880. Yet along with contributing to the family economy with their hard labour in the home and on the farm, they were contributing to the community, both in the charitable acts we see in Moodie's "A Walk to Dummer" and Traill's "The Bereavement" and in their early involvement in education. While Anne Langton began a school in her home as a charity for local children,[7] other women, such as Mrs. J. V. Noel, were also operating small private schools in their homes as essential money-making ventures, and, of course, writing became for some a source of essential revenue; like teaching, this work could be done at home. Moodie augmented the family income importantly with her contributions to the *Literary Garland*. Given the few choices for women were obliged to earn money, writing was an attractive option. Popular novelist Ellen McGregor Ross, twice widowed, both times with two small children, first took in boarders to support her family—another of the options that did not require leaving the family hearth. Then she began writing novels. Her first novel, *Violet Keith. An Autobiography* (1868),[8] was a bestseller. Published first in Montreal, it was republished in New York by William Carleton, the publisher of many of the most popular American writers.[9] From then on, her three-decker novels kept bread on the table.

Alcoholism was widespread in the immigrant and pioneer conditions of early British North America. Because of its drastic effect on family life, women were at the fore in attempting to do something to resolve the problems caused by it, and their attempts led them into the public sphere. As a Methodist Sunday School teacher, Letitia Youman saw the effects of alcoholism on the lives and families of many of her pupils: domestic violence, family breakdown, immorality, and crime. She first began a non-denominational temperance group for children, and then founded the first Canadian branch of the Women's Christian Temperance Union in Picton, Ontario, in 1874.[10] Later she became the first president of the Ontario and then of the national Women's Christian Temperance Union. Alcoholism and its effects figure in several of the stories in this volume. Moodie's "The Walk to Dummer" graphically portrays the tragic situation of the family of an alcoholic: an abused wife and virtually starving children, deserted by the formerly considerate and gentlemanly retired officer whom alcohol has turned into a dishonest, debt-ridden, and abusive addict. The effects of drunkenness play a part in Crawford's "A Rose in His Grace," and Sadlier's "A Peep into the Dominions of Pluto," as well.

In both art and life, *Pioneering Women*'s authors and works demonstrate the importance of female bonds in a male world. The concern of women for each other in a pioneer setting is central to Traill's "The Bereavement" and Moodie's "The Walk to Dummer," and female bonds among friends and family are stressed in stories by Cheney, Herbert, Fleming and Leprohon. Women writers were themselves linked and sustained by bonds of blood. Catharine Parr Traill and Susanna Moodie were sisters, and Mary Eliza Herbert's sister, Sarah Herbert, was also a writer. Sisters Eliza Cushing and Harriet Cheney worked together as editors, and received early inspiration to write from their novelist mother. Ellen Vavasour Noel followed in the foot-steps of her mother, Mrs. J. V. Noel, and Isabella Valancy Crawford's mother, Sydney Crawford, was her greatest supporter. Mary Anne Sadlier also had a writer–daughter, Anna Teresa Sadlier. Given that these women were pioneers in both gender and genre in an emerging country and in an evolving literary form, these female bonds were of great importance.

In gender relations and in other ways, therefore, the stories written by women in Canada at this early period bear witness to the rapidly transforming historical, social, and publishing conditions of Canada. The stories by Traill and Moodie were written just after the Rebellion of 1837 in Upper Canada, while Leprohon, the Noel mother and daughter, and Crawford wrote in the decade after Confederation. The stories by Moodie, Traill, Cushing, and Cheney, written in the years between 1839 and 1852, remind us that at this period British North America embraced both the backwoods of Ontario and the more sophisticated cosmopolitan centres whose history dates back to the French regime. While Moodie and Traill give us the rigours of the bush, Cushing presents with perfect confidence the intricate courtships of young women in the more developed region about Montreal. Yet, as Cheney's "The Emigrants" (1850) makes us aware, even storied and sophisticated Montreal was part of a grim immigrant reality of poverty and disease. The Irish setting of two stories in this anthology—Sadlier's "A Peep into the Dominions of Pluto" and Mrs. J. V. Noel's "A Night of Peril!"—as well as the Irish dialect placed in the mouths of characters in the stories by Moodie, Ellen Vavasour Noel and others, testify to the hold of the Old World on the speech and imaginations of many of the inhabitants of the New World.

The realities of life in early nineteenth-century British North America influenced form as well as plot. Carl Ballstadt, Carole Gerson and Kathy Mezei, among others, write of the importance of the sketch form, which was then enjoying a vogue in English and American literature, in early Canadian writing.[11] The sketch, with its colloquialism and focus on description of a selected scene or incident rather than plot or character, meshed well with the need of early women writers to imaginatively occupy a new country. Traill's "The Bereavement" and Moodie's "The Walk to Dummer," with their vivid and detailed descriptions of the bush and the intimacy of first-person narration, exemplify the form. Still in the process of settlement in many regions, pre-Confederation British North America was an exotic land to many readers, especially to the British readers, to whom much of the early writing was directed. Traill and Moodie focussed on a formidable and untamed landscape, recording the physical and imaginative settlement of a new land. The documentary quality of Canadian creative writing, pointed out by Dorothy Livesay, comes through vividly in the sketches of these two writers, as well as in Cheney's depiction of a Montreal epidemic in "The Emigrants."[12]

Women's diaries, journals, and letters, as well as stories and sketches of professional writers, such as Traill and Moodie, provide important historical documentation of this era. Recent years have seen the recovery of some of these non-fictional private records, giving us a new perspective on Canadian history. As Margaret Conrad, Toni Laidlaw, and Donna Smyth remark in their introduction to *No Place Like Home*, "Diaries and personal records turn traditional history inside out."[13] Langton's *A Gentlewoman in Upper Canada: The Journals of Anne Langton* (1950)[14] records details in the domestic lives of three women—a daughter, a mother, and an aunt—pioneers in the Ontonabee area of Ontario in the early nineteenth century. The three women cope with the challenges of backwoods living with initiative and imagination, and participate in the development of a community, the same community, in fact, in which the Moodies and Traills were struggling to eke out an existence, and which they were recording in their sketches. The more recently published *No Place Like Home*, a selection from Nova Scotia women's diaries from 1771 to 1938,[15] reveals life experiences of Maritime women and their responses to them; in the words of the authors, such documents record "history as it is experienced by most men and women," rather than wars and revolutions which have traditionally been seen as history. These writings are graphic and moving, as are the more polished sketches of the professional writer–sisters, Traill and Moodie. Like them, these diarists reveal the centrality of family and community relationships. Later writers, such as Frances Herring and Kate Simpson Hayes, included in *Aspiring Women*, detail in equally realistic fashion the settlement of the West. Such sketches, based on real-life experience, blurring the line between fiction and non-fiction, contain documentary elements, which make them closer to women's letters and journals of that time than to the improbable sentimental fiction being published alongside them.

By contrast with Traill and Moodie, writers Fleming, Leprohon, and Mrs. J.V. Noel draw upon the novelty of more cultivated Canadian settings. In "The Philopena," Fleming gives details of winter sports in Canada for a New York readership, and describes a general sophistication of life alien to the experiences on which Traill and Moodie base their sketches. Leprohon and Mrs. J.V. Noel provide details of the comfortable homes and lifestyles of wealthy Montrealers for their Canadian magazine readers. Life among the elite in Montreal and Quebec at this time was in stark contrast to that in rural Ontario. Leprohon's novels of Quebec of one hundred years earlier reveal the sophistication of Montreal life in the 1760s. Her description in *The Manor House of De Villerai* (1859) of richly furnished homes with oil paintings, capacious libraries, a social life of balls and outings, and other elements of a sophisticated and cultured lifestyle in Montreal of the 1750s, reveals a way of life far different from that of Moodie and Langton in Ontario almost one hundred years later. At a time when Langton was using her home as a classroom in which to teach local children, Leprohon was being educated in the Montreal convent of the Congregation of Notre Dame, learning, among other subjects, biology, philosophy, and chemistry. Fleming, too, the product of the bustling, prosperous, and long-established port of Saint John, New Brunswick, was educated in the 1840s and 1850s by the

Sisters of the Sacred Heart, reputed for their excellent teaching. These women's Canadian experience, reflected in their stories, stands in remarkable contrast to that of their Ontario sisters.

Some of the elements of local colour popular in American fiction of the late nineteenth century can be observed in the stories of *Pioneering Women*. The sentimentality, humour, eccentric characters, and dialect, which characterize local-colour writing generally, stemmed largely from nostalgia for a lost or fading way of life. We see it in Sadlier's portrayal of Irish village life in "A Peep into the Dominions of Pluto." Its simple but likeable characters, Irish dialect, and Jansenist clergy would all be familiar to Montreal's Irish immigrant readers. Leprohon, whose earlier "Alice Sydenham's First Ball" was set in an England and a society the author had never known, as was much of the popular writing in Canada at the time, later shifted her attention to her own country. Her novels of New France and of the early years of British rule (*The Manor House of De Villerai*, and *Antoinette de Mirecourt* [1864]) provide elements of local colour in their description of the snowshoe parties, Christmas festivities, and other activities of a way of life one hundred years earlier.

Suggestive of the evolving form of the modern story, a more fully developed plot can be observed in some of these earlier stories, as in Cheney's "The Emigrants," for example, in contrast to the episodic sketches of Traill and Moodie. Such stories point to the increasing emphasis on plot and character in women's stories later in the nineteenth century. Although the sketch continued to appear in Canadian writing, works in this volume written after 1860, more often present story rather than sketch. For example, the botanical interests of the characters in Leprohon's "My Visit to Fairview Villa" (1870) are diversionary and superficial, and are a source of amusement for both characters and readers, in contrast to the carefully accurate botanical observations in Traill's sketches. By the time of Crawford's "A Rose in His Grace" (c.1880), we have the generalized description of the seashore of popular magazine fiction, a quicksilver backdrop for the romance plot, rather than the careful documentation of the earlier writers of climate and landscape.

Not surprisingly, many of our writers used the romance plot. Crawford's story is a romantic confection of the sort savoured by the popular magazines of the day. Cushing's "Grace Morley: A Sketch from Life," the first story in *Pioneering Women*, is a classic example of the genre. In some instances, writers used the conventions and rewards of the romance plot playfully or ironically, their narrators playing upon the readers' awareness of the tensions between life and art in the area of marriage and romance. May Agnes Fleming's "My Folly" is charged with the tensions between the conventions of romantic feeling and the reality of the female protagonist's emotions; in "The Philopena," her heroine is finally enmeshed in the courtship rituals she once coquettishly manipulated. The narrator of Leprohon's "Alice Sydenham's First Ball" laughs at such staple settings as the hidden nook near the ball room and mocks convention when her downcast heroine, far from refusing food, heartily devours cold chicken and hot coffee.

While England was the favoured setting for much of the popular romance writing, writers sometimes shifted their setting to other regions of interest to their readers. Herbert's New England setting of "Light in the Darkness" would have been of particular interest to her Maritime readers, for whom New England was not only a commercial centre but for most the home of emigrated family or friends. The Irish countryside of Mrs. J. V. Noel's "A Night of Peril" would have appealed to the many Canadian readers of Irish extraction, as would Sadlier's Irish mining town of "A Peep into the Dominions of Pluto."

From bush lot to drawing room, from the Maritimes to Upper Canada, *Pioneering Women* reveals the variety to be found in stories by an intrepid group of women of early British North America. Many—Fleming, Herbert, and the two Noels, for example—are only now being rediscovered and reexamined, while a few, notably Moodie and, to a lesser extent, her sister, Traill, have enjoyed longer prominence, but even they were recovered only with the revival of interest in Canadian literature in the 1960s. Certainly the diversity and output of these women writers is remarkable at such a comparatively early era in both literary and women's history in Canada.

Editorial note: Spelling and punctuation of the original stories have been retained; typographical errors are silently corrected. Unless otherwise noted, stories are reprinted here as first published.

Notes

1 For a discussion of early publishing, see George Parker, *The Beginnings of the Book Trade in Canada* (Toronto: University of Toronto Press, 1985).

2 See Klay Dyer, "A Periodical for the People: Mrs. Moodie and the *Victoria Magazine*." M.A. thesis, University of Ottawa, 1992.

3 See Gwendolyn Davies, "'Dearer than Her Dog': Literary Women in Pre-Confederation Nova Scotia." In *Gynocritics/Gynocritiques*, edited by Barbara Godard, 111–129. (Toronto: ECW Press, 1987).

4 See "Tales of the Olden Times: A Collection of European Traditions," *Literary Garland*, December 1845, 576.

5 "Women's Social Position," *Anglo-American Magazine* (Toronto), 2 June 1853, 572–573.

6 "List of 'Woman's Rights' Which Have Been Sadly Overlooked," *Canadian Illustrated News* (Hamilton), 25 July 1863, 128.

7 See H. H. Langton, ed., *A Gentlewoman in Upper Canada: The Journals of Anne Langton* (Toronto: Clarke, Irwin, 1950).

8 Mrs. [Ellen McGregor] Ross, *Violet Keith. An Autobiography* (Montreal: John Lovell, 1868).

9 See Jeffrey Wollock, "Ellen Ross (1816?–1892): Violet Keith and All That Sort of Thing," *Journal of Canadian Fiction*, 1974, no.3.

10 Alison Prentice, et. al., *Canadian Women: A History* (Toronto: Harcourt, Brace, Jovanovich, 1988), 172–173.

11   Carole Gerson and Kathy Mezei, eds., *The Prose of Life: Sketches from Victorian Canada* (Toronto: ECW Press, 1981) and Carl Ballstadt, "Susanna Moodie and the English Sketch," *Canadian Literature*, 1972, 51, 32–37.

12   Dorothy Livesay, "The Documentary Poem: A Canadian Genre." In *Contexts of Canadian Criticism*, edited by Eli Mandel, 267–281. (Chicago: University of Chicago Press, 1971).

13   Margaret Conrad, Toni Laidlaw, and Donna Smyth, *No Place Like Home: Diaries and Letters of Nova Scotia Women, 1771–1938* (Halifax: Formac, 1988), 1.

14   H. H. Langton, ed., *A Gentlewoman in Upper Canada: The Journals of Anne Langton* (Toronto: Clarke, Irwin, 1950).

15   See Conrad, Laidlaw, Smyth, eds., *No Place Like Home: Diaries and Letters of Nova Scotia Women, 1771–1938* (Halifax: Formac, 1988.)

Eliza Lanesford Cushing (1794–1886)

GRACE MORLEY:
A SKETCH FROM LIFE (1839)

Eliza Lanesford Cushing, with her sister Harriet Cheney
(see page 89), was an important early editor and creative
writer in Montreal during the 1830s, 1840s, and 1850s. The
two women founded the children's periodical *Snow Drop*,
the first of its type in British North America, and Cushing
edited the landmark literary magazine the *Literary Garland*
in the last two years of its existence. Cushing was not only
a staple contributor of poetry and fiction to the *Garland*,
she also wrote dramatic sketches and plays now viewed as
marking "the beginning of playwriting as a literary art form
in English-Canada itself."[1]

Eliza Lanesford Foster Cushing was born in
Brighton, Massachusetts, on 19 October 1794, one of three
daughters of the pioneering American novelist Hannah
Webster Foster and Unitarian minister John Foster. Eliza
and her younger sister Harriet early collaborated on a series
of Sunday school sketches for children. Before her marriage
to Dr. Frederick Cushing in 1828 and their removal to
Montreal in 1833, Cushing pseudonymously published two
historical novels—*Saratoga: A Tale of the Revolution* (1824)
and *Yorktown: A Historical Romance* (1826). Cushing's literary
interests were reinforced by economic imperatives when her
husband died in 1846 of ship fever (typhus) while treating
some of the scores of poverty-stricken, diseased Irish immigrants at the Montreal Emigrant Hospital. Of the *Snow
Drop*, which survived from 1847 until 1852, historian Susan
Mann Trofimenkoff wrote: "... girls seem to have been the

---

1. Anton Wagner, "Introduction," *Women Pioneers, Canada's Lost
Plays*, vol. 2. Toronto: Canadian Theatre Review Publications,
1979, p. 5.

object of most of the moral lessons which again imbued all the tales: they were the ones who had to learn truthfulness, reliability, goodness, obedience, filial respect, perseverance, thrift, orderliness, integrity and self-reliance. As future guardians of the morals of their families, perhaps they did have the most to learn."

The importance of self-abnegation, unselfishness, goodness and maternal feeling to young women is equally evident in "Grace Morley: A Sketch from Life" (1839), one of Cushing's early stories for the *Garland*. The story has the blend of pastoral and genteel setting so favored by the *Garland*. The triumph of the "rosebud" Clara's unselfishness and maternal feeling over the selfishness and Circe-like spell of the "half-blown rose" Grace Morley is made abundantly clear.

Another Cushing story, "Deaf Molly" (*Literary Garland* [1848]), a grim tale of a hot-headed, misanthropic servant woman is a similar rebuke to selfishness, especially in women. Some of Cushing's stories have a historical setting: "The Indian Maid: A Traditionary Tale" (*Literary Garland* [1846]) is a story of colonial Virginia, where a sympathetic Indian maid spends her life caring for the grave of the noble white adventurer she loved and tried to save from death at the hands of her people.

Cushing's plays, for which she is perhaps best known today, often have a Biblical theme, such as in *Esther, a Sacred Drama* (1840). According to Anton Wagner, her best play is *The Fatal Ring*, set in sixteenth-century France and published in the *Literary Garland* in 1839–40. Its theme is that of a woman destroyed by the wiles of a worldly society, which is also a theme in her serial novel "The Neglected Wife," a dark tale of adultery and death published in the *Garland* in 1843.

Cushing's literary art and moral concerns were largely focussed on the character and destiny of women and their overriding need to embrace qualities of self-sacrifice, modesty, self-control, stoicism, and positive maternal feeling—all qualities exalted in the nineteenth-century image of the maiden, wife, and mother.

∽

Suggested Reading:

Cushing, Eliza Lanesford. "The Fatal Ring." In *Women Pioneers, Canada's Lost Plays*, vol. 2, edited by Anton Wagner, 22–91. Toronto: Canadian Theatre Review Publications, 1979.

Gerson, Carole. "*The Snow Drop* and *The Maple Leaf*: Canada's First Periodicals For Children." In *Canadian Children's Literature*, 18–19 (1980), 10–23.

Trofimenkoff, Susan Mann. "Eliza Lanesford (Foster) Cushing," *Dictionary of Canadian Biography*, vol. 11, 321–322.

Grace Morley: A Sketch from Life

Eliza Lanesford Cushing ("E.L.C.")

> She knows no sympathy with childhood's joys,—
> No touch of pity for its bursting griefs;
> And I would have the maiden of my choice,
> She who should sit beside my household hearth,
> And o'er my home shed the soft light of love,
> A child in heart, with feelings that gush'd forth,
> Like a glad fount, at childhood's ringing laugh
> And the fair infant's smile.

"And so the children are to have a pic-nic tomorrow," said Charles Castleton, a young naval officer, approaching a table, at which his cousin Clara Ilsley sat copying a cluster of rose-buds, that stood in a vase beside her.

"Yes, should the weather continue fine," answered Clara,—"It is Henry's birth-day, and mamma has promised them to celebrate it in the woods,—so they are to drive to old Pompey's cottage, and rove to their heart's content among the sweet dells and dingles, and dine in the old wood on the banks of the beautiful river, and return home by moonlight, over the wild mountain road, that you used to love so well, Charles, before you saw fairer and more classic lands on the shores of the blue Mediterranean."

"More classic, Clara, but not fairer, and surely not dearer; you cannot think that. But for this pic-nic, are we not to share the privileges of the children, and be included in its delights!"

"Doubtless, if you wish it; I dearly love these little rural festivals; but we feared you and Grace might not fancy the boisterous mirth of the children, which, on this annual day of liberty and enjoyment, we make it a point never to restrain; unless, indeed, which is seldom the case, it far 'o'erstep the modesty of nature.'"

Clara looked up from her drawing, with a glance of soft inquiry as she spoke, for she desired much that her cousin might choose to join this excursion; she wished to share the pleasure of the children, and she could not, neither did she seek to conceal from herself, that his presence would greatly enhance her happiness; Charles had recently returned from a three years cruise in the Mediterranean, and found Clara, whom he left a child, grown up into a blooming and beautiful woman, not dazzling, but lovely, lovely in person and still more so in mind and character; and with the enthusiasm peculiar to his profession, he had yielded unreservedly to the influence of her attractions. During the month that he had now passed at Oakland, he had breathed words of love into her ear, and if she listened to them in silence, it was not with a reluctant or untouched heart; for that, had thrilled to every whispered accent, and not a word or tone that had fallen from his lips, nor a look that had beamed from his dark and eloquent eyes, but she had garnered them there, and brooded ever over them, with woman's voiceless, yet impassioned tenderness.

But recently a gay and celebrated belle, who was on a visit at Oakland, had shared, Clara sometimes thought, too largely in the attentions and admiration of the young sailor; though as she now raised her sunny eyes to his, she almost forgot the shadows that for a week past had darkened her glowing and happy heart; for there was something in the fond gaze that met hers, which told a tale too dear and flattering to be disbelieved, and she reproached herself for the doubts she had permitted to disturb her peace, and for the wrong she had done her cousin, in supposing for a moment, that all beautiful and courted and admired as was Miss Morley, he could be so vascillating, as already to have transfered, even to her thronged and brilliant shrine, the homage of a heart, that he had so recently proffered to herself.

Clara's eye drooped, and her cheek glowed, as these thoughts passed rapidly through her mind; nay, it burned painfully, when made conscious that he noticed her confusion, as touching her cheek with one of the rose buds, that he had stolen from the vase, he suddenly exclaimed:

"What thoughts are those, dear Clara, that tinge this pure cheek, with such a brilliant hue!—why this bursting bud looks pale beside it, and I could almost fancy it pining with envy to be thus outvied in loveliness. Would I could look into your mind, fair cousin, that temple of bright and sweet images, and see what is now passing in its innermost recesses."

"Ah, Charles, do not wish so; all that you beheld there might not appear to you so pure and stainless as should beseem a maiden breast. Remember we are yet of earth, and even with our holiest affections, our highest and noblest aspirations, mingles a taint of human frailty and imperfection. But a truce to moralizing, and give me back my rose bud."

"Nay, I must keep this, dear Clara, it is now associated in my mind with the cheek to which I compared it," and he plead so eloquently that although, she said it was the prettiest in the bunch she was attempting to copy, she suffered it to remain in his possession.

"And now let us make arrangements for this pic-nic, Clara, since I am resolved to be included among the children, and I can answer for Miss Morley, who so loves the country and its simple pleasures, that she will be delighted to join us."

"Does she love them Charles?" asked Clara in a somewhat doubting tone.

"Yes does she, fair sceptic, as truly and as fervently as yourself," cried a gay voice, in a tone of blended rebuke and playfulness, and Grace Morley entered through the glass

20   ELIZA LANESFORD CUSHING

door from the terrace, followed by a merry troop of children, dragging forward a huge Newfoundland dog, which they had literally loaded with flowers. But the animal burst from them the moment he saw Clara, and trailing the broken garlands after him, bounded forward and laid his shaggy head, with a whine of joy, in her lap. The children too, clustered around her, each talking with delight of the morrow, and begging that she and cousin Charles, would go with them and share their holiday.

"You include Miss Morley, also!" said Clara.

"No, we do not," answered Lucia, in a subdued voice; "she does not like us, sister, she says we make her head-ache, and was angry, and left the garden because Neptune sprinkled her dress when he leaped from the water."

Clara could not repress a smile, though she hastened to silence the little girl, lest the object of her complaint, might overhear it and be vexed. But they prattled on upon some other theme, while Clara caressed and listened to them, or seemed to listen, though her attention was in reality attracted by Miss Morley, who had thrown herself listlessly upon a sofa and called Charles to come and fan her. And there he now stood, gently waving the painted feathers, and speaking, as he bent over her, in the softest and most subdued tone, while with her radiant face upturned to his, she looked, so Clara thought, unutterable things.

She was in truth a creature of matchless beauty, perfect in form and faultless in feature—such an one as Phidias might have chosen for the subject of his chisel. She had a dazzling complexion, a brow like polished ivory, dark, eloquent eyes, that could bewitch at will, that were lovely in tears, and resistless when half veiled by their long silken fringes, and by those snowy lids which made one involuntarily recall that expressive line of Shakespeare:

"As sweet as were the lids of Juno's eyes."

No woman ever understood better than did Grace Morley the management of the eye—and when it was her pleasure so to do, she could make it discourse most eloquently, and in a language not to be misunderstood—as she now lay half reclining on the damask cushions of the sofa, her white dress and ebon hair contrasting with their crimson hue, Clara fancied she had never before seen her look so beautiful—her colour was heightened by exercise, and a half blown rose, which she had gathered in her walk, was placed with careless grace among the soft ringlets that shaded her brow. "How," thought the humble Clara, "when viewed in comparison with this radiant creature, can I hope to retain my empire over the heart of one who so loves beauty, as does my cousin," and instinctively she raised her eyes towards an opposite mirror—but it reflected back so lovely an image, a figure so delicate and sylph-like, a face of such pure and childlike, yet *spirituel* beauty, that she blushed with conscious pleasure as it met her view.

Her brother Henry, a fine boy of ten, caught her eye in the glass, and laughingly exclaimed:

"Do you blush, sister, because you are so pretty? well then I will make you blush again, by telling you what I thought this morning, as I read of the three goddesses who quarrelled for the golden apple, that if you had been there they would neither of them have got it."

"Bravo, Hal!" shouted Charles Castleton from the other end of the drawing room; "as gallant a speech that, my boy, as ever knight of the tourney whispered in the ear of his lady love, and a goodly promise it gives to the rising fair, of your manhood."

"You have no need to laugh, Mr. Castleton," said one of the younger boys, with the air of a champion; "because Henry told Clara she was pretty, for I am sure no one can look at her twice without knowing it, thought she is above making a boast of it herself," and he glanced significantly at Miss Morley.

"And she is good too," lisped little Kate, climbing up and throwing her arms round the laughing but confused Clara; "she never frowns upon us when we teaze her, and if I had torn her dress as I did Miss Morley's this morning, she would not have sent me away crying—would you, sissy dear?"

ELIZA LANESFORD CUSHING

"Yes, Kate, if you had been naughty," returned Clara, striving by a sign to silence the clamourous little group, and bending down her lovely face, so as almost to hide it in the clustering ringlets of the child.

"No, you would not—would she be cross, cousin Charles?" and the persevering little questioner appealed to Castleton, who at that moment crossed the apartment towards her.

"Never, Kate, her nature is all sweetness," he answered in a fervent tone, and taking the little creature from Clara's arms, he pressed her fondly in his own.

Glad to make her escape, Clara glided away towards the sofa, where Grace still reclined—but this little scene had not produced a very amiable effect upon her temper—she saw that the children's remarks were not lost upon Charles, and she was excessively annoyed to have Clara represented to him, in a light so much more attractive than herself. Clouds overshadowed her bright and beautiful brow, and when Clara, hoping to turn her thoughts into a pleasant channel, spoke of the pic-nic, and kindly asked her if she would like to join the excursion, she coldly replied:

"That if her head continued to ache as it did then, she should be incapable of any enjoyment, and fit only for her pillow—but she begged not to interfere with the plans of others, or be the means of marring any one's pleasure, especially that of the children, by detaining Clara from them, who seemed—" and her lip slightly curled, "to be so essential to their happiness."

"They would certainly prefer my accompanying them," said Clara, with her accustomed gentleness of tone and manner; "but even little Kate is old enough to sacrifice her wishes unrepiningly to the comfort of others, and I doubt not, all of them will abundantly enjoy the day, even should I remain at home, which I shall cheerfully do, unless you are able and inclined to join the party. But let me do something for your head, dear Grace; I will send these noisy children away, and bathe it in eau de Cologne, and I doubt not it will be quite well tomorrow."

"Let me kiss you before I go, sister," said Kate, stooping down from Castleton's arms, who stood by holding her in silence, and stretching out her dimpled hands towards Clara. The embrace was given and returned, and as she slid down to go away, she cast an arch glance at Grace, and roguishly plucking the rose from her hair, threw it at Charles, and ran laughing from the room. Miss Morley started and endeavoured to smile, but it was plain to see how much she was annoyed by the wild freedom of the artless child. But her fair face assumed a more complacent expression, when Charles, as though it were a precious deposit, placed the stolen flower in his bosom, and finding herself again the sole object of thought and attention, her animation and good humour by degrees returned. Charles sat on a low ottoman assiduously fanning her, while Clara's little soft hand bathed her temples with eau de Cologne, and thus ministered to, and amused, she became once more the brilliant and fascinating beauty, whose faults were lost in the assumed sweetness of her manners and disposition, or forgotten in the charm of her varied and lively conversation.

The following morning dawned bright and cloudless, and the gay voices and busy feet of the children were heard from their apartment, even before the shrill note of chanticleer proclaimed its approach. Miss Morley too, rose with renovated health and spirits, declaring herself well enough to join the pic-nic, and looked forward with much pleasure to the promised enjoyments of the day. She wished to go on horseback, and Charles and Clara, who were experienced equestrians, gladly acceded to the proposal. Mr. and Miss Grey, some friends of Clara's, also rode with them, while Mr. and Mrs. Ilsley, with Mrs. Darracot and her sister, occupied one carriage, and the children of the two families, with their nurses, the other. It was still early when the party set out, and Mr. Grey, who was an admirer of Clara's, immediately attached himself to her, nor could she avoid feeling wounded, at the willingness with which her cousin Charles yielded her entirely to his care. For himself, he seemed completely fascinated by Miss Morley, and beautiful indeed she

ELIZA LANESFORD CUSHING

looked, as gracefully she managed her high spirited steed, and bent her bright glowing face gaily towards Castleton, conversing as she rode with unaffected ease and vivacity.

"Could I be thus absorbed by another," thought Clara, "and he within hearing of my voice?" and a pang shot through her heart as she asked herself the question. "Oh, man knows nothing of the intensity and fervour of that sentiment which springs up in the heart of woman—nothing of its self devotion, its concentration of thought and feeling and purpose—looking with fond desire but to one end, circumscribing its enjoyments and hopes within one magic circle, which however limited it may be, is broad enough for the wide expansion of those tender sympathies and emotions that constitute her felicity."

Such were the thoughts of Clara Ilsley, as she contrasted her lover's conduct with what would have been her own, under similar circumstances. But hers was a well disciplined mind, fortified by principles, that could alone sustain her under life's many and varied trials, and which enabled her gratefully to enjoy the blessings of her lot, even if deprived of one dear and cherished source of happiness. She dearly loved the innocence and gaiety of childhood—too dearly, not now to sympathise in its pleasures, and was too fervent a votary of nature, not always to derive exquisite delight from the boundless and exhaustless beauty of its rich and ever varying scenes.

Their road lay through winding lanes, overgrown with shrubbery, and fragrant with the breath of wild roses and the rich scent of clover fields, or along the elevated banks of a broad river, from whence they caught lovely views of mountains blue in the distance, farm houses standing in the sheltered nooks of wooded hills, with the rich vegetation of early summer glowing around them in the varied hues of the different grains, that were clothing the earth with beauty, and promising an abundant harvest to the rejoicing husbandman. How those dear children enjoyed their drive, and how sweetly in unison with their ringing voices and merry faces, were those natural melodies that floated unseen but felt, on every breeze that fanned their rosy cheeks, and lifted the silken curls from their young and laughing brows. In the exuberance of their glee, they mimicked the wild notes of the birds and the bleating of the lambs that clustered in snowy groups on the emerald meadows; and they shouted with joy at the sight of a golden oriole that darted from its leafy covert, and passed like a ray of light before their eager eyes. Sometimes they were enamoured with a graceful birch, whose silver trunk seemed starting from the bank in which its old roots were imbedded, to bend almost horizontally over the bright water, as though it sought in that mirror to gaze upon its reflected image and lave its pensile boughs in the cool and limped wave—or they stretched forth their hands as they passed on, to pluck the wild briar roses that grew in rich luxuriance on the banks, and stood on tip-toe, heedless of the prohibition of old John, and the warnings of the terrified nurses, to grasp the snow-white blossoms of the cornel, or the feathery branches of the larch, that loaded with its small and delicate cones, stretched its fantastic arms across the road, as if to crave companionship with the statelier trees that bordered the opposite side.

And so they passed on, quaffing that cup of happiness which the lip of childhood only tastes—for man poisons it with vain regrets for the past, and hopes as vain for the unseen future—regardless of that present, which may perchance comprise all that ought to constitute his earthly felicity. Let him learn of happy childhood a lesson, and enjoy as they are bestowed, the rich blessings strewed in his path by a bountiful Providence—leaving with child-like confidence the events of the future to His disposal, who orders all things in wisdom. Clara's heart shared in the overflowing delight of the little ones, and reining up her gentle Thetis beside their carriage, she echoed all their joyous exclamations, and spurred her steed up many a tangled bank to pluck for them the coveted privet or the tempting wreath of wild convolvulus, that waved its purple bells in air. Mr. Grey vainly strove to follow where she led—her quick and graceful movements put him continually at fault, and often when

ELIZA LANESFORD CUSHING

he had struggled through a dense thicket in pursuit of her, and gained with indefatigable pains the top of a high bank, whither she had preceded him, her "silver footed Thetis" would suddenly re-appear bearing the laughing girl, on the very spot from whence they had commenced their ascent— she having forced her way down another path, before he had succeeded in gaining the summit she had left. These little *contretemps* of Mr. Grey's, furnished the children with much amusement, and Clara in seeing their happiness, ceased to dwell upon her own sources of disquiet.

In a couple of hours the little party reached the cottage of old Pompey, an aged black, whose youth had been spent in the service of Mrs. Ilsley's father, but who, with a partner as ancient as himself, had for several years tenanted this quiet spot, overseeing a small farm belonging to Mr. Ilsley, and spending the long evening of his life in ease and comparative indolence. The small dwelling, scarcely discernible through the vines and trees that embowered it, stood midway up a richly wooded hill, overlooking a wide stretch of fertile country, that was bounded by a chain of mountains, lying far off on the horizon, and towering towards heaven, till their faint and shadowy outline was lost in the ethereal hue of the atmosphere. Below spread out a broad and rapid river, studded with clusters of minute but exquisite islands, than which the far famed Cyclades, that gem of the classic Ægean could not boast a rarer degree of beauty. Gently swelling hills rose on either side, and groups of venerable trees, cultivated farms, and every object essential to the perfection of a lovely landscape, were here embraced within the range of vision.

Old Dinah's wrinkled face lighted up with pleasure when she saw the children—she had nursed their mother in her arms, and the faithful creature loved them as her own. With what gracious hospitality she brought the richest milk from her little dairy to regale them—delicious beer of her own brewing, cakes, that Peverelly might not have been ashamed to own, and strawberries—such strawberries! rich and ripe, and actually smothered in cream! Rare and dainty was that rural refection, and dainty would it have been, even without the aid of Spartan appetites to heighten its flavour. And then how cheerfully the old couple allowed those little fingers to pluck their choicest roses and carnations—aye, and even to steal some clusters of the sweet scented honey suckle, that climbed over their one low casement, and filled their little room with such an exquisite fragrance—and Pompey himself led them round his small neat garden, and loaded their young hands with all that their eyes coveted, and seemed to feel his own youth return in ministering to the happiness of those gay and guileless beings. But the day was wearing on, and as they were to dine in a beautiful wood of tall beech trees, that formed a verdant point in the river, they bade farewell to their kind entertainers, and repaired to the place of encampment.

The servants had already conveyed thither, the various contents of the carriages—hampers, and baskets, and boxes innumerable—dolls and toys, and bows and arrows, and guitars and flutes, and books, aye, even books, that nothing might be wanting, as Mrs. Ilsley said, for comfort, pleasure or improvement—and so, as if they had indeed come hither for study, a score or more of volumes lay strewn upon the turf. Each one, in selecting them, had suited their own taste, or aimed to please that of another, and to say nothing of Mother Hubbard, and Cock Robin, and Peter Parley, there were rival reviewers lying in friendly neighbourhood, and rival poets amicably reposing side by side. Clara had brought only a volume of Miss Mitford's "Village," which she loved for its simplicity, and fidelity to nature. "Childe Harold" was Miss Morley's choice, and as for Charles Castleton, like a true sailor, as he was, he drew forth a volume of Cooper and of Marryatt, and laid them on the grass, with old Isaac Walton in the middle, to keep them, as he said, from quarrelling.[1] And there they all lay undisturbed,

---

1. Izaak Walton (1593–1683), William Cowper (1731–1800) and sea novelist Frederick Marryat (1792–1848) all wrote works that deal in some way with life on the water, appropriate reading for the sailor Charles Castleton.

ELIZA LANESFORD CUSHING

for little was read throughout that lawless day, excepting what was conned from the human heart, and from the wide spread and ever glorious book of nature. It was a picturesque scene which that old wood presented on this happy holiday—all strayed or sat at will among its shades, and the joyous children roved in every direction, and came bounding through the trees, laden with wild flowers, and stained with wood strawberries—their glad shouts waking the silent echoes, and their flying feet chasing the nimble squirrel, that looked down as if in triumph, from the top of a swinging bough, on the noisy group whom he had baffled.

Clara gave zest to their enjoyment, by the gaiety with which she shared their sports, and she was just giving them a lesson in archery, while they all gathered round to witness and imitate her skill, except little Kate, who sat upon the turf nursing her doll—when Charles Castleton, with Grace hanging on his arm, approached the spot and begged to join in the diversion. They had been absent for a long time, walking apart by themselves, and Clara, who was in the act of shooting, felt her hand tremble as they drew near. But she conquered her emotion, and the arrow sprang from the relaxed string and pierced the distant mark at which she aimed. Every little voice shouted applause, as casting down her bow, she turned, with a heightened colour, to greet her cousin and Miss Morley. But the glow left her cheek, when she marked the rose that on the preceding evening had graced Miss Morley's hair, fading on Charles' breast. 'Was it then so cherished because she had worn it?' thought Clara—'and where was the bud that had been her gift, and which he had plead so earnestly to obtain!' Charles marked her changing colour, and the direction of her eye, and he felt his cheek burn at the silent reproach that look unintentionally conveyed to his heart. But at that instant Miss Morley took up the bow to try her skill, and Clara's wounded feelings were forgotten in his eagerness to watch the gestures of her rival.

Conscious, as she was, of her surpassing beauty, Grace stood long, slowly adjusting her arrow, and taking deliberate aim, in an attitude well calculated to exhibit to their utmost advantage, her personal superiority over her less brilliant but more lovely friend. Clara saw through the studied purpose of Grace, but she was a stranger to envy, and she gazed with unqualified admiration upon her beautiful and graceful figure. Charles however dreamed not that there was any art in this display—the fabled spells of Circe, never more completely changed the outward form, than had the wit, the beauty, the evident devotion of this modern enchantress, wrought upon, and for the time, transformed the mind, and blinded the perceptions of Castleton. He had been startled on the preceding evening by her brief display of an unamiable temper—but during this day of close companionship, she had expressed sentiments so beautiful, and discovered tastes and inclinations so perfectly in unison with his own, that every unpleasant impression was effaced, and he yielded to her fascinations, to the almost total neglect of one, whose loveliness of person and mind had hitherto gratified alike his pride and his affection. Whether, had Miss Morley in reality possessed that purity of heart, and those endearing traits of character, which Charles loved in Clara, the transient admiration which she had awakened, would have ripened into a warmer sentiment, it is impossible to say—but as it was, she could not long maintain over a mind like his, the influence she had struggled so hard to obtain. It was an unusual thing for a day to pass without some development of her real disposition, and, guarded as she had now been, circumstances surprised her into a display, which rent the flimsy veil her art had cast over the eyes of Charles, by the force of contrast and enhanced in his estimation the loveliness of Clara, and firmly reestablished her dominion over his affections.

Several minutes elapsed before Miss Morley affected to be satisfied with the correctness of her aim—aware that the gaze of Castleton was upon her, she stood drawing out, and then relaxing the silken string of her bow, till even his patience was almost exhausted by her delay. The children gathered around her, each bright eye intently watching for the arrow's flight, and each little foot placed in advance, all eager to start in the race and be the first to pick it up, the

ELIZA LANESFORD CUSHING

moment it should have fallen to the ground. But alas! for the beautiful serenity of Grace, Henry Ilsley, in his eagerness to be foremost, accidentally touched the elbow of the fair archer, at the very moment she was in the act of letting her arrow fly, when the sudden motion sent it whirring from the string in a direction much more wide of the mark than she had meditated. Instantly she threw down her bow with a gesture of angry impatience, that petrified Charles with astonishment, but she seemed for the instant to have forgotten his presence,—Clara's innocent laugh rang in her ears, and vexed beyond endurance, that any one should presume to find a subject of mirth in her annoyance, she lost all self-control, and exclaimed with a look and accent, that at once and forever dispelled her enchantments over the heart of Castleton.

"Indeed, I see nothing to be amused at, Miss Ilsley, and cannot but marvel that a person so correct and elegant in her habits and tastes as you are reputed to be, should at all pretend to admire, or even endure the mad frolics of these lawless children. For my part, when next we come into the woods for pleasure, I hope they will be left in their nurseries—I confess I am not philanthropist enough to have my enjoyment enhanced by their presence."

"Dear Grace, pardon me for laughing; but indeed I could not help it," said Clara, still struggling to suppress the mirth that dimpled her sweet mouth; "and as for those gay young creatures," she added, "how can you be vexed at their wild glee? it is delightful to see their happiness, and hear their gushing laughter ring through these old woods. I am sure the day would have been a dull one to me without them," and she checked a rising sigh, and looked down with a flitting blush as she inadvertently uttered these last words, fearful lest Charles might think her so far wanting in maidenly modesty as to have intended them for a reproach to him.

"They are amusing enough for a short time, but to have one's comfort spoiled for a whole day by their noisy mirth, is too great a trial for the patience of any one less patient than yourself," answered Grace pettishly, and she turned away with a still frowning brow, when she encountered the piercing eye of Charles Castleton, fixed upon her with an expression, ah! how changed from that which a few minutes before had told so flattering a tale. She started, as the too probable consequences of her self indulgence flashed upon her, and anxious, if possible, to retrieve her error, she affected a sudden playfulness of manner, as she gaily asked:

"And am I to expect no sympathy from you either, Mr. Castleton, in this provoking defeat of my skill, when I had taken such a careful and true aim! or do you too," she continued, piqued by the stern seriousness with which he regarded her, "see so much to admire in the rude gambols of these children, that with Clara, you esteem every thing connected with our own comfort a matter of secondary importance?"

"As it is their holiday, Miss Morley," said Charles coldly, "and we are only self-invited guests, I think we have no right to complain of any annoyances, to which we have voluntarily exposed ourselves. And you must pardon me, if I agree with Clara in seeing far less cause for anger, than for mirth in the little incident that has now discomposed you."

"I bow submissively to your wisdom," said Grace, with an air of vexation, that she endeavoured vainly to conceal; "and when I have been long enough instructed by your sage precepts, with Clara's example to enforce them, I trust I shall become as all enduring and equable, as her serene and faultless self."

Charles bowed with a somewhat scornful smile as he replied:

"I presume not to utter precepts for Miss Morley's guidance, but I can wish of her no better boon, than that she may become in all things like my cousin Clara."

Clara's colour went and came at these words, and not trusting herself to meet the tender glance that she felt to be resting on her, she turned away to hide her emotion. But it was difficult indeed for Grace Morley's proud spirit to endure in silence this scarcely veiled rebuke—yet she did

ELIZA LANESFORD CUSHING

command herself so far as to utter no reply, though her haughty air, her kindling eye, and the mock humility with which she curtsied her thanks, gave certain indication of the deep resentment that was awakened in her heart. But still hoping to recover her influence over Castleton, and finally to triumph, by winning him from Clara, she resolutely suppressed the bitter expression of her anger, and smilingly resumed the bow to try once more her skill in archery. Clara made some playful remark, foreign to the unpleasant circumstance that had disturbed their enjoyment, and Charles was selecting for her a light and well balanced arrow, when Henry Ilsley came up to say the boats were ready for a sail, and Mr. Grey had sent him to desire they would come down immediately.

They instantly obeyed. Charles gave an arm to each of the ladies; cheerfulness was restored and they hastened, gaily talking and laughing, to the river. One boat, laden with the elder members of the party, was just pushing off as they arrived there, and Mr. Grey was waiting for them in the other, and forcibly keeping out the children, who were crowded together on the bank, impatient to embark. The ladies were soon seated, together with the elder children, but as there was no room for the nurses, it was thought best to leave the little ones behind. Their entreaties and cries, however, melted Clara's tender heart, and declaring that she would herself take charge of them, she placed them about her, greatly to her own inconvenience, and looked perfectly happy when she saw their little faces brighten up, and heard them lisp forth their innocent delight. Grace at first looked rather annoyed, but she marked Castleton's eye beaming tenderly upon Clara, and in imitation of so beautiful an example, she condescended to take Rosa Dorracott under her especial care, promising to be answerable for her safety.

She, however, soon repented of her benevolence, if it be possible so to term any action that is prompted by a purely selfish motive—for the child was restless, as children ever are, continually reaching over the edge of the boat to grasp the water lilies that floated on the surface of the waves, or clapping her little hands and dancing with delight, as they sailed among the fairy islands, and saw their banks gay with wild roses, and tufts of winter green with its bright glossy leaves and clusters of exquisite, wax-like flowers. Obliged thus to bestow her attention almost exclusively upon her young charge, Grace became heartily weary of her self-imposed task, and would not have attempted to conceal her chagrin had she not been conscious that Charles was observing her—for he had again renewed his devotion to her, and she flattered herself that her empire was becoming firmly established. But she dreamed not how greatly to her disadvantage was the parallel which all that time, he was drawing between her undisciplined, and selfish and exacting mind, and the self-sacrificing, serene, and benign spirit of his lovely cousin.

That day's experience had indeed rivetted fast the golden links of affection that bound his heart to Clara, and though he still rendered external homage to Miss Morley, his eyes continually strayed from her dazzling beauty, to the speaking face of Clara, as, beaming with kind and tender emotions, it looked down on the little dependent beings, who clung with such fond and trusting confidence around her. She seemed indeed as guileless, and as childlike in her sweet simplicity as themselves, and as Charles thought what a fountain of deep and pure and holy feeling dwelt within her heart, he wondered at his own strange infatuation, that had pledged him, though but for a day, to the service of another—and yet he blessed his folly, since it had shewn him more strikingly than ever, the true value of the gem, that he might else have cast away, for one that sparkled indeed, and attracted by its outward brilliancy, but could boast no intrinsic virtue to render it precious.

Long before their sail terminated, Miss Morley had grown very weary of her little protegé, and so far relaxed in care and vigilance, as frequently to alarm Clara for the child's safety. Grace, however, ridiculed her fears, and by assuring her that she kept a firm hold of the little girl's clothes, made her tolerably easy. But as they again came into shallow water on their return to the shore, Rosa's anxiety to obtain the water lilies revived, and Grace exhibited much impatience in endeavouring to restrain her efforts. The little girl, notwithstanding, continued to persevere, and in an unlucky moment, when Miss Morley's attention was given to Castleton, she lost her balance, as having fairly grasped one of the lilies she was striving to drag it up, and fell over the side of the boat. Grace screamed, and all started with dismay to their feet, but Clara's watchful eye had marked her danger, and her ready hand caught her as she fell, and snatched her back from death.

"Good heavens! how these children terrify one!" exclaimed Miss Morley, pale with mingled terror and anger.

"God bless you, my sweet Clara," cried Charles, "but for your presence of mind, the child had surely been lost!"

Clara could make no reply; but these words uttered in a tone of impassioned tenderness, were not even in that moment heard without emotion, and clasping the terrified little creature closely in her arms, her agitated feelings found relief in tears. There were few words spoken during the brief moments that elapsed before the boat touched the shore, excepting indeed the clamourous exclamations and unceasing prattle of the children. When they had all landed, Grace, as if instinctively aware that her reign of power over Castleton was finally ended, took Mr. Grey's offered arm, and walked away, her beautiful features clouded by an expression of chagrin and vexation, that she no longer endeavoured to conceal. The children bounded away to where the sylvan board seen through the trees, was spread for their repast, and Charles and Clara followed at a slower pace, and by a more circuitous path—and then it was that Castleton made the fond avowal of his love, and as Clara listened with a downcast eye and glowing cheek to the tale of his heart's wanderings, for he sought to conceal nothing from her, and heard how every roving thought had at length returned to its true allegiance, acknowledging only the influence of her sweetness and purity, she felt that the self denial and patient forbearance of years, would have been more than repaid by such moments of happiness as those.

From regard to Miss Morley's feelings, nothing would have been said of Rosa's danger, had not the little girl told the tale herself, and when Clara appeared, she was overwhelmed with the mother's grateful thanks, whose expression, however, served not to heighten Grace Morley's good humour, though she had so far recovered her spirits, as already to have commenced a flirtation with Mr. Grey.

The dinner in that old woods was a joyous one, and it was not till the tall beeches were tinged with the golden light of declining day, and their lengthened shadows fell far across the green-sward, that the blithe revellers arose from their repast, and thought with regret of bidding adieu to that scene of rural happiness. The ladies repaired to Pompey's cottage to resume their riding dresses, which, in the morning, they had there exchanged for garments better adapted to the woods, and all were soon in readiness, and the equestrians mounted for their return. Grace fell into the rear with Mr. Grey, hoping to pique Charles by her coquetry, but he and Clara, happy as affianced lovers always are, or ought to be, rode, together with Miss Grey, beside the children's carriage. It looked almost like a triumphal car, so laden was it with green boughs and wild flowers—every little hat too was garlanded with briar-roses, and even the horses heads were crowned with the bright blossoms of the woods. Some of the merry things, worn out with the day's pleasure, had fallen asleep, but most of them were as gay and as frolicsome as on their first setting out in the morning. They carolled forth their baby songs in full chorus, and little Kate's joyous voice rose shrill above the rest, as they sung that pretty rhyme which is familiar in many a nursery, and cherished in many ripened minds with the fond and happy associations of childhood, and which, as it is now nearly out of print, we shall insert for the benefit of our readers:

> "Lady-bird, lady-bird, fly away home,
> The field mouse has gone to her nest,
> The daisy's have shut up their sleepy red eyes,
> And the bees and the birds are at rest.

ELIZA LANESFORD CUSHING

"Lady-bird, lady-bird, fly away home,
The glow-worm has lighted her lamp,
The dew's falling fast, and your fine speckled wings,
Will be wet with the close clinging damp.

"Lady-bird, lady-bird, fly away home,
The fairy bells tinkle afar;
Make haste, or they'll catch you, and harness you fast,
With a cobweb, to Oberon's car.

"Lady-bird, lady-bird, fly away now,
To your house in the old willow tree,
Where your children so dear, have invited the ant,
And a few cozy neighbours to tea."

Clara was still child enough to join in the song, and when Charles and Miss Grey also lent the aid of their voices, the children were enchanted with the melody. Its last words were concluded, just as the carriage reached the termination of the avenue at Oakland, and as each little foot sprang out upon the piazza, their sad voices were heard exclaiming, "and this is the end of the pic-nic."

But when the long sweet days of another June returned, Charles and Clara passed one of the earliest days of their bridal in that old beech wood—and of all, who had now returned with them from that pleasant spot, none were then absent except Grace Morley—she had not yet forgotten the humiliations of the last pic-nic, for she had preferred Charles Castleton to all her admirers, and she wished not to witness Clara's happiness—a happiness, which she felt might have been hers, had she early learned the task of self-discipline, and sought to cherish, as peculiarly became her sex, the kindly and gentle affections of her nature.

୭

Literary Garland (August 1839), 405–412.

Catharine Parr Traill (1802–1899)

THE BEREAVEMENT (1846)

Catharine Parr Traill, in company with her sister Susanna
Moodie (see page 51), is one of the best-known nineteenth-
century Canadian women writers. As a creative writer and
a gifted amateur botanist of Canadian wildflowers, Traill
imaginatively documented a pioneer Upper Canada with
a keen, sensitive, and optimistic eye.

One of the six literary Strickland sisters, Catharine
Parr Traill was born in Kent, England, on 9 January 1802,
the daughter of Elizabeth Homer and Thomas Strickland.
Catharine grew up in Norwich, Norfolk, and at Reydon
Hall, Southwold, Suffolk, part of a large and genteel family
educated by their intellectual parents to be sensitive to the
beauties of the rural scene. Her father's financial reverses
and death in 1818 prompted Catharine, like her sisters
Agnes, Elizabeth and Susanna, to turn her developing
literary talents to profit. Thanks to the intervention of a
friend of the family, *The Tell Tale: An Original Collection of
Moral and Amusing Stories* was published in 1818. Her sisters
Agnes and Elizabeth remained in England and became well
known for their writings, especially on British royalty. For
her part, Catharine married in 1832 Lieutenant Thomas
Traill, a half-pay officer, and the couple resolved on a new
life in British North America.

By 1833, the Traills were struggling on a bush
lot in Douro Township near Peterborough, not far from
Catharine's brother Samuel. Her sister Susanna and her
husband later settled nearby. *The Backwoods of Canada*
(1836), published in London, is Traill's epistolary account
of these years—part chronicle, part settler's handbook. This
classic work of Canadian literature attests to the rigours of
backwoods life, to Traill's resolute optimism, and to her
gifts as a writer and observer of nature and a new society.

In 1839, Thomas Traill sold the farm and he and the family moved to Peterborough. Settlement life was more congenial but the Traills continued to be plagued by financial difficulties. In the spring of 1846, the Traills moved to Rice Lake, living at "Oaklands" from 1849 until the farmhouse was destroyed by fire in 1857. By 1847, Traill had given birth to nine children, seven of whom survived infancy. She continued writing, publishing in the *Literary Garland*, and, with the help of her sister Agnes, in English periodicals. Her children's story *The Canadian Crusoes: A Tale of the Rice Lake Plains* (1852), an account of children lost in the wilderness and helped by Indians, became a staple work for Victorian Canadian children. Less popular was *Lady Mary and Her Nurse: or, A Peep into the Canadian Forest* (1856).

Traill was successful with her compendium *The Female Emigrant's Guide, and Hints on Canadian House-keeping* (1855). The book's varied contents—from recipes to narrative sections—mirrors the multifaceted demands on women of early Canadian life. After her husband's death in 1859, Traill settled in Lakefield. She collaborated with her niece Mary Agnes Fitzgibbon to crown her interest in Canadian flora with *Studies of Plant Life in Canada; or, Gleanings from Forest, Lake and Plain* (1885), a work of interest to both scientific and literary historians. Though troubled with deafness and the death of five of her children in her own lifetime, Traill valiantly continued to write throughout the latter stages of her life. In her nineties she published *Pearls and Pebbles; or, Notes of an Old Naturalist* (1894) and, with the help of Mary Agnes Fitzgibbon, published *Cot and Cradle Stories* (1895). Traill died on 29 August 1899 at Lakefield.

"The Bereavement" (1846), a story written for the *Literary Garland*, is an interesting contrast to Moodie's "The Walk to Dummer" (See page 55). Both stories are first-person narratives about an errand of mercy, and both effectively describe the Canadian landscape. The physical and emotional hardships experienced by women in a pioneer society underlie both stories. Nevertheless, the different personalities of the two writers are revealed in the contrast in settings (dead of winter versus early spring), in tone, and in the shadings of social consciousness. Traill is the more optimistic and the more interested in nature of the two sisters, and the tone of her story is gentler than Moodie's. Traill also wrote stories of English country life on the love themes so popular with *Literary Garland* readers.

∽

Suggested Reading:

Ballstadt, Carl P. A., "Catharine Parr Traill." In *Canadian Writers and Their Works*, Fiction Series, vol. 1, edited by Robert Lecker, Jack David, and Ellen Quigley, 149–194. Toronto: ECW, 1983.

Peterman, Michael A. "'Splendid Anachronism': The Record of Catharine Parr Traill's Struggles as an Amateur Botanist in Nineteenth-Century Canada." In *Re(Dis)covering Our Foremothers: Nineteenth-Century Canadian Women Writers*, edited by Lorraine McMullen, 173–185. Ottawa: University of Ottawa Press, 1990.

Traill, Catherine Parr. *The Backwoods of Canada* (1836). Toronto: McClelland and Stewart, 1929.

_____. *The Canadian Crusoes: A Tale of the Rice Lake Plains*. Edited by Agnes Strickland. London: Virtue, 1852.

_____. "Helen." In *Literary Garland* (September 1842), 476–479.

♒

THE BEREAVEMENT
Catharine Parr Traill

It was one of those soft warm mornings in April, that we not infrequently experience in this country during the melting of the snow, when the thermometer indicates a degree of temperature not less than summer heat. The air was filled with insects which had either revived from their winter torpor or been prematurely awakened to the enjoyment of a bright but brief existence. A few sleepy, dusty looking flies had crept from their hiding places about the window—while some attenuated shadowy spider made vain attempts at commencing a web to entangle them. Without all was gay and cheerful—a thousand spring-like sounds filled the air—flocks of that pleasant warbler, the Canadian song-sparrow, mingled with the neat snow-bird (*fringilla nivalis*) flitted about the low wattled fence of the garden; at the edge of the cedar swamp, might be heard from time to time the rapid strokes of the small spotted wood-pecker, full of energy and animation, the mellow drumming of the Canadian partridge, (or ruffed Grouse,) mingled not unharmoniously with the wild cry of that bold but beautiful depredator, the blue jay. There too was the soft melancholy whispering note of the little chickadee, (*parus palustris,*) as it restlessly pursued its insect prey among the feathery branches of some old gnarled hemlock—the murmuring melody of the breeze stirring the lofty heads of the pines, with the "still sweet sound of waters far away," combining made sweet music to the ear.

Bright and blue as was the sky above, warm and genial as was the air around, and inviting as were the sounds of nature abroad, I yet found myself obliged to be an unwilling prisoner; the newly melted snow had rendered the surface of the ground porous as a sponge; half decomposed ice and pools of water, made the roads and paths impassable. The luxury of India rubbers had scarcely at that time reached our settlement; they were among the rare things heard of but seldom seen. How I envied the more fortunate flocks of wild geese and ducks that were revelling in the azure pools, that lay so invitingly open to them, on the ice-bound lake in front of our log house. Sorely tempted as I was by the bright sunshine, and all spring's pleasant harmonies, to go forth into the newly uncovered fields—yet I dared not risk wetting my feet, having but recently recovered from a severe fit of illness.

I was still lingering at the open door, watching the graceful manœuvres of the wild fowl on the lake, when my attention was attracted to a bare-footed, bare-headed, uncouth looking girl, who was hurrying towards the wicket, and panting from the speed which she had used. The little damsel, as soon as she could speak, told me she had been sent by her mistress, (a nice young Scotchwoman, wife to the overseer of a neighbouring saw-mill,) to entreat me to go and see her baby, a lovely infant of eight weeks old— which lay dying as she feared. I hesitated. Of what use could I be in a case of such emergency? I asked myself. The road lay through a tangled cedar swamp, the mudholes would be opened by the soft air—and I cast a glance at the wide pools of water, and the honey-combed ice. The bare-legged little messenger seemed to read my thoughts.

"Ye 'll no find the path sae vera bad, gif ye 'll gang the same gait wi' me. The mistress is greeting, greeting sairly a' the time, about the sick wean—she'll weary till she sees ye coming."

The simple entreaties of the little lassie prevailed over the dread of swamps and mudholes, wet feet and draggled garments. If I could afford no aid to the suffering child, I might yet support and console the afflicted mother—it was worth some little risk. Joy sparkled in the eyes of my little conductress as she watched me adjusting my tartan shawl; and as a reward for my compliance, she declared that I looked "like a bonny Scotch leddy."

My rough but warm-hearted little guide set off at a good round trot before me—heedless of mud or mire, stone or log; plunging most independently through the first, and scrambling fearlessly over the second—more than one high pile of logs she invited me to cross, after having set me the example with the agility, if not with the grace, of a squirrel— I might as well have followed a Will-o-the-Wisp, as little Maggie Freebairn.

Half an hour's quick walking brought me to the dwelling of the young mother and her sick infant. The babe had been ill several days, and many improper remedies had been successively adopted; among the most pernicious of these whisky punch, (the country people, by-the-bye, call all mixtures of spirits and water punch,) and bad port-wine had been forced down the babe's throat. It now lay, convulsed and evidently dying, on the lap of the weeping, sorrowing mother, a pale and wasted shadow of what had been so lovely only a single week before disease had seized it. The hand of Death had set its seal upon it—and "life's young wings were fluttering for their flight!"

By the advice of my sister-in-law, who happened to call in a few minutes after my arrival, we put the babe into a warm bath, and applied gentle friction to its body and extremities; but alas! it was beyond the reach of human skill or human care. It seemed almost cruel to torment it with unavailing remedies. It was sad to see the anguish of the poor mother, as she hung in tearful agony over its pale unconscious face. It was her first-born—her only one, and the bare possibility of parting from it was too bitter a grief to be dwelt upon. With what tender solicitude did her sad eyes wander towards it continually, as it lay upon my knees, while she almost unconsciously performed those household tasks which her situation rendered imperatively necessary,

CATHARINE PARR TRAILL

having to cook for some ten or twelve workmen, belonging to the saw-mill. How often would she throw herself upon her knees beside me to take its cold damp hands and place them on her bosom, or bathe them with her scalding tears—and ask with despairing accents, if I thought it could yet recover—and with what eager looks did she listen to the assurances of the compassionate millwrights and lumberers, that the infant would surely live—they had seen many young children brought as low and yet grew up fine stout boys and girls. I felt as if it were cruel to deceive her.

Towards night, the convulsion fits became more frequent, and, yielding to the passionate entreaties of the poor young woman, not to leave her alone with her dying babe, I consented to take share in her painful vigil. The little Scotch lass was again sent forth on a message to my household, and I prepared to act the part of nurse and watcher, while poor Jessy laid down to sleep—that heavy sleep, that the weary in heart and body alone know. Alone, in silence—I watched, by the flickering light cast by the pile of logs that had been carefully built up in the ample chimney (for candle there was none,) the last faint glimmerings of life in the unconscious form that lay upon my lap. No sound but the crackling and settling of the burning logs upon the hearth, the shrill chirp of the crickets, and the deep breathing of the tired slumberers in the loft above, met my ears within the dwelling; the ever moving waters of the river, as they rushed along their rocky bed, was the only sound abroad: and thus I passed the long night.

The first grey dawn found me still watching—I had not the heart to rouse the worn-out mother. I knew she could only waken to renewed anxiety. I felt the chill air of the early frosty morning blow bleak through the wide chinks of the imperfectly framed apartment. The infant appeared to have sunk into a tranquil sleep, and cramped with having maintained one posture for many hours, I now placed it in the cradle, and looked forth upon the face of Nature—and a lovely sight it was! The frosty earth was gemmed with countless diamonds—the mimic picture of those bright orbs above, which were still gleaming down from the clear blue sky; the saffron tint of early dawn was streaking the East. A light curling mist was gathering on the face of the rapid river, which lay before my eyes in all the majesty of its white crested waves, darkly shaded by the then unbroken line of forest on the opposite bank.

The little hamlet with its rude shanties and half erected dwellings and mill, lay scattered before me on the wide area in front—it was a scene of quiet and of freshness, save the rapid restless river rushing over its ledge of limestone rock, and hurrying away beneath the newly erected bridge in its downward course. It recalled to my mind Moore's lines written at the falls of the Mohawk river:

> From rise of morn till set of sun,
> I've seen the mighty Mohawk run—
>
> *   *   *   *   *
>
> Rushing alike untired and wild
> Thro' rocks that frowned and flowers that smiled.

From the contemplation of things like these, I turned with a subdued and humbled heart to look upon human suffering and human woe. Without all was beauty and magnificence, for I gazed upon the works of God. Within was sorrow and death—the consequence of man's sin.

On my re-entering the house, I found Jessy sitting beside the cradle—her hopes had risen with the new day.

Her profound sleep had refreshed both body and mind, and she came to her labour of love with renewed spirits. She was anxious to get breakfast for me, but I preferred the reviving influence of the morning air to anything she could offer me, and promising to return in a few hours, I set forth on my solitary walk homeward.

There is no season when gratitude seems more naturally to fill our hearts, than at early dawn—it is the renewal to us of our existence, we feel that we have been cared for and preserved, and we lift our hearts to Him, from whom all blessings flow. How indeed, can we listen to the chorus of thanksgiving poured forth at sunrise, without being assured that an instinctive feeling of gratitude animates all things living—nay, even the very flowers, and trees, and herbs seem to rejoice in their freshness. Do not the Heavens declare the glory of God, and the firmament shew his handy-work!

The day was now risen, and the silent woods seemed suddenly to become eloquent with melodious notes, heard at no other time. The ground was white and crisp with frost, a comfortable change from the soft mud and half melted ice of the preceding day—the breeze blew sharp and cold from the river, but it seemed to revive my exhausted spirits and wearied frame. The wood-peckers were at their ceaseless work, hammering away at the pines and hemlocks—the red squirrels were out crossing my path in every direction, now stopping to regard me with furtive glance, now angrily erecting their beautiful feathery tails and darting up the stem of some rough barked tree, pausing from time to time in their ascent, to chatter forth some indignant remonstrance at my unseasonable intrusion on their privacy at such an hour—seldom, I ween, had lady fair been seen at dawn of day among the deep solitudes of these hemlock and cedar shades, through which I then winded my way. I was lost in a train of reflections to which the novelty of my situation had given birth, when a heavy tread upon the frozen ground near made me look round, and I perceived my husband advancing among the trees to meet me. He had risen thus early to escort me home.

I had not been home more than two hours, before the little Scotch maid came over to tell me that the babe was dead. The deep sleep, in which I had left it, was its last—it breathed its little life away so peacefully, that it might indeed be said, that it fell asleep and wakened in Heaven. The golden bowl was broken, and the young spirit, wearied with this earthly strife of pain, had returned to God who gave it!

It was evening when I renewed my visit to the house of the afflicted mother. Exhausted with weeping, she lay stretched upon her bed, fevered and ill at ease in body, and bowed down with the grief that belongs to human nature, when deprived of the object of its love. It was her first-born, her only one. It was piteous to hear her sad wailing, as she cast her eyes down upon her arm, and exclaimed:

"It used to lie here—just here, but it will never rest upon my arm again. It is gone—gone—gone!"

I did not then know the pangs of a bereaved mother, mourning for a dear babe, but I have often thought of poor Jessy, since that day—and felt how natural was her sorrow.

It was the third day, after this last sad visit, that I again re-entered the house of mourning. It was a day of sunny brightness. The sounds of business and labour had ceased—the axe no longer made the woods echo to its heavy strokes, the rush and whirl of the mill-wheels was stopped—it was the Sabbath morning, and silence and repose reigned over that busy spot. The door of the dwelling stood open, and I entered unbidden. A solemn feeling came over me, as I stepped across the threshold, from the broad glare of daylight into the dim religious light of the darkened room. In the centre was a table, decently covered with a snow white damask cloth; beside it sat the father of the child, his hat craped and tied with the simple white riband, symbol of the youth and innocence of the dead; his head was bent down over the big Bible, that rested on his knees; he was habited in decent mourning. As I entered, he raised his head, and bowed with an air of deep reverence, but spoke no word, and I passed on, unwilling to intrude upon his wholesome meditation. The father was gathering strength from the Book of peace and consolation.

At the further end of the apartment stood the mournful mother, her face bowed over the pale shrouded form of the idol of her heart. Her fair hair, gemmed with tears, fell in long soft ringlets over her face, and swept the pallid brow and tiny ice-cold hands of the dead infant; they were wet with the holy weeping of maternal love.

The sound of my steps made her look up, and forgetting all distinctions of rank, and alive only to the sympathy

CATHARINE PARR TRAILL

that had been shewn to her in her hour of deep distress, she threw her arms about my neck, and wept—but her grief was softened and subdued. She had schooled her heart to bear the sad reality, and she now sorrowed, as one not without hope.

Silently, she drew from within the folds of her muslin handkerchief, a small packet, carefully fastened with a thread of black silk—it was the fair hair of her lost treasure. She regarded it with a look of inexpressible tenderness, kissed it and replaced it in her bosom—then imprinting a last passionate kiss upon the marble brow and cheek of the dead babe, she suffered me to lead her quietly away, while the men approached to screw down the coffin, and throw the white pall over it.

With tearful earnestness did poor Jessy entreat of me to join in the procession that was about to form, but the burial ground was three or four miles off, on the opposite side of the river, and I was unequal to so long a walk.

I watched the funeral train, as it slowly crossed the bridge, and ascended the steep banks of the river, till the last waving of the white pall and scarfs of the mourners was no longer visible among the dark pines. I turned to retrace my steps, and felt that it was better to go into the house of mourning, than the house of mirth.

'Tis a sweet quiet spot, that burial ground in the woods. A few rudely sculptured stones—a heap piled here and there—a simple cross of wood, or a sapling tree planted by some pious hand, are the only memorials, to point out where rest the poor forgotten emigrant or his children. But the pines sigh above them a solemn requiem, the wild birds of the forest sing their lullaby, and the pure white lily of the woods and the blue violet, grow as freely on their green mossy graves, as though they slept within the holy shadow of the sanctuary. Their resting place is indeed hallowed, by the tears and humble prayers of their mournful relatives.

There is one that sleeps there among the children of the soil, unknown and uncared for, save by one who sadly remembers his guileless childhood, his early promise, and the bright example of a talented, but too indulgent father, and of a doting mother—

> "But thoughtless follies led astray
> And stained his name."

Cut off in the reckless levity of youth's mad career, he fills an early grave; and I might say of him in the words of the old Scotch ballad:

> "Ah! little did thy mother think
> The day she cradled thee,
> Through what lands thou should's travel,
> And what death thou should'st die!"

∽
Literary Garland (February 1846), 69–72.

Susanna Moodie (1803–1885)

THE WALK TO DUMMER (1847)

Susanna Moodie is the best-known Canadian female
writer of the nineteenth century. She dealt powerfully and
incisively with the society and landscape of Ontario in its
formative decades. Despite having had an upbringing, a class
consciousness and an inclination unsuited to backwoods life,
she nonetheless left us memorable and sophisticated sketches
and fiction of that pioneer world. As woman and writer,
moreover, Moodie has seized the imagination of later
Canadian women writers, such as Margaret Atwood and
Carol Shields.

Born in Bungay, Suffolk, England, on 6 December
1803, Susanna Moodie was the youngest daughter of
Elizabeth Homer and Thomas Strickland. Educated at
home by her parents and five older sisters, Susanna was
shaped by the genteel, bookish milieu of the Strickland
family. Affected by the financial travails of her father, who
died when she was only fifteen, Susanna, like her older sisters
Agnes, Elizabeth and Catharine, wrote to supplement the
family income. She contributed to the flourishing giftbooks
and periodicals of the England of the day, and also wrote for
the Anti-Slavery Society. Like her sister, Catharine Parr
Traill (see page 39), Susanna Moodie married a half-pay
British officer— John Wedderburn Dunbar Moodie.
Susanna's conversion to Congregationalism and a period
of residence in London to further her literary career were
contemporaneous with the marriage in 1831. A year later,
the Moodies' poor economic prospects led the couple to
emigrate with their infant to British North America. They
experienced the rigours of transatlantic travel, the fear of
cholera on arrival, and the hardships of bush life, first on a
cleared farm at Cobourg and then in the bush in Douro,
near Peterborough, not far from her brother Samuel, sister
Catharine and their families. The rigours of the Moodies'

life before their removal to Belleville in 1840 formed the basis for Moodie's *Roughing It in the Bush*.

Once in Belleville, where her husband had been appointed Sheriff of Victoria County to reward his military service in the Upper Canadian Rebellion of 1837, Moodie devoted herself to the work of editor and writer, as well as of wife and mother, in the face of frequent financial hardships. By now the Moodies had seven children, two of whom died in Belleville in the 1840s, one by drowning. She turned out a stream of poems, stories, sketches and novels, publishing in the Montreal *Literary Garland*, whose publisher John Lovell knew of her pro-British poems at the period of the Rebellion of 1837, as well as in English publications. In 1847–48, Susanna and Dunbar Moodie edited the *Victoria Magazine*, during which time Moodie corresponded with Louisa Murray, encouraged Rosanna Leprohon (see page 151) and serialized one of her own stories, "Rachel Wilde," in the struggling magazine.

At times ill, and often short of cash, Moodie was widowed in 1869. She then left Belleville to live with relatives in Seaforth and Toronto, returning to Belleville in 1870–71 to board with friends. A spirited and strong-minded woman to the last, Moodie died in Toronto on 8 April 1885.

Moodie's novels include *Mark Hurdlestone; or, The Gold Worshipper* (1853), *Flora Lyndsay; or, Passages in an Eventful Life* (1854) and *Matrimonial Speculations* (1854). As Carl Ballstadt has put it, most of her pure fiction is "religious romance marked by melodramatic and gothic excesses." In the popular *Roughing It in the Bush*, however, and to a lesser extent in its sequel, *Life in the Clearings Versus the Bush* (1853), Moodie wrote her finest work. *Roughing* documents the interaction and the tension between a polished woman and an inchoate, crude new country. The work is narrated by a complex and incisive female narrator full of irony and ambivalence about the new land and her place in it. Moodie published sections of the work in the *Garland* and elsewhere, and worked and reworked the shape of the book, a process well documented by recent scholars such as

Ballstadt and Alec Lucas. "The Walk to Dummer" was the second of six such "Canadian Sketches" published in the *Literary Garland*. These sketches are typical of the genre in their predilection for chronicle and vivid characters, and are interesting to compare with Traill's *The Backwoods of Canada* (1836) and Anna Brownell Jameson's *Winter Studies and Summer Rambles* (1838).

Ballstadt (1990) has established on the evidence of a letter by Moodie to her husband that the walk by Moodie to Dummer, upon which this sketch is based, took place in January or February 1838. He sees a parallel between the vicissitudes of the abandoned wife's life and certain aspects of Moodie's own circumstances of the day. That is to say, Moodie was isolated and poor, had to care for children alone while her husband was away (in military service), and became herself the recipient of neighbourly charity. For Lucas, the work establishes the narrator as a woman of "competence and human sympathy."[1] Certainly there is much of Moodie in both the narrator and the object of her sympathy, and the sketch suggests the encounter between emigrant self and wilderness nature experienced by Moodie in her first years in Upper Canada. Dummer, the scene of misery brought on by poverty and drink, is a moral and physical wilderness, a *terra incognita* which the narrator and Emilia reach to perform acts of mercy only after a cold and desolate journey worthy of Bunyan's *Pilgrim's Progress*.

〰️

Suggested Reading:
Ballstadt, Carl, Elizabeth Hopkins, and Michael Peterman, eds. *Susanna Moodie: Letters of a Lifetime*. Toronto: University of Toronto, 1985.

---

1. Alec Lucas. "The Function of the Sketches in Susanna Moodie's *Roughing It in the Bush*." In *Re(Dis)covering Our Foremothers: Nineteenth-Century Canadian Women Writers*. Edited by Lorraine McMullen. Ottawa: University of Ottawa Press, 1990.

McMullen, Lorraine, ed. *Re(Dis)covering Our Foremothers: Nineteenth-Century Canadian Women Writers*. Ottawa: University of Ottawa Press, 1990. See especially essays by Carl Ballstadt, Bina Friedwald and Alec Lucas.

Moodie, Susanna. *Roughing It in the Bush*. Edited by Carl Ballstadt. Ottawa: Carleton University Press, 1988.

Peterman, Michael. "Susanna Moodie (1803–1885)." In *Canadian Writers and Their Works*, vol. I. Edited by Robert Lecker, Jack David and Ellen Quigley, 62–99. Toronto: ECW, 1983.

THE WALK TO DUMMER

Susanna Moodie

> We trod a weary path, through silent woods,
> Tangled and dark, unbroken by a sound
> Of cheerful life. The melancholy shriek,
> Or tossing into waves the green pine tops,
> Of hollow winds careering o'er the snow—
> Making the ancient forest groan and sigh,
> Beneath their mocking voice, awoke alone
> The solitary echoes of the place.

> Author.

Reader, have you ever heard of a place called Dummer? Ten years ago it might not inaptly have been termed the last clearing in the world—nor, to this day, do I know of any in that direction which extends beyond it. Our bush farm was situated on the border line of a neighboring township, only one degree less wild, less out of the world, or nearer to the habitations of civilization, than the far-famed "English Line," the boast and glory of this terra incognita. This place, so named by the emigrants who had pitched their tents in that solitary wilderness, was a long line of clearings, extending for several miles along the forest road, and inhabited chiefly by Cornish miners, who, tired of burrowing like moles under the ground, had determined to emigrate to Canada, where they could breathe the fresh air of heaven, and obtain the necessaries of life, upon the bosom of their mother earth. Strange as it may appear, these men made good farmers, and steady, industrious colonists, working as well above ground as they had in their early days beneath it. All our best servants came from Dummer, and although they often spoke a language difficult to be understood, they were faithful and obedient, performing the tasks assigned to them, with the patient perseverance of the Saxon race—good food and kind treatment always rendering them cheerful and contented.

My dear old Jenny, that most faithful and attached of humble domestic friends, came from Dummer, and I was wont to regard it with complacency for her sake. But Jenny was not English,—she was a generous, warm-hearted daughter of the Green Isle,—the emerald gem set in the silver of ocean. Yes, Jenny was one of the poorest children of that impoverished but glorious country, where wit and talent seem indigenous to the soil, springing up spontaneously in the wildest and most uncultivated minds, shewing what the land can bring forth in its own strength, unaided by education and unfettered by the conventional rules of society. Jenny was a striking instance of the worth and noble self-devotion which is often met with, and alas! but too often disregarded, in the poor and ignorant natives of that deeply injured and much abused land. A slight sketch of my old favorite may not prove uninteresting, and as it is drawn from life, I shall not hesitate in presenting it to my readers.

Jenny Buchanan, or, as she called it, Bohanon, was the daughter of a petty exciseman, who, at the time of her birth, resided near the old town of Inniskillen. Her mother died a few months after she was born, and her father, within the twelve months, married again. In the meanwhile the poor orphan babe had been adopted by a kind neighbor, the wife of a small farmer in the vicinity. In return for coarse food and scanty clothing, the little Jenny became a servant of all work; she fed the pigs, herded the cattle, assisted in planting potatoes, and digging peat from the bog, and was undisputed mistress of the poultry yard. As she grew up into womanhood the importance of her labor increased with her size. A better reaper or footer of turf could not be found in the district, or a woman more thoroughly acquainted with the management of cows, and the rearing of young cattle. But here poor Jenny's accomplishments terminated. Her usefulness was all abroad. Within the house, she made more dirt than she had the inclination to clean away. She could neither read, nor knit, nor sew, and though she called herself a Protestant, she knew no more of religion, as revealed to man through the word of God, than the savage who daily perishes in his ignorance. But God had poured into the warm heart of this neglected child of nature, a stream of the richest benevolence. Honest, faithful and industrious, Jenny became a law unto herself, and practically illustrated the golden rule of our Saviour, "To do unto others as we would they should do unto us." She thought it was impossible that her poor services could ever repay the debt of gratitude which she owed to the family who had brought her up, although the obligation for years past must entirely have been upon their side. To them she was greatly attached, for them she toiled unceasingly; and when evil days came and they were no longer able to meet the rent day, or to occupy the farm, she determined to accompany them in their emigration to Canada, and formed one of the stout-hearted band that fixed its location in the lonely and unexplored wilds now known as the Township of Dummer. During the first years of their settlement, the means of obtaining the common necessaries of life became so precarious, that, in order to assist her friends with a little ready money, Jenny determined to hire out into some wealthy house as a servant.

Jenny's first pecuniary speculation was a complete failure. For five long years she served a master, from whom she never received a farthing of her stipulated wages. Still her attachment to the family was so strong that the poor creature could not make up her mind to leave them. The children she had received into her arms at their birth, and whom she had nursed with maternal tenderness, were as dear to her as if they had been her own, and she continued to work for them, although her clothes were worn to tatters, and her friends were too poor to replace them.

Her master, Captain ——, a handsome, dashing officer, who still maintained the carriage and appearance of a gentleman, in spite of the mental and moral degradation arising from a constant state of intoxication, still promised to remunerate her services at some future day, and Jenny, willing to believe him, worked on and hoped for that better day to arrive.

And now a few words respecting this master: Allured by the bait that has been the ruin of so many in his class, the offer of a large grant of wild land, he had been induced to form a settlement in this remote and untried township; laying out much, if not all of his available means, in building a log house, and clearing a large extent of barren and unproductive land. To this uninviting home he conveyed a beautiful young wife, and a small, but increasing family. The result may easily be anticipated. The want of society, the total absence of all the comforts and decencies of life, produced inaction, apathy, and at last despondency, which was only alleviated by a constant and immoderate use of intoxicating spirits.

As long as Captain —— retained his half pay he contrived to exist. In an evil hour he parted with this, and quickly trod the down hill path to ruin.

It was at this disastrous period that Jenny entered his service. Had Captain —— adapted himself to the circumstances in which he was now placed, much misery might have been spared both to himself and his family; but he was a proud man—too proud to work, or to receive with kindness the offers of service tendered to him by his half civilized, but well meaning neighbors.

"Damn him!" cried an indignant English settler, whose offer of drawing him wood had been rejected with unmcritcd contempt; "wait a few years, and we shall see what his pride will do for him. I am sorry for his poor wife and children—but curse him! I wish him no good."

This man, who had been uselessly affronted, at the very moment when he was anxious to perform a kind and benevolent action, now seemed to take a malignant pleasure in watching his proud neighbour's progress to ruin. The year after the sale of his Commission, Captain —— found himself considerably in debt.

"Never mind," he said to his anxious wife; "the crops will pay all."

The crops were a failure. Creditors pressed him hard; he had no money to pay his workmen, and he would not work himself. Disgusted with his location, but unable to change it for a better, without friends in his own class, to relieve the monotony of his existence with their society, or to afford him advice and assistance in his difficulties, the fatal whiskey bottle became his constant refuge from gloomy thoughts.

His wife, an amiable and devoted creature, well born, well educated, and deserving of a better lot, did all in her power to wean him from the growing vice. But, alas! the pleadings of an angel, in such circumstances, would have had little effect upon the mind of such a man. He loved her as well as he could love anything, and he fancied that he loved his children, while he was daily reducing them, by his vices, to beggary and ruin.

For a while he confined his excesses to his own fireside, but this was only for as long a period as the sale of stock and land would supply him with the means of his criminal self-indulgence. After a time, all these resources failed, and all his lands had been converted into whiskey, save the one hundred acres upon which his house and barn stood, and the small clearing from which the family derived their scanty supply of wheat and potatoes. For the sake of peace, his wife gave up all her jewels and household plate, and the best of a once ample and handsome wardrobe, in the hope of hiding her sorrows from the world, and keeping him at home.

The pride which had made him so obnoxious to his humbler neighbors, yielded at length to the inordinate cravings for drink, and the man who had held himself so high above his honest and industrious fellow-settlers, could now unblushingly enter their doors to ask for a drop of whiskey.

The feeling of shame once subdued, there was no end to his audacious mendicity. His whole time was spent in wandering about the country, calling upon every new settler in the hope of being asked to partake of the coveted poison. He had even been known to enter the windows of an absent emigrant's cabin, and remain drinking in the house while a drop of spirits could be found in the cupboard. When driven forth with contempt, by the angry owner of the dwelling, he wandered on to the distant town of P——, and remained for days drinking in some low tavern, while his wife and children were starving at home.

"He is the most breachy beast in the township," said the neighbor I before mentioned, to me. "It would be a good thing for his wife and children if his worthless neck were broken in some of his drunken frolics."

Though this might be deemed a melancholy fact, it was not the less dreadful on that account. The husband of an affectionate wife, the father of a lovely family, and his death to be a matter of rejoicing!—a blessing instead of an affliction,—an agony not to be thought upon without the deepest sorrow.

It was at this melancholy period of affliction and distress that poor Mrs. —— found a help in Jenny in the hour of need. The heart of the faithful creature bled for the misery which involved the innocent wife and children she dearly loved; their want and destitution called all the generous sympathies of her ardent nature into active operation, and they were indebted to her labour for every morsel of food which they consumed. For them she sowed, she planted, she reaped. Every block of wood which shed a cheering light and warmth around their desolate home, was cut from the forest by her own hands, and brought up a steep hill to the house upon her back. For them she coaxed the neighbors, with whom she was a general favorite, out of many a mess of eggs for their especial benefit; while her cheerful songs and hearty, hopeful disposition, dispelled much of the cramping despair which chilled the heart of the unhappy mother in her deserted home.

SUSANNA MOODIE

For several years did this great poor woman keep the wolf from the door of her beloved mistress, toiling for her with the strength and energy of a man; but when was man ever so devoted, so devoid of all selfishness, so attached as this uneducated Irish woman? But a period was at length put to her unrequited services. In a fit of intoxication, her master beat her severely and turned her from his doors. She forgave this outrage for the sake of the helpless beings who depended upon her care. He repeated the injury, and the poor creature, almost heart-broken, returned to her former home.

Thinking in a few days that his spite would have subsided, Jenny made a third effort to enter his house in her usual capacity, but Mrs. —— told her, with many tears, that her presence would only enrage her husband, who had threatened her with the most barbarous treatment if she allowed her to enter the house. Thus ended her five years service to this ungrateful master. This was all the thanks that she received for her unpaid labours of love. Oh! drink! drink!—how dost thou harden into stone the human heart!

I heard of Jenny's worth and kindness of heart, and sent for her to come to me. She instantly accepted the offer, and I found her a good and faithful servant.

The smiles and dimples of my loving, rosy, curly-headed Donald, a baby boy of fifteen months old, seemed to console Jenny for the separation from her darling Ellie, and the good will with which all the children regarded the kind old woman, soon reconciled her to her new home. Her accounts of poor Mrs. —— soon deeply interested me in her fate; and Jenny never went to visit her friends at Dummer, without an interchange of good wishes passing between us.

The year of the Canadian Rebellion came, and brought with it sorrow into many a bush dwelling. My dear husband was called away to help to defend the frontier, and I and old Jenny were left alone in the depths of the dark forest with four little children, to help ourselves in the best way we could. Men could not be procured for love nor money, and I now experienced the usefulness of Jenny's manlike propensities. Daily she yoked up my oxen and brought down from the bush fuel to supply our fires, which she chopped with her own hands. She fed the cattle and kept all things snug about the doors, not forgetting to load her master's two guns, in case the rebels should attack us in our lonely retreat.

The months of November and December had been unnaturally mild for that season of the year; but the middle of January brought an unusually severe spell of frost and snow. We felt very lonely, crouching round the blazing fires, that yet scarcely chased the cold from our miserable log dwelling; but this dreary time was cheered by the presence of a beloved friend, who came to spend a few days with me in my forest home. She brought her own lovely baby boy with her, and an ample supply of buffalo robes, not forgetting a treat of baker's bread and sweeties for the children. Oh! dear Emilia!—best and kindest of women, though absent in your native land, long, long shall my heart cherish with affectionate gratitude, all your visits of love, and turn to you as to a sister, tried, and found most faithful in the hour of adversity.

Great was the joy of Jenny at this accession to our family party; and after my friend was well warmed and had partaken of a cup of tea, we began to talk over the news of the place.

"By the by, Jenny," said she, turning to the old servant, who was busy undressing the little boy by the fire, to put him to bed; "have you heard lately from poor Mrs. ——? We have been told that she and her family are in a dreadful state. That worthless man has left them for the States; and it is supposed, has joined M'Kenzie, on Navy Island—but whether this is true or not, he has deserted his wife and children, leaving them without money or food."

"The good lord! what will become of the creatures?" responded Jenny, wiping her wrinkled cheek, with the back of her hard brown hand. "An' they have not a soul to chop or draw them fire-wood; an' the weather so uncommon severe. Ochone! what has not that *baste* of a man to answer for—!"

"I heard," said Mrs. S——, "that they have tasted no food but potatoes for the last nine months, and scarcely enough of them to keep life together; that they have sold their last cow—and the poor young lady and her brother bring all the wood for the fire, from the bush in a hand-sleigh."

"Oh, dear! oh, dear!" sobbed Jenny, "and I not there to help them—and poor Miss Mary! such a tender thing. Ah! it is hard, terribly hard upon the creatures, and they not used to the like."

"Can nothing be done for them?" said I.

"That is what we want to know," said Emilia, "and was one of my reasons for coming up to Douro. I wanted to consult you and Jenny on the subject. For you, who are an officer's wife, and I, who am both an officer's wife and daughter, might, perhaps, devise some plan of rescuing this unfortunate lady and her family from ruin."

"Oh! if we could help her, it would give me the deepest pleasure—"

"Well! you see the ladies of P—— are all anxious to do what they can for her; but they first want to learn if the miserable circumstances in which she is said to be placed, are true. In short, my dear friend, they want you and I to make a pilgrimage to Dummer, and to see the poor lady herself, and then, they will be guided in their movements by our report."

"Then let us lose no time in going to see her—"

"Oh! my dear heart! you will be lost in the woods," said Jenny; "it is nine long miles to the first clearing, and that through a lonely blazed path. After you have passed the Beaver Meadow, there is not a single hut to rest and warm yourself in. It is too much for you; you will be frozen to death on the road."

"No fear!" said my benevolent friend. "God will take care of us, Jenny; it is on His errand we go—to carry a message of mercy, to one about to perish."

"Well! the lord bless you, for a darlint, as you always were," said Jenny, devoutly, kissing the little fellow, whom she had let fall asleep upon her lap, in her anxiety about her old mistress. "May your own purty child never know the want and sorrow which is around her, poor dear! and her little children!"

Well, we talked over the Dummer expedition, until we went to sleep; and many were the plans we thought of, for the relief of the unfortunate family. Early the next morning, my brother-in-law, Mr. T——, called upon my friend, Emilia. The subject next to our heart was immediately introduced; and he was called into the general council. His feelings, like our own, were deeply interested; and he proposed that we should each provide something for the immediate wants of the family, and he would bring his cutter early the next morning, and take us as far as the edge of the great swamp, which would shorten four miles of the journey. We joyfully acceded to his proposal, and set cheerfully to work, to prepare some provisions for the morrow. Jenny baked four loaves of her very best bread, and boiled a large piece of beef; and Mr. T—— brought with him the next day, a fine cooked ham, in a sack, into the bottom of which he stored the beef and loaves, besides some sugar and tea, which his own kind wife had sent. I had some misgivings as to the manner in which these good things could be introduced to the poor lady, who I had heard, was reserved and proud.

"Oh! Jenny," I said; "how shall I be able to ask her to accept provisions from strangers? I am afraid of wounding her feelings."

"Och, darlint, never fear that. She is proud, I know, but 'tis not a stiff pride. She will be very thankful for your kindness, though she may have no words to tell you so. Say that ould Jenny sent the bread for her dear wee Ellie, for she knew that she would like a loaf of Jenny's baking."

"But the meat!"

"Och! maybe you'll think of something to say about that, when you get there."

"I hope so, but I am a sad coward with strangers. I will put a good face on the matter. Your name, Jenny, will be no small help to me."

All was now ready, and kissing our little bairns, and telling Jenny for the hundredth time to take care of them, we mounted the cutter, and set off, under the care and protection of Mr. T——, who determined to accompany us on the journey.

It was a black, cold day. No sun, a grey dark sky, a keen cutting wind, and hard frost. We crouched close to each other. "Good heavens! how cold it is," whispered Emilia; "what a day for such a journey!"

She had scarcely ceased speaking, when the cutter went bump upon a stump, which lay concealed in the drifted snow, and we, together with the ruins, were scattered around.

"A bad beginning," said my brother-in-law, as with rather a rueful aspect, he surveyed the wreck of the conveyance, from which we had promised ourselves so much benefit.

"There is no help for it, but to return home."

"Oh, no!" said Emilia, "let us go on; it will be better walking than riding such a dreadful day."

"But, my dear madam, consider the distance, the road, the dark dull day, and our want of knowledge of the path; I will get the cutter mended to-morrow, and the day after we may be able to proceed."

"Now, or never!" said the pertinaceous Emilia; "if Mrs. —— will go, I will. We can stop at Col. C——'s and warm ourselves, and you can leave the cutter at his house until our return."

"It was only upon your account, that I spoke," said the good T——, taking the sack, which was no inconsiderable weight, upon his shoulder, and driving his horse before him into neighbour W.'s stable; "where you go, I am ready to follow."

Colonel C—— and his family were at breakfast, of which they made us partake, and after vainly endeavouring to dissuade us from our Quixotic expedition, Mrs. C—— added a dozen fine white fish to the contents of the sack, and sent her youngest son to help Mr. T—— along with his burthen, and to bear us company on our desolate road.

Leaving the Colonel's hospitable house on the left, we again plunged into the deep woods; and after a few minutes' brisk walking, found ourselves upon the brow of the steep bank, that overlooks an extensive Beaver Meadow, which contained within its area several hundred acres. There is no scenery in the bush which presents such a novel appearance as these meadows; surrounded by dark, intricate forests, and high rugged banks, covered with the light, airy tamarack and silver birch, they look like a lake of soft rich verdure, hidden in the bosom of the barren and howling waste. Lakes they certainly have been, from which the waters have receded, "aye, ages long ago," and still the whole length of these curious level valleys is traversed by a stream of no inconsiderable dimensions. The waters of the narrow, rapid stream, which flowed through the meadow we were about to cross, were of sparkling brightness, and icy cold. The frost-king had no power to check their swift, dancing movements, or stop their perpetual song. On they leaped, sparkling and flashing beneath their ice crowned banks, rejoicing on their lonely way. In the summer, this is a wild and lovely spot, the grass is of the richest green, and the flowers of the most gorgeous dyes. The gayest butterflies float above them, upon painted wings; and the Whip-poor-will pours forth from the neighboring woods, at close of dewy eve, his strange, but sadly plaintive cry. Winter was now upon the earth, and the once gay meadow looked like a small forest lake, covered with snow.

The first step we made into it, plunged us up to the knees in snow, and we toiled on without saying a word, following hard upon Mr. T—— and his young friend, who were breaking with their feet a sort of track for us. We soon reached the Cold Creek, but here a new difficulty presented itself. It was too wide to jump across, and we could see no other way of passing to the other side.

"There must be some sort of a bridge hereabouts," said young C——, or how can the people from Dummer pass constantly to and fro? "I will go along the bank and hollo, if I find one."

In a few minutes he raised his hand, and on reaching the spot, we found a round slippery log flung across the stream by way of a bridge. With some trouble, and after various slips, we got safely to the other side.

To wet our feet would have ensured their being frozen, and, as it was, we were not without serious apprehensions on that score.

After crossing the bleak snow plain, we scrambled over another brook and entered the great swamp, which occupied two miles of our dreary road.

It would be vain to attempt giving any description of this tangled maze of closely interwoven cedars, fallen trees, and loose scattered masses of rock. It seemed the fitting abode of wolves and bears, and every other unclean beast. The fire had run through it during the summer, making the confusion doubly confused. Now we stooped, half doubled, to crawl under fallen branches which hung over our path, which to lose would have been certain destruction; then again we had to clamber over fallen trees of great bulk, descending from which, we plumped down into holes in the snow—sinking mid-leg into the rotten trunk of some treacherous decayed pine tree. Before we were half through the great swamp we all began to think ourselves sad fools, and to wish ourselves safe again by our own fire-sides. But a great object was in view, the relief of a distressed fellow creature, and like the "full of hope, unshamed, forlorn," we determined to overcome every difficulty, and toil on.

It took us an hour at least to clear the swamp, from which we emerged into a fine wood, composed chiefly of maple trees. The sun had, during our immersion in the dark shades of the swamp, burst through his leaden shroud, and cast a cheery gleam along the ragged boles of the lofty trees. The squirrel and chipmunk occasionally bounded across our path; the dazzling snow which covered it reflected the branches above us in an endless variety of dancing shadows. Our spirits rose in proportion. Young C—— burst out singing, and Emilia and I laughed and chatted as we bounded along our narrow road. On, on for hours, the same interminable forest stretched away to the right and left, before and behind us.

"It is past twelve," said my brother T—— thoughtfully; "if we do not soon come to a clearing we may chance to spend the night in the forest."

"Oh! I am dying with hunger," said Emilia. "Do C——, give us one or two of the cakes your mother put into the bag for us, to eat upon the road."

The ginger cakes were instantly produced. But where were the teeth to be found that could bite them? They were frozen as hard as stones. This was a great disappointment to us tired and hungry wights; but it only produced a hearty laugh. Over the logs we went again, for it was like a perpetual stepping up and down, crossing the fallen trees which strewed the path. At last we came to a spot, from which two distinct roads diverged.

"What are we do to now?" said Mr. T——.

We stopped, and a general consultation was held, and without one dissenting voice we took the branch to the right —which, after pursuing for about half a mile, led us to a log hut of the rudest description.

"Is this the road to Dummer?" asked I of a man who was chopping wood outside the fence.

"I guess you are in Dummer," was the answer.

My heart leaped for joy, for I felt dreadfully fatigued.

"Does this road lead through the English Line?"

"That's another thing," returned the woodman. "No; you turned off from the right path, when you came here." We all looked very blank at each other. "You will have to go back, and keep the other road, and that will lead you straight to the English Line."

"How many miles is it to Mrs. ——'s?"

"Some four, or thereabouts," was the cheering rejoinder; "why, 'tis one of the very last clearings on the line. If you are going back to Douro tonight, you must look sharp."

Sadly and dejectedly, we retraced our steps; and the other road soon led us to the dwellings of man. Neat, comfortable log-houses, well fenced, and surrounded with small patches of clearing, now arose on either side of the road. Dogs flew out and barked at us; and children ran shouting in doors to tell their respective owners that strangers were passing their gate; a most unusual circumstance, I should think, in that location.

A servant, who had lived two years with my brother, we knew, must live somewhere in this neighbourhood, at whose fireside we hoped not only to rest and warm ourselves, but to obtain something to eat. On going up to one of the dwellings, to enquire where Hannah J—— lived, we happened fortunately (as we thought) to light upon the very person we sought. With many exclamations of surprise, she ushered us into her very neat and comfortable log hut.

A blazing fire, composed of two huge logs, was roaring up the chimney; and the savory smell which issued from a large pot of pea-soup, was very agreeable to our cold and hungry stomachs. But the refreshment went no further— Hannah most politely begged us to take a seat by the fire, and warm ourselves. She even knelt down and assisted in rubbing our half frozen hands; but she never once said, "Do take a little hot soup," a cup of the warm tea, which was drawing upon the hearth stone, or even a glass of whiskey, which would thankfully have been received by our male pilgrims.

Hannah was not an Irish woman, no, nor a Scotch lassie, or her first request would have been for us to take something to eat. Hannah told us that the soup was waiting for her husband and two men, who were chopping for him in the bush; and she feelingly lamented their want of punctuality in keeping her so long without her dinner. All this was very tantalizing; as neither of us had thought of bringing any money in our pockets, (always a scarce article in the bush, by the bye,) we could not offer to pay for our dinner, and too proud to ask it of the stingy owner of the house, who was one of the wealthiest farmer's wives in the township, we wished her good morning, and jogged on.

Many times did we stop to enquire the way to Mrs. ——'s, before we ascended the steep bleak hill, upon which the house stood. At the door Mr. T—— out of delicacy, deposited the sack of provisions, and he and young C—— went across the road to the house of an English settler (who, fortunately for them, proved more hospitable than Mrs. J——,) to wait until our errand was over.

The house before which Emilia and I were standing, had once been a large and tolerably comfortable log dwelling, surrounded by dilapidated barns and stables, which were uncheered by one solitary head of cattle. A black pine forest stretched away to the north of the house, and the hill terminated in front in a desolate swamp, the entrance to the dwelling not having been constructed to face the road.

My spirits died within me. I was fearful that my visit would be deemed an impertinent intrusion. I knew not in what manner to introduce myself, and my embarrassment was greatly increased when Emilia declared that I must break the ice, for she could not go in. I tried to remonstrate, but she was firm. To hold any long parley was impossible; we were standing in the very bite of the bitter freezing blast, and with a heavy sigh I knocked slowly, but decidedly, at the door. I saw the head of a boy glance against the broken window. There was a stir within, but no one answered our summons. Emilia was rubbing her hands together, and beating a rapid tattoo with her feet upon the snow, to keep them from freezing.

Again I knocked with a vehemence which seemed to say "We are freezing good people,—in mercy let us in." Again there was a stir, and a sound of whispering voices from within, and after waiting a few minutes longer, which, cold as we were, seemed an age, the door was slowly opened by a handsome dark-eyed lad of twelve years of age, who, carefully closing it after him, stepped out upon the snow and asked us what we wanted. I told him "that we were two ladies from Douro, who wished to speak to his mamma." The lad, with the ease and courtesy of a gentleman, told us "that he did not know if his mamma could be seen by strangers, but he would go in and see." So saying he abruptly disappeared, leaving behind him the ugliest skeleton of a dog I had ever beheld; which, after expressing his disapprobation at our presence, in the most unequivocal manner, pounced like a wolf upon the sack of good things which lay at Emilia's feet, and our united efforts could scarcely keep him off.

"A cold, doubtful reception this," said my friend, turning her back to the wind and hiding her face in her muff; "this is worse than the long, weary walk."

I thought so too, and began to apprehend that our walk had been all in vain, when the lad again appeared, and said that we might walk in, for his mother was dressed. Emilia went no further than the passage. In vain were all my entreating looks, and as there was no help for it, I entered the apartment which contained the family, alone.

I felt that I was treading upon sacred ground, for a pitying angel hovers round the abode of suffering virtue, and hallows all its woes. On a rude bench before the fire sat a lady dressed in a thin muslin gown, the most inappropriate garment for the rigor of the season, but in all probability the only decent one which she retained. A subdued melancholy looked forth from her large, dark, pensive eyes, and she appeared like one who knew the extent of her misery and had steeled her heart to bear it. Her face was most pleasing, and in early life, though she was still young, she must have been very handsome. Near her, her slender form scarcely covered with her scanty clothing, sat her eldest daughter, a gentle, sweet-looking girl, who held in her arms a baby brother, whose destitution she endeavored, as much as she could, to conceal. It was a touching sight, that suffering child, hiding against her young bosom the nakedness of the little creature she loved. Another fine boy, whose neatly patched clothes had not one piece of the original stuff apparently left in them, stood behind his mother with glistening eyes fastened upon me, as if amused, and wondering who I was, and what business I had there. A pale, but very pretty little girl, was seated on a low stool by the fire. This was poor Jenny's darling Ellie, or Eloise. A rude bed in the corner of the room, covered with a coarse coverlid, contained two little boys, who had crept under the clothes to conceal their wants from the eyes of strangers. On a table lay a dozen pealed potatoes, and a small pot was on the fire to receive this their scanty and only meal.

There was such an air of patient and enduring suffering in the whole group, that, as I gazed heart-stricken upon it, my eyes filled with tears.

Mrs. —— first broke the silence, and asked to whom she had the pleasure of speaking? I mentioned my name, and told her that I was so well acquainted with her and the children, through Jenny, that I could not consider her as a stranger; that I hoped she would look upon me as a friend. She seemed surprised and embarrassed; and I found no small difficulty in introducing the object of my visit, but the day was rapidly declining, and I knew that not a moment was to be lost. At first, she rather proudly declined all offers of service, and said, she wanted for nothing.

I appealed to the situation of her children, and implored her not to refuse the help of those who felt for her distress,—and would do all in their power to relieve it. Her maternal feelings triumphed, and when she saw me weeping, for I could not restrain my tears, her pride yielded, and for some minutes, not a word was spoken. I heard the large tears as they slowly fell from her daughter's eyes, drop upon her garments. At last the poor girl said: "Dear mamma! why conceal the truth from Mrs. ——? You know that we are nearly starving!"

Then came the sad tale of domestic woes—the absence of the husband and eldest son—the uncertainty of where they were, or what had become of them—the sale of the only cow, which used to provide the children with food. It had been sold for twelve dollars—part to be paid in cash, and part in potatoes. The potatoes were nearly exhausted; and they were allowanced to so many a day. But the six dollars remained. Alas! she had sent the day before, one of the boys into P—— to get a letter out of the post-office from her husband. They were all anxiety and expectation—but the child returned late at night, without the letter, which they had longed with such feverish impatience to receive. The six dollars, upon which they depended for a supply of food, were in notes of the "Farmer's Bank," which at that time would not pass for money. Oh! imagine ye, who revel in riches, who can throw away six dollars on the merest toy, the cruel disappointment, the bitter agony of this poor mother's heart, when she received this calamitous news, in the midst of her starving children.

For the last nine weeks they had lived upon potatoes. They had not tasted animal food for eighteen months.

"Then, Ellie," said I, anxious to introduce the sack, which had lain like a nightmare upon my mind; "I have a treat for you. Jenny baked some loaves last night, and sent you four with her love."

The eyes of all the children grew bright. "You will find the sack, which contains them, in the passage," said I, to the tall, black-eyed boy. He rushed joyfully out, and returned with Emilia, and the sack. Her bland and affectionate greeting restored us all to tranquillity.

The delighted boy opened the sack. The first thing he produced was the ham.

"Oh!" said I, "that is a ham, my sister sent to Mrs. ——. She thought it might prove acceptable." Then came the white fish; "Mrs. C—— thought fish might be a treat to Mrs. ——, so far from the great lakes." Then came Jenny's bread, which had already been introduced. The beef and tea and sugar fell upon the floor, without any comment.

"And now, ladies," said Mrs. ——, with true hospitality, "since you have brought refreshments with you, permit me to cook you something for dinner."

The scene I had just witnessed had produced such a choking sensation about my throat, that all my hunger had vanished. Before we could accept, or refuse Mrs. ——'s offer, Mr. T—— arrived, to hurry us off. It was two o'clock when we descended the hill, in front of the road, and commenced our homeward route. I thought the four miles of clearing would never be passed. The English Line appeared to have no end; at length we entered the dark forest. The setting sun gleamed along the ground—the necessity of exerting our utmost speed, and getting through the swamp before dark, was apparent to us all. The men strode vigorously forward, for they had been refreshed at the cottage in which they had waited for us—but the poor Emilia and I, faint, hungry and foot sore,—it was with the greatest difficulty we could keep up. I thought of Rosalind, as our march up and down over the fallen trees, recommenced; and often mentally exclaimed, like her—"Oh, Jupiter! how weary are my legs!"

Night closed around us, just as we reached the Beaver Meadow. Here our ears were greeted with the sound of well known voices; James and Henry C—— had brought the ox-sleigh to meet us at the edge of the bush. Never was splendid equipage welcomed with such delight. Poor Emilia and I scrambled into it, and lying down on the straw in the bottom, covered our faces in the buffaloes, and actually slept, until we arrived at the Colonel's hospitable door. Dear Mrs. C—— had an excellent supper of hot fish and fried venison smoking on the table, and other hot cheer, to which we did ample justice. I, for one, never was so hungry in my life. We had fasted for twelve hours, and walked upwards of twenty miles, during that period. Never, never shall I forget that weary walk to Dummer—but a blessing followed it.

It was midnight when we reached home. Our good friends the oxen being put again in requisition to carry us there. Emilia went immediately to bed, from which she was unable to rise for several days. In the meanwhile, I wrote to my husband, an account of the scene I had witnessed; and he raised a subscription among the officers of the regiment, for the poor lady and her children, which amounted to forty dollars. Emilia lost no time in making a full report to her friends at P——, and before a week passed away, Mrs. —— and her family were removed thither by the benevolent gentlemen of the place. A neat cottage was hired for her—and to the honor of Canada be it spoken, all who could afford a donation, gave cheerfully. Farmers left at the door, beef and pork, flour and potatoes. The store-keepers sent goods to make clothes for the children. The very shoemakers contributed boots for the boys, while the ladies did all in their power to assist and comfort the gentle creature thus thrown by Providence upon their bounty. While Mrs. —— remained in the town she did not want for any comfort. Respected and beloved by all, it would have been well for her if she had never left the place in which for several years she enjoyed tranquillity, and a respectable competence from her school; but in an evil hour she followed her worthless husband to the Southern States, and again suffered all the woes which drunkenness inflicts upon the wives and children of its degraded victims.

෴

Literary Garland (March 1847), 102–109. (A revised version was included in *Roughing It in the Bush*, 1852.)

Mary Anne Sadlier (1820–1903)

A Peep into the Dominions of Pluto (1847)

An energetic author, editor, and publisher, Mary Anne
Madden was the daughter of Irish merchant Francis
Madden. Born at Cootehill, County Cavan, Ireland, on
31 December 1820 and educated at home, Mary Anne was
contributing poetry by the age of eighteen to the London
La Belle Assemblée. In 1844, at twenty-three, following her
father's death, she immigrated to Canada with her family.
Here she helped support the family with her writing,
publishing poems and stories in the *Literary Garland*, and
in 1845, by subscription, published a book, *Tales of Olden
Times: A Collection of European Traditions*. Like many women
of her day, Sadlier felt compelled to apologize for seeking
the public stage, pleading that "necessity rather than choice
brings [me] before the public":

> If truth must be told—and it is somewhat of a
> secret, gentle Reader—had it been my fate to
> belong to that fortunate class which is happily
> exempt from the necessity of working, I should in
> all probability, never have presented myself before
> you; at least it seems so to me now; for, after all,
> authorship is a perilous craft—ay! and an irksome
> one too, seeing that there are so many masters to
> be pleased. It is foreign to a woman's nature, more-
> over, to 'move in the uncongenial glare of public
> fame'—hers are, or should be, the quiet shades of
> retirement, and woe to her who steps beyond their
> boundary, with the hope—of finding happiness.[1]

---

1. Excerpt from the preface to *Tales of Olden Times* published in the
Literary Garland (December 1845), 576.

In 1846 Mary Anne married James Sadlier, of the Catholic publishing firm D. and J. Sadlier. The brothers Denis and James had immigrated to New York with their widowed mother in 1830, and established their business there. The Sadlier firm was highly successful, publishing Bibles, books, and school texts, and became a major bookseller as well. The Montreal branch of the firm was a big sales outlet. In both New York and Montreal the firm catered to the large Irish Catholic population.

Sadlier became the lifelong friend of the Irish–Canadian patriot Thomas D'Arcy McGee, whom she met in 1850. That year she published the serialized novel *The Blakes and Flanagans: A Tale Illustrative of Irish Life in the United States* in McGee's New York periodical *The American Celt*. This highly successful chronicle of two Irish families that immigrate to the United States established her reputation with a wide North American audience. She also published in the other widely read Catholic paper, the Boston *Pilot*.

In 1857 the Sadlier firm bought *The American Celt*, and continued it until 1881 as the New York *Tablet*. When, in 1860, Sadlier, her husband and six children moved to New York, she took over the running of the *Tablet*. By this time she had published eight novels. Undeterred by her domestic duties as wife and mother and her professional duties as publisher and editor, Sadlier published twenty-three books between 1860 and her husband's death in 1869. Most were immigrant novels characterized by religious piety and sentiment or historical romances celebrating the Irish past. From 1853 her books appeared under the Sadlier imprint. Returning to Montreal in 1885, on the death of her brother-in-law, Denis Sadlier, she continued for another ten years to be actively involved in the publishing company, assisted by her daughter Anna Teresa (1854–1932), a writer in her own right, primarily of pious religious stories and children's books. In the last years of her life, no longer in control of the family business, Sadlier suffered from financial difficulties that required her to move from the family home and accept assistance from a fund established for her by friends in Montreal. Nevertheless, in these last years she received signal honours in recognition of her achievements, both literary and religious.

A leading member of the Irish Catholic community in New York and Montreal, Sadlier was especially concerned with religious issues, Irish history and culture, and the trials and difficulties of Irish immigrants to North America. Besides writing about such issues, Sadlier's social concerns led her to establish A Home for the Aged, A Foundling Asylum, and A Home for Friendless Girls.

In many of her early stories for the *Literary Garland*, Sadlier dealt with Irish themes, often with the folk culture of the simple Irish peasantry; at times adroitly handling her topics with irony and indirection. In "The Fortunes of Brian Mulvany and His Wife Oonagh," a story appearing in the *Literary Garland* (June 1848) that is only superficially amusing, Sadlier indirectly but realistically reveals the harshness, poverty and fundamental injustice of Irish peasant life. With "Autobiography of an Irish Earl," also in the *Garland* (June 1851), Sadlier shifts to a very different stratum of society with fictional letters of a dissolute Irish nobleman that allow him to recount the misery he has caused in his life and his resultant remorse and unhappiness.

In the story that appears here, "A Peep into the Dominions of Pluto," published in the *Garland* (November 1847), Sadlier handles her topics with some irony, poking fun not only at the naïvete and simplicity of the uneducated, but at the much respected Irish clergy: "If neither endowed with grace of manner nor eloquence of speech, the clergy-man of whom we speak was a man of dignified demeanor," observes the narrator. The unexpected results of a practical joke, which is the core of the story, undercut the dour message about hell so insistently preached by the Irish clergy, of which the narrator comments, "There are few sermons in which, in one portion or another, the terrors of hell are not held up as a menace before the unrepentant sinner." Although Sadlier was given to writing of the dire results of drinking, as were many of the women writing at the time, in this story her criticism of drunkenness and its effects is mitigated by the humour that arises from the incident.

∾

Suggested Reading:

Sadlier, Mary Anne. *The Blakes and Flanagans: A Tale Illustrative of Irish Life in the United States*. New York: P. J. Kenedy, 1850.

Sadlier, Mrs. J. *Elinor Preston: or Scenes at Home and Abroad*. New York: D. and J. Sadlier, 1861.

Lacombe, Michèle. "Frying-Pans and Deadlier Weapons: The Immigrant Novels of Mary Anne Sadlier," *Essays on Canadian Writing* 29 (Summer 1984), 96–116.

~⚬~

A Peep into the Dominions of Pluto

Mary Anne Sadlier

In one of the inland counties of Ireland there was discovered a vein of silver, probably not sufficient to cover the expense of drawing it forth, however, for it is now many years since the search for the mineral was given up, and the mouth of the excavation closed. Whether the work would eventually have repaid those who embarked their capital therein, I cannot determine, nor is it at all necessary for me to do so, as my story refers merely to the time when the mine was being excavated; with its real value, therefore, I have nothing to do.

It was in the grey light of a morning in spring, that a party of the miners were on their way to the mine, when one of them suddenly called out:

"Hollo, boys! what have we here?" pointing as he spoke to a dark object which lay upon the road-side at some distance before them. On a nearer approach, the same man exclaimed:

"Be the powers! but it's Darby the piper:—He has been in his cups over night, an' fell asleep here on his way home."

The men all gathered round, when Micky Lynch, a wild, harum-scarum young fellow, cried out:

"Be this an' be that, but we'll play ould Darby a trick —we'll carry him off with us into the mine, an' then when he comes to, we'll have music for nothin', for we'll make him play whether he will or no.—What do you say boys?"

"Oh! faith, we're all willin' enough, for the ould fellow 'ill be in the divil of a fright when he finds himself down in the cavern, an' it was a chance, sure enough, to light upon him this mornin', for we were just in want of a good laugh."

So saying they hoisted the piper on their shoulders, and having placed himself and his pipes in the bucket, by means of which they ascended and descended, Darby was speedily deposited in the very depths of the cavern. It was no part of the plan to awaken Darby, so leaving him to enjoy his sleep unbroken, they proceeded to make fires and go on with their work. After some time honest Darby awoke, and on opening his eyes, the first object that presented itself to his astonished sight, was a huge fire, the miners having taken care to light one in his immediate vicinity. He next cast a look around the dark cavern, whose limits were lost in the distance, and whose gloom was rendered still more intense by fires placed at intervals, appearing as though they shot up from the bowels of the earth.

Darby's first care (albeit in no way remarkable for piety on ordinary occasions—but this was no ordinary occasion,) was to raise his hand and bless himself devoutly. He then began to soliloquize as follows:

"Och; then, an' is it come to this so soon? Sure enough, I was often tould that sooner or later it 'id happen me, but och! murthur, murthur! sure I could'nt expect it this many a long year, becase I'm not an ould man, an' I thought I'd have time for repintance. Och! och! och! but it's the sorrowful sight I see. I suppose they'll be comin' presently to put me on this big fire to roast. Och, Johnny Hannigan! Johnny Hannigan! but it was the unlucky hour that I sat down in your house to drink, for I'm sure I died drunk, an' that's what brought me here!"

It was no sooner perceived that the piper was awake than a crowd gathered around him, and as he gazed on their black faces his heart sank within him. Determined to remain quiet as long as they would permit him to do so, he looked from one to the other with such a look of terror, mingled with entreaty, that a general laugh was heard to ring through the vault.

"Och! the merciless divils!" sighed the terrified piper, "sure it's laughin' they are at the fine sport they'll have roastin' me in that blue blaze!"

Having enjoyed for some time the fears of poor Darby, one of the men (our friend Micky,) called out,

"What the divil are you muttherin' there between your teeth, you poor unfortunate wretch of a piper?"

"Och! your honor!" returned Darby, in the most fawning accents, "sure it's admirin' the fine place I am, that my good fortune brought me into, and I hope your worship 'ill take no offence, for I'm a poor, harmless piper, Darby McBride by name, an' the whole parish can tell your honor's glory that I never did ill to man, woman or child. Och! sure you'll not have the heart to burn me, gintlemen!—sure you'll not?"

"Burn you, you pitiful wretch! is it burn you we'd do? —no, faith! you're not worth the trouble we'd have. But any how, up with you and give us a tune, an' play your best or you know what 'ill happen you. It isn't every day we have music here. So begin at once."

It may well be believed that Darby instantly complied; at first with a very bad grace, it must be confessed, but under the inspiration of his own music, he soon became animated; and, forgetting his fright in the wild excitement of the moment, he called out:

"Up an' at it, your souls! Why don't you dance?"

"Be the powers o' pewter, but he's right; it's a pity to lose the music!"

And, so saying, they all commenced dancing with might and main—the tones of the bag-pipes waxing louder and louder, and Darby himself calling out, from time to time,

"Hurra, boys! faix it's yourselves can do it. Hurra for our side!"

The dancers at length gave over, when one of them drew near Darby, with a well-filled black bottle of capacious dimensions in one hand, while the other contained a glass, which he filled and handed to Darby.

"Here, piper! we liked your music well, and here's something to warm your heart."

"Many thanks to your worship!" replied Darby, as he took the glass, which he emptied without a moment's delay.

Having wiped his mouth with the sleeve of his coat drawn across it, he indicated his approval of the liquor by a loud smack. Raising his eyes knowingly to the face of his companion, he asked:

"You call this place *hell*, don't you?"

"What the deuce else would we call it?" returned the other.

"Och! then, musha! if this is hell, where you keep sich stuff, the sorra heaven ever myself 'id wish for!"

A loud laugh followed, and Darby having drank off a second glass of the so-much vaunted beverage, became, under its genial influence, somewhat more courageous.

"Sure myself thought," he remarked, "that you had nothin' to do here in the wide world, but to shovel coals on the fires an' keep them agoin'—and now I see that every one o' you is busy diggin' away for the bare life. May I be so bould as to ax what your worships are diggin' for?"

"Why, you ould fool! did'nt you know that the day of judgment is comin' soon, an' as there is'nt room enough for all the souls that 'ill be sent here, you see we're jist makin' the place big enough to hould them all."

Darby stood aghast on hearing this announcement.

"Arrah! do you tell me so?" he earnestly inquired. "An' will your honor plase to tell me will there be many sent here from the parish o' Killsheridan—becase that's my parish, an' I'd wish to know what'll become of the owld neighbours?"

"Tarnation to the one among them but'll be here," returned the supposed imp gravely; "not one from Jack McCarty, the rich meal-man, down to Owen Malone, the blind beggar-man."

"Och, murther in Irish!" ejaculated Darby. "Can that be thrue? an' do you tell me that Phil Mahony that I was drinkin' with in Johnny Hannigan's the night I died, that he'll be sent down here?"

"Not a doubt of it," replied his informant.

"Well, afther all!" went on Darby, communing with his own thoughts; "I wish poor Phil so well that I can't be much sorry for his comin' here, becase I know he loves a good glass, and so if they only get some way to land him here in safety, why, myself 'ill be the first to welcome him."

When our friend Micky and his companions had sufficiently enjoyed their practical joke on poor Darby, they plied that worthy disciple of Orpheus with the contents of the black bottle, until he relapsed into the state of unconsciousness in which they had found him; whereupon they placed him again in the bucket, and having hoisted him up once more into open day, deposited him with his pipes in the self-same spot wherein he had first attracted their attention. It was then drawing towards the evening, so that Darby had every chance to pass the night where he had spent the previous one. Alas! poor Darby! His "lodging was on the cold ground."

∽

It was late next morning when Darby awoke, and as it was then Sunday, the people were hurrying in crowds from every direction towards the parish chapel. Darby shook himself up, and without having any definite end or object in view, determined to follow the general example. The sight of the chapel (which name is applied in Ireland, to the temples of the Roman Catholics and Dissenters—the term Church being reserved for those of the Establishment,) recalled Darby's wandering ideas; and, entering with the multitude, he found the priest engaged in performing divine service. At its conclusion the priest turned to address his congregation. If neither endowed with grace of manner nor eloquence of speech, the clergyman of whom we speak was a man of dignified demeanor—he had a pale, thin countenance, shaded on the temples by a few scattered locks of snowy hair, and his whole appearance was rather impressive. He was heard, of course, with respectful attention, merely interrupted from time to time (as is usual in country chapels in Ireland,) by various exclamations of admiration, of fear, or of horror, as the subject varied. Now it was "Och! och! och!" then again, "Oh! wirra, wirra!" and still oftener, that singular sound heard only (at least I think so,) in an Irish congregation, and which can scarcely be expressed by written characters, being produced by striking the tongue quickly and repeatedly against the palate of the mouth. There are few sermons in which, in one portion or another, the terrors of hell are not held up as a menace before the unrepentant sinner, and the priest in question having found it necessary to enlarge on the subject, concluded by saying:

"Oh! my brethren! have ever before your eyes the fear of that place of great torment, where there is nought but 'weeping and wailing, and gnashing of teeth'—where—"

He was here interrupted by a voice from the body of the church.

"Jist stop there now, Father Felix! for you've gone far enough. Now I'm listenin' to you off an' on these twenty years, an' I often had my doubts about what you tould us about heaven an' hell, an' all them things, but now I know you're not sayin' the thing that's true, becase I'm only jist come from the place below, an' I tell you to your face that I never was betther thrated in my life. Divil a dacenter set o' people ever I seen than the very same divils—faith they thrated myself like a lord. So, if you were the priest over again, you should mention them with respect, for it's myself can tell you that they desarve it. An' another thing, Father Felix! I wish you may have no worse luck than to go there when you die!—and so, the back of my hand to you, for I'm entirely ashamed of you, for backbitin' the dacent people in the low counthry."

Whereupon honest Darby (for it was himself,) marched off with a most majestic air, leaving priest and people alike bewildered, but one and all under the impression that the poor piper had lost his senses.

That worthy individual, however, if crazed he was, had at least "method in his madness"—for on leaving the chapel, he proceeded to take his station on a high wall, so as to command the attention of all who should pass. He had not been long on his "airy perch," when the congregation began to issue from the church, and as all were alike desirous to hear still more of Darby's ravings, as they deemed them, he had, in the course of a few minutes, a great part of the population of the parish assembled as his auditors.

Silence prevailed for a few minutes, during which the people awaited Darby's address, while he, on his part, was leisurely engaged in looking out amongst the crowd for some particular person. At length a voice called out:

"Arrah then, Darby *a-hagur*, tell us what news from the place we won't mention?—you know it yourself."

"Musha, then boys! but it's myself has the great news entirely for yees all. Sure the day o' judgment is close at hand, an' becase the place below was too confined for all that's expected there, why they're all hard at work makin' room for the company."

"Musha no, then, Darby! is that thrue?"

"Faix it is every word thrue as thruth, an' sure they tould me below there, that the sorra a man, woman, or child, in the whole parish, but what 'ill be sent down. Now maybe yees think this bad news, but I can tell you that it 'ill be the blest an' happy day that they'll let you in, for onst yees get there, yees 'ill never want a good glass or a male's mate."

"It's thrue for you, Darby *astore*," returned a wag in the crowd. "The good glass or the good male's mate 'ill be but little consarn to us."

"Arrah then, Paddy Phillips, sure I know well enough what you mane with your jibin', an' that's all you're good for, sure the world an' Garrett Reilly knows that.* An' in troth it's a pity sich a lazy good for nothin' fellow as you, 'id be sent to sich a dacent place, but I suppose it can't be

---

* A by-word in some parts of Ireland. [Author's note.]

helped. But did any o' yees see Phil Mahony, or was he at mass the day?"

An answer was returned in the negative, when Darby descended at once from his elevated position to go in search of his friend, leaving the assembled crowd in roars of laughter, for by this time the true version of the story had become known by means of some of the miners who had chanced to be present. It was long, however, before honest Darby could be persuaded that it was in the mine he had been, and even then, he was wont to say with a shrug of the shoulders:

"Troth an' more's the pity that it wasn't in hell I was, for that 'id be a far betther place than Father Felix's hell."

Poor Darby! he has long since "crossed that bourne whence no traveller returns;" but of his *second* journey to the world of spirits no revelations have reached us, so that, none can say whether his notions of the happiness of a future state have or have not been realized. Alas! the times when such doings were practicable in Ireland, have now almost passed away, and yet increase of knowledge has brought but small increase of happiness or prosperity.

∽

Literary Garland (November 1847), 504–506.

Harriet Vaughan Cheney (1796–1889)

THE EMIGRANTS (1850)

Born in Brighton, Massachusetts, the daughter of writer
Hannah Webster Foster and Unitarian clergyman John
Foster, Harriet Cheney inherited intellectual legacies from
both parents: she was to become an adherent of the Unitarian
Church of Montreal, making a moral commitment evident
in her fiction, and she was to emulate the literary pursuits of
her mother, author of an early American novel, *The Coquette;
or, The History of Eliza Wharton* (1797). Harriet and her
older sister Eliza Cushing (see page 15) early collaborated on
The Sunday School or Village Sketches (1820), pious stories for
children. The Foster family had business and personal ties
with Montreal, where Harriet married hardware merchant
Edward Cheney in 1830. Cheney spent much of the rest of
her life in Montreal, writing, mothering four children and
ultimately dying there on 14 May 1889. Literary historian
Mary Lu MacDonald tells us that, during her career,
Cheney published four novels with a Boston publisher,
among them, *The Rivals of Acadia, an Old Story of the New
World* (1827).

As "H.V.C.," moreover, Cheney was a staple
contributor of stories to Montreal's *Literary Garland*,
which favoured the genteel and moralistic, and was given
to featuring instructive stories of love and loss, often in a
society setting. In company with her sister, Cheney founded
and edited an early periodical, *The Snow Drop* (1847–1852),
Canada's first children's magazine, which provided young
girls with instruction and amusement through stories,
history, games, and nature lessons, all aimed at "progress
and instruction."

Cheney's religious nature infuses her fiction.
So strong were her ideas about fiction that in 1850
she published a sketch in the *Literary Garland*, "Early
Authorship," full of precepts for the eager young female

author. Aspiring young girls possessed by "the scribbling mania" were cautioned to be consistent and realistic in plots and settings and to eschew stimulating "the diseased appetite for novelty and excitement." Rather, the female writer was to write polished and plausible fiction for magazines whose aim was "to elevate the popular taste, and give an intellectual and high moral tone to the community."

"The Emigrants" is typical of Cheney's fiction in its interest in historical event; other Cheney stories, such as "A Legend of the Lake" (*Literary Garland* [1851]), present a romanticized New France. By contrast, "The Emigrants" evokes the cholera epidemics in British North America in the 1830s and 1840s precipitated by the overcrowding and poor sanitation of such centres as Montreal, Kingston, Quebec City and the immigrant station of Grosse Île, venues of misery for thousands of Irish immigrants fleeing famine. Such epidemics had touched Cheney's own life: her sister's husband, a physician, died of typhus in 1846 while ministering to immigrants. The story valorizes female domestic and spiritual virtue. The narrator admonishes her women readers to take pity on the poor and unfortunate. The admonishment is a kind of forerunner of maternal feminism in Cheney's invocation of the importance of Christian charity and the early establishment of "houses of refuge" for the orphaned and indigent. The story echoes Moodie's *Roughing It in the Bush* (1852), which also touches on Irish emigration and the cholera epidemics of the period. The story's epigraph—from Thomas Gray's "Elegy in a Country Churchyard" (1750)—foreshadows its grim events. Other Cheney stories, such as "Cousin Emma" (*Literary Garland* [1850]), enjoin women's fidelity and strength.[1]

---

1. Another Montreal writer, Jessie Georgina Sime, was to pen an equally striking picture of Montreal in the grip of an epidemic. The conclusion to Sime's novel *Our Little Life* (1921) is set in the great influenza epidemic of 1918–19.

~

Suggested Reading:

Cheney, Harriet Vaughan. "Early Authorship," *Literary Garland* (May 1850), 231–234.

Gerson, Carole. "*The Snow Drop* and *The Maple Leaf*: Canada's First Periodicals for Children," *Canadian Children's Literature* 18–19 (1980), 19–23.

MacDonald, Mary Lu. "Harriet Vaughan Cheney," *Dictionary of Literary Biography*, vol. 99, 71–72.

THE EMIGRANTS

Harriet Vaughan Cheney ("H.V.C.")

> "Let not ambition mock their useful toil;
> Their homely joys, their destiny obscure,
> Nor grandeur, hear with a disdainful smile,
> The short and simple annals of the poor."
>
> [Thomas Gray,
> "Elegy in a Country Churchyard," 1750]

The eventful summer of 1832, will be long remembered by everyone who witnessed its devastation. None can forget the gloomy despondency which brooded over this fated city, when the first half suppressed rumour went abroad, that pestilence had rolled in with the tide of emigration from the mother land. None can forget the shrinking fear which paralyzed the stoutest hearts, when the truth could be no longer concealed, that cholera in its most malignant form, that dreaded and mysterious disease which had long revelled in the luxuriant East, and destroyed its thousands in the fairest portions of the civilized world, had winged its flight to this cold, distant region of the North. Neither age nor sex were exempted from the general calamity; it darkened the chamber of the wealthy, and extinguished the last earthly hopes of the poor and destitute.

The first Sabbath which succeeded the appearance of the cholera was marked by the greatest number of its victims; many an eye which welcomed the light of that sacred morning with unclouded brightness, before the midnight hour lay closed in its last sleep. The houses of public worship were unopened, for even in the presence of his Maker, man feared the dreaded encounter of the destroying angel. No sound was heard through the desolate streets, save the timid footsteps of the few whom necessity called abroad to procure medical assistance for themselves or their friends, and the heavy tread of those who carried their fellow mortals to a hasty and unhonoured burial. Hearses, often without even a solitary mourner to attend them, constantly passed and repassed the portals of the grave-yard, and the scarcely cold remains of hundreds were hurried away in carts, and thrown into one common receptacle. Night closed in, and twilight lingered in its purple loveliness, upon the mountain and the wave, and the moon looked down in brightness, and the stars sparkled in their nightly course as gloriously as if the city slumbered in serene repose, and no voice of death, no cry of lamentation, arose upon the midnight air. A few solitary individuals still flitted like shadowy forms along the silent streets, the physicians worn out with anxiety and fatigue, exhausting their art to conquer a disease which baffled their utmost skill, and the ministers of religion who were never weary nor their hearts faint in the performance of Christian duties.

Amidst the general desolation there were none, perhaps, who suffered more severely than the Emigrants. Avoided as the source of public calamity, from their privations and exposures peculiarly susceptible to the attacks of disease, the hard earnings which they had saved to bring them to a land they believed a home of freedom and abundance, consumed by harassing delays and unforeseen accidents, and unable to procure employment in a season of universal distress, they were reduced in many instances to extreme and hopeless misery. Happily for them they found among strangers, hearts to pity and hands to relieve their distress. A ripe and pleasant Autumn succeeded that desolating Summer, the city was gradually purified from contagion, and the citizens of every class returned to their customary occupations and amusements. It was only in the bereaved domestic circle, in the bleeding heart which mourned its broken ties and disappointed hopes, that the fell destroyer had left the traces of his short but frightful reign.

Among the humbler ranks who were exposed to the severest physical sufferings, the benevolent found ample scope for the exercise of their humane and charitable exertions. Many a tale of sorrow was poured into the ear which kindly listened to receive it, and those who are conversant even in a slight degree with the variety of suffering to which that class is subject, may feel an interest in the simple story of an obscure and nameless family. It is unmarked by any marvellous event or romantic incident, but it may serve to shew that the passions and emotions of human nature are the same in every condition, that the heart beats with equal truth and sincerity, beneath the tattered grey cloak of the emigrant, as under the richer garments of wealth and fashion. It may teach some to realize, that it is only by placing themselves in contact with those whom they are too apt to view merely with pity or disgust, that they can learn to regard them as their fellow creatures, and to feel that circumstances alone have made them to differ from each other.

It is indeed difficult in the squalid abodes of abject poverty, amidst the filth that disfigures and the vice which too often disgraces it, to recognize the immortal spirit which infinite goodness has implanted in every human form. But that it does exist there, however obscure or imperfect, should be a sufficient incentive to every benevolent mind to use the utmost exertion to rescue it from degradation, and render it worthy its glorious destination. Fallible man too often confounds the outward circumstances with the inward state of the mind, and is too ready to believe that vice is the certain attendant upon poverty, and that the evils of the poor are entailed by their own misconduct. The all seeing eye alone can penetrate the heart and discern the good which is concealed beneath the pressure of external evil.

HARRIET VAUGHAN CHENEY

William Dermot rented a few acres of ground in the north of Ireland, and when he welcomed his fair young bride to his neat but humble cottage, he felt that he had received a blessing which would ensure prosperity and comfort to his earthly lot. With more providence than is generally characteristic of his countrymen, he had deferred his marriage till he could command a little sum to defray the first expenses of housekeeping, and secure himself from the danger of incurring debt. Mary was gentle, modest, prudent, trained by an excellent mother in early habits of piety, industry and self denial; she had also received from her, many lessons of worldly wisdom, and more learning and mental discipline than is usual even among the better class of Irish peasantry. Their simple annals afforded no striking events for many successive years. Industry and economy presided over their little domicile, and if they sometimes found it hard to supply the wants of a rising family, patience and perseverance surmounted every difficulty, and mutual affection sweetened their daily toil. The spirit of emigration to America was at that time prevailing throughout the British dominions, and William began to feel that a new world of hope and enterprise was opened before him. All his exertions became directed to the sole purpose of conveying his family to that land of promise, where he believed the path to riches and independence was short and easily attained. Mary was less sanguine in her feelings. "We are happy and contented here" she said "and why, William, should we leave this pleasant home, to meet, we know not what, of danger and disappointment. If our bread is hardly earned our children are fast growing up to labour with us and relieve us of our burdens." "Yes," returned William; "they too will toil, and their children after them, not to increase their own stock of comfort, but to pour it into the hands of a greedy landlord, who exacts every tithe, and grinds the face of the poor to pamper his own extravagance. There we shall at least be free, and, whatever we earn, shall have no one to account to for it." Mary as usual yielded to her husband's wishes, and it was finally agreed that the coming year should be devoted to the most rigid industry and self denial, hoping they might be enabled to leave the ensuing Spring, with a comfortable outfit and a little stock laid by for the emergencies of their new situation. Sandy, a younger brother of William, had already preceded them, and his letters were cheerful and full of encouragement. He had obtained a situation as gardener in the vicinity of Montreal, and his wages at the end of the year would, he hoped, enable him to stock a small farm which he could purchase on credit, and by prudence and good management in a few years free it from incumbrance.

About the middle of April 1832, William and his family embarked at Dublin and bade a final adieu to their native country. They were accompanied by Catherine, Mary's only sister, who had early received the plighted affection of Sandy, and his promise to marry her, whenever circumstances would permit their union. The ship was crowded with emigrants although the captain had stipulated not to exceed a certain number, and in consequence, it soon became excessively uncomfortable. For a few days the weather was favorable and their progress rapid. With characteristic improvidence, the greater number lavished their small stock of provisions, determined to revel in idleness when not obliged to labour, and utterly indifferent to the representations of the more careful, that delays might impede their progress, and subject them to severe privations. A large proportion were grossly ignorant on every subject connected with their undertaking. They had been blindly urged on by the example of others, by persuasions of the interested, and in many instances, bribed by those who were anxious to relieve themselves of the burden of supporting the inmates of almshouses, and the mendicants of the streets. Numbers were soon reduced to their last morsel, and obliged to subsist on the charity of others, when they could no longer satisfy the exorbitant demands of the captain, for what he chose to furnish them from his own stores. After six tedious weeks, embittered by contention, sickness, and the loss of several lives, they gained the entrance of the noble Gulf of St. Lawrence.

HARRIET VAUGHAN CHENEY

William and his family, who had prudently econo-
mized their little stores and kept themselves aloof from the
bickerings of their fellow passengers, sat apart on the deck
enjoying the tranquillity of the scene around them. Life
seemed to revive even in the torpid and inert. The sky was
pure and transparent, and the breeze, too light to swell the
canvas, came loaded with refreshing sweetness from the distant shore. The morning sun rose gloriously from the crim-
soned waves, and at eve went down cradled in gorgeous
clouds, throwing a blaze of splendour across the lonely
islands, then just tinged with the tender verdure of early
June. Birds of various forms and plumage, whirled their
rapid flight around the vessel, and immense shoals of por-
poises bathed on the surface of the slumbering deep. The
unwieldy whales, which frequent these northern waters, displayed their clumsy gambols and spouted their briny
columns to the astonishment of all beholders and the fanci-
ful appearance of the Mirage was a source of never tiring
wonder. This singular phenomenon, which has puzzled the
wisest philosophers, seemed nothing short of enchantment
in the eyes of the ignorant and unlettered; cities, battle-
ments and castles, often floated before the vision, in all the
distinctness of reality, and then faded away like the "baseless
fabric of a dream." The cry of "Quebec, we are near
Quebec!" often passed from mouth to mouth, when they
were still many scores of leagues distant from it. As they
approached the mouth of the river, the mountains on the
north assumed a bolder and more lofty aspect, while southern shore, sprinkled with white cottages, with occasionally a
glittering church spire, rising from a circle of fresh budding
trees, presented a pleasing picture of rural comfort and
repose. There are few who do not feel some sympathy with
the beautiful in nature, though they may not view it with a
painter's eye or express it in a poet's language; and after the
dull monotony of a dull and tedious voyage even the animal
spirits exult in the prospect of recovered freedom, and the
earth seems to put on a robe of loveliness till then, unseen
or unadmired.

On arriving at Grosse Isle, the emigrants were dismayed by intelligence that the cholera had made its appearance, and that a strict quarantine was enforced on every vessel which came into the harbour. There was no evading this regulation; they were restricted to narrow limits, the healthy and robust mingled with the sick, the infected, and the dying, compelled to breathe a tainted atmosphere and subject to severe distress. Many, very many, who landed in perfect health fell victims to this unwise regulation, others found all their little means wasted away, and were compelled to throw themselves upon the charity of strangers.

William and his family, though they had suffered many privations, and much loss both of time and money, proceeded, immediately on their release, to Quebec, and from thence to Montreal. On reaching the latter place they were much disappointed to find, that Sandy had left it the preceding week. Impatient of waiting for their arrival, the Summer fast advancing, and his time unemployed, he had gone to take a survey of the country and select the best position for his future settlement. Every thing in Montreal was unfavorable to their views and wore a gloomy aspect. All business was suspended, the labouring classes found little employment, and fear and want added their countless victims to swell the rank of the destroyer. With much difficulty William found a decent shelter for his family, but his resources were greatly diminished, his hopes of immediate exertion frustrated, and it was indispensable to adopt some means for their present support. He yielded reluctantly to the necessity of leaving his family, even for a short time, under such painful circumstances, but felt obliged to follow his brother, who had left directions where he might be found, with the gentleman who had lately employed him.

Mary, whose expectations had never been so sanguine as her husband's, felt her heart die within her as she received his last embrace, and found herself alone in a world of strangers; for the first time since her marriage deprived of the protection and assistance of her husband, and with sickness and suffering abounding on every side of her. Several of their fellow lodgers fell victims to the cholera, and William's absence was prolonged, week after week, till poor Mary's spirits were almost exhausted by the agony of anxiety and suspense. The children, who had always been accustomed to fresh air and wholesome food, suffered severely from their confinement in a crowded room, in the tainted atmosphere of one of the meanest suburbs, and as their mother's scanty means became every day more precarious she saw, with a pang which a mother only can feel, their healthy looks and cheerful spirits exchanged for the pallid hues and languid motions of incipient disease, and actual want. She was at last obliged to limit their allowance to the merest necessaries of life.

Both Mary and Catherine used every endeavor to procure work of any kind to assist them in this extremity. But strangers as they were, and in a season of general alarm and distress their efforts were unavailing. At length Catherine, through the recommendation of an acquaintance, obtained some plain sewing which she finished so neatly, that she received from the lady who furnished it, the promise of constant employment. The remuneration was small, but it kept them from actual want and was gratefully received. The children sick, petulant, and unhappy, required all their mother's attention through the day, and it was not till their wearied eyes were closed in the balmy sleep that seldom deserts the couch of childhood, that Mary had leisure to sit down and assist Catherine in her labor. Their task was often protracted till past the hour of midnight, and stricken in heart, it was generally pursued in melancholy silence. The absent husband and lover were ever present to their thoughts, but they feared to increase each others misery by dwelling on the apprehensions which constantly weighed on them.

"Why," said Catherine, one evening after an unbroken silence, "why did we ever leave our dear home to come to this wretched place? we were happy there, oh why would not William be contented with his lot?"

Mary burst into a flood of tears, the first she had yet indulged,—a vision of her neat cottage, the home of her childhood, the scene of her maturer joys, rose before her eyes. She saw her children, healthy and happy, sporting before her door, and her husband, with a light heart and cheerful smile, returning from his daily labour to partake her evening meal. The recollection was too vivid, and it was many moments before she had power to reply.

"Do not Catherine," she at last said, "do not speak of past happy days, and above all do not say a word to reproach my poor William; God knows he did all for love of us, and whatever may yet betide us, no word of upbraiding shall ever pass my lips, nor a thought of unkindness find place in my heart towards him."

At that moment a sound of foot-steps ascending the stairs arrested their attention. It was unusual at that late hour, when the wearied inmates of their miserable abode were commonly buried in profound repose. Some one tapped lightly at the door, and Catherine rose to open it with a sickly sensation at her heart, believing she was called upon to assist in the last duties to some suffering fellow mortal. The next instant she was clasped in the arms of Sandy. Mary rose to welcome him, but her eyes were fixed on the still open door, expecting another and still dearer, her husband. He came not, she looked at Sandy, his haggard and altered face alarmed her, she grasped his arm with an imploring look. Her pale lips were rigid, and her tongue refused its office.

Sandy had not courage to reveal the fatal truth, but poor Mary read it in his averted looks, his tearful eyes and unbroken silence. "He is dead, dead," she murmured and sunk senseless on the floor. It was long before the unhappy wife returned to a state of consciousness. One fainting fit followed another, and before morning she became the mother of a helpless child whose feeble cries for kindness and protection were long unanswered by a thrill of maternal tenderness. Exhausted by previous suffering and continued anxiety, poor Mary had not strength to sustain this last infliction, she sank

HARRIET VAUGHAN CHENEY

into a state of complete despondence from which nothing could arouse her. She then exacted from Sandy repeated and minute accounts of her husband's illness and death, and dwelt constantly and with a melancholy interest on the painful detail. William had written twice to his wife informing her of his proceedings, but she had only received one short letter, saying he had been disappointed in meeting Sandy at the place where he expected to find him, and that he should immediately proceed to Kingston, feeling certain he awaited him there. He was still sanguine and full of hope though the journey had been a more expensive one than he anticipated, and his money was almost exhausted. Sandy, in the mean time, had selected a farm which he could purchase on easy terms and only awaited his brother's sanction to conclude the bargain. He had but twenty-five pounds to pay in ready money, and a long credit for the remainder. That sum, Sandy had saved from his years wages, and placed it in the hands of a friend, who gave him a note on interest, payable on demand. The brothers met at Kingston, and it was agreed that William should proceed to the farm and make the necessary arrangements, while Sandy returned to Montreal to procure his funds, and convey the family to their destination. But on the evening of their separation William was seized with the cholera which in a few hours terminated his existence, and Sandy, after seeing him decently interred, returned alone and disconsolate, the messenger of sad tidings to his afflicted family.

Mary's extreme illness required the most unintermitting attention and careful nursing. Catherine bore her heavy burdens with a fortitude and cheerfulness which few, so young, would have exhibited. Even from her lover she concealed the extreme misery and want to which she was often reduced. She well knew he had little to impart, but he saw enough to feel most painfully his inability to place her immediately in a more comfortable situation. The person to whom he had lent his money had left town during the prevalence of the cholera, and as that disease was now greatly abated, it was supposed he would shortly return, and

Sandy received from Catherine a promise to become his wife as soon as Mary's health allowed to her venture on a fatiguing journey. Catherine felt that her sister's life depended on a removal from her present abode, and her heart bled for the poor children, emaciated by confinement and the deprivation of proper food.

"We must all work now Catherine," said Sandy, "but with God's blessing on our labors, I hope a few years will make us comfortable and independent of the world; exercise and fresh air will soon make the little ones robust again, and they will, at least, have clean straw to lie down upon and plenty of food, though it may be of the coarsest kind." These unambitious anticipations of humble and homebred comfort, reciprocated by affectionate and confiding hearts, beguiled many a weary day of toil and self denial. But alas! they were destined never to be realized. Sandy had found occasional employment in the service of a gardener to whom he was well known, and returned home one evening, wet, exhausted and oppressed with indescribable languor which was soon succeeded by more alarming symptoms. Medical assistance was procured, but in vain. Early in the morning Catherine, at his request was summoned to attend him. She arrived only in time to receive his last blessing, and the comfortable assurance that he died at peace with God and in charity with all mankind. He was one of the last victims of the cholera.

This melancholy event aroused Mary from her state of despondence, and necessitated her to renewed exertion. With a fortitude that was natural to her, though for a time paralyzed by sickness, sorrow, and want, she returned cheerfully to the performance of her duties, and again shared the labors which had lately fallen heavily and solely on her sister. Many and bitter were the tears which they shed together as they reviewed the past, and looked forward to the hopeless future. But the truths of the Gospel which had been from childhood their rule and guide, were now their consolation and support, and the blessed assurance, "He will never leave thee nor forsake thee," fell like balm upon their

HARRIET VAUGHAN CHENEY

wounded spirits. Winter was fast approaching, the children shivered around the scanty fire, and the long nights were mostly consumed in toiling at the needle, which scarcely defrayed their small expenses and furnished them with a bare subsistence. Every article of comfort which was not indispensable, even many of their clothes, were sold, often at a great sacrifice, to pay their monthly rent, and purchase food. The lady from whom Catherine first procured employment, had been absent during the sickness, but hearing of her return she went to carry home some work which had been left with her to finish. The lady was much struck with the change in Catherine's appearance, and with great kindness enquired the cause, and her sympathy, so soothing to the wounded feelings of the poor girl, elicited a full disclosure of her situation. The next day the lady visited their cheerless abode, and her heart was wrung with compassion at the misery which she witnessed. Mary, worn to a shadow, sat over a few embers nursing her feeble infant, whose premature existence had been with difficulty prolonged, and busily employed in finishing a piece of work on which depended their precarious subsistence for another day. Three elder children were gathered around her, eagerly watching the motions of Catherine who was at that moment engaged in preparing their scanty repast. In spite of their extreme poverty there was an air of cleanliness, almost amounting to comfort, in the small and desolate apartment. The floor, the table, every article of furniture was scrupulously neat;—the children were perfectly clean, and their clothes though coarse and threadbare, were mended with the utmost neatness. Want and penury were certainly there, but without their common and most dreadful attendants, foulness, idleness, and vice. Every thing bespoke an innate purity of character, a remnant of brighter and happier days. The lady gazed upon the little ones, their hungry looks, their pale emaciated countenances, marked with the traces of early care and sorrow, and her heart was deeply touched.

Alas, the children of the poor! it is on them the weight of their parent's misery falls with tenfold force; their gay and buoyant spirits, crushed by nipping penury, early called to bear the yoke of toil, to feel the degradation of beggary, initiated in duplicity, before they can discern good from evil, outcast from society, and associated only with the vicious and profane. What but the fruits of evil can mature from such seed? Thousands of such, now swarm from the suburbs of this city, transported from the hot-beds of European vice, to become the future populace of these rising colonies. Mothers! ye who watch with tenderest solicitude the downy couches in which repose the objects of your fondest love, who fear lest the breeze of Heaven should too roughly wave the silken curtains, which shade their cherub loveliness, who with maternal rapture watch the dawning and expansion of their intellectual powers, and with Christian watchfulness guard the purity of their immortal spirits, turn your thoughts from your own happy fire-side to the contemplation of the unhappy offspring of poverty, of vice and misery, subject to the contagion of bad examples, and destitute of the means and instructions of religion, and let your aid, your influence, your example co-operate with the endeavours of active benevolence to bring these "lost lambs into the fold of Christ," to rescue them from physical suffering, from moral depravity and intellectual blindness.

In the course of a few days the situation of Mary and her family was materially altered. The sympathy of the lady who visited her was followed by marks of substantial kindness. The children were comfortably fed and clothed. Mary's little debts were paid off, and herself and Catherine enjoyed a few days respite from the incessant labour which had almost exhausted their health and spirits, and with a painful experience of her childrens sufferings, she gratefully received the pecuniary aid which was offered her, but she could not consent to remain the pensioner of individual charity. She looked to a long and dreary winter, the wants of her little ones must be provided for, her feeble infant required the most constant care and watchfulness, and her wasted strength no longer admitted of unremitting labour. Catherine's single efforts could not sustain the family, nor

HARRIET VAUGHAN CHENEY

was she able to endure the continued fatigue which for the last few weeks had harassed her. In this extremity Mary thought it no degradation to apply for admission to the "Ladies Benevolent Institution," a charitable asylum which had been recently established by a few ladies, whose compassion was excited by the great distress resulting from the cholera, and the utter destitution to which many widows and children were reduced by that awful visitation. There Mary and her children were received among the earliest inmates. Neatness and order prevailed throughout the Institution, and they had "food to eat and raiment to put on," daily instruction for the children, and the privilege of attending on religious worship. Her heart overflowed with gratitude, and health and serenity again beamed from her countenance.

Catherine was retained in the service of the lady who had so kindly assisted them, she had liberal wages, which were carefully reserved for the benefit of her sister's family, as she hoped the return of Spring would open to them some plan which would reunite them, and give them the means of earning an independent living. They had one brother, a very young man, who would gladly have accompanied them to Canada but the master to whom he was bound, till of age, refused to release him from his engagement. James had expressed his determination to follow them as soon as he was at liberty to do so, which would be early in the following Spring. Catherine had written him an account of William and Sandy's death, and she feared those melancholy events, with the general derangement and distress of the preceding season, might discourage him from the undertaking. But she was happily disappointed. He came in one of the earliest vessels which arrived at Quebec, resolved to hazard every thing to secure the comfort of his sisters. The meeting may be more easily imagined than described. Many plans were suggested for their future course of life, but the one most agreeable to the wishes of the sisters was finally adopted as also the most eligible.

James had been bred a farmer, and as the land which Sandy had selected was still untenanted, he took immediate measures to become the purchaser. Sandy had placed his pocket-book in Catherine's hand during their last interview, intimating that she would find in it a sum sufficient to defray his funeral expenses, she had opened it only once to take out the money appropriated to that purpose, and laid it sacredly aside as a memento of the dead, without a thought that it contained any thing else of value. But on relating the circumstance to James, he requested to look at it, and found the note for twenty-five pounds, which Sandy had undoubtedly intended for her use, had he had power to express his wishes. This sum which was readily obtained from the person who borrowed it, according to the original intention, was advanced to pay the first instalment on the farm. The little which James brought with him, together with Catherine's earnings defrayed the expense of removing the family, and furnished the necessary stock, and few implements of husbandry wanted. A year from their arrival in Montreal after so many painful vicissitudes and so much of actual suffering, this little family of emigrants were quietly domesticated in their new abode. It was a lonely and uncultivated spot almost in the primitive wildness of the native forest, but it was to them a shelter from the storms of life, a home where they could unite together in training the little ones to industry and virtue, and where they were secure of the necessaries of life, with a reasonable prospect of future support and independence.

"I have saved nothing from the wreck of my better fortunes" said Mary "but my mother's Bible, but this has been to me of more value than gold and silver, 'a pearl of great price,' which I shall bequeath to my children as the richest legacy which a parent could bestow. But for the holy precepts, and blessed promises it contains, I should have sunk under the weight of sorrow and poverty, and in my destitute and forlorn state, I might have yielded to despair and become, myself, an outcast from society, and left my children to beggary and its attendant vices."

The industry and good management of James and his sisters have been crowned with signal success. Four years of patient industry converted the fallow ground into fruitful fields, the seed and the harvest were multiplied, the produce of the dairy brought in exchange, all the necessaries which their simple habits required. Neatness and order prevailed in every department within doors and without, and the children repayed the care and anxiety bestowed on them, by their diligence and activity, in the performance of their allotted duties.

Let no one who may read this simple tale suppose it entirely a fiction of the imagination. It has had many a parallel in the humble annals of the Emigrants, particularly during that season of almost unequalled distress. Many have been reduced even from a higher station, and have suffered the same afflictions, want and deprivation. But few perhaps have shown the moral courage and the firm religious principle which actuated Mary and her sister, which urged them to a course of virtuous exertion, and finally raised them to respectability and comfort. As there is no human being so depraved as to be beyond the hope of mercy, so there is probably no situation in life so utterly destitute and forlorn, that it may not be improved by honest labour and persevering industry.

∽

Literary Garland (June 1850), 275–281.

May Agnes Fleming (1840–1880)

THE PHILOPENA (1860)

MY FOLLY (1863)

May Agnes Fleming, Canada's first international bestselling author, began her career at the age of fifteen when she sent a story to the *New York Mercury*, one of the most popular story papers of the time. (Papers consisting of short stories and serialized novels, published weekly or biweekly, attained great popularity in the mid-nineteenth century.) Fleming continued to write short stories and, within a few years, serialized novels, often writing for three or four papers at the same time.

Born in the Saint John area of New Brunswick on 14 November 1840, Mary Agnes Early was the daughter of Irish immigrants Mary Doherty and Bernard Early. In 1865, by then a successful novelist, she married John Fleming. Marriage and motherhood (she had four children) did not slow her career. With increasing success came increasing wealth. In 1868 she began writing solely for the Philadelphia *Saturday Night*, and in the 1870s she transferred to the widely circulated *New York Weekly*, arranging for simultaneous publication in the *Journal* (London, England), followed by hardback publication in both Great Britain and the United States. By this time she was making at least $15,000 yearly, a princely sum at that time.

Fleming was a prolific writer. Most of her novels may be termed sensation novels, designed, with their convoluted plots, melodramatic incidents, mysterious incidents, and gothic atmosphere, to keep readers in suspense from one week to the next. Her popularity is indicated by the wide sale of her novels and the continuing publication of editions many years after her death on 24 March 1880. Fleming left four children between the ages of four and twelve. She provided well for them. Some years before her death she had separated from her alcoholic husband. Her will protected her children by providing for guardians, and included a proviso preventing their father from interfering with their inheritance.

Most of Fleming's short fiction was written in the early years of her career, from 1857 to 1863. She used the pseudonym "Cousin May Carleton" for most of her fiction before 1868. By 1863, she was primarily writing serialized novels. For the most part, her short fiction is based on the romance plot. On the whole, Fleming resists the conventional happy closure with the marriage of the lovers. In stories such as "Nora; or, Love and Money," (*Sunday Mercury* [26 June 1859]), and "Maggie's Love," (*Sunday Mercury* [23 September 1860]), the young woman, deserted by her lover, remains unmarried. In "For Spite" the protagonist marries an older, ugly, but wealthy suitor whom she does not love. "Love's Young Dream," (*Sunday Mercury* [20 November 1859]) puts a different spin on the romance plot: the country girl jilts the young man who has educated her, marries his wealthy father, and becomes a worldly sophisticate; her disillusioned lover remains unmarried. On a happier note, "Ned's Wife and Mine," (*Sunday Mercury* [8 April 1860]) uses a male narrator to satirize some of the conventions of the romance plot, such as suicide by rejected lovers, while recounting two young men's unexpectedly rapid courtship and marriage, just as they are about to embark on a carefree life.

"The Philophena" (*Sunday Mercury* [7 October 1860]) is, like "Ned's Wife and Mine," a lighter story. In the pattern of Shakespeare's Beatrice and Benedict, the flirtatious young American woman enjoying the activities of a Canadian winter meets her French Canadian Benedict. The story is reminiscent of Leprohon's "My Visit to Fairview Villa" (page 189) in its tone, witty dialogue, social setting, and use of eavesdropping to further the plot. It has the added interest, unusual in a Fleming story, of a Canadian setting. Fleming's skill in dialogue is already apparent in this early story. "The philopena" (from the Greek "philo" [love] and "poena" [penalty]) refers to a game in which a man and a woman who have shared the twin kernels of a nut each try to claim a gift from the other as a forfeit at their next meeting by fulfilling certain conditions (as, in this story, by being the first to exclaim "philopena"). The game provides an effective closure for the game of love as played in this story.

Fleming's penchant for weaving in apt quotations suitable to the protagonist's situation is evident in both stories appearing here—in "The Philophena," with its quotations from Shakespeare's comedies and in "My Folly," where "Ellen Adair," a folk song of the deserted woman, provides echoes of the theme. "My Folly," which appeared in the *Sunday Mercury* (5 July 1863), recalls "The Philophena," but without the conventional romance closure. It focusses on the feelings of the narrator–protagonist, whose mocking, ironic tone is evident from the first sentence: "Everybody said it was an excellent match, and you know what everybody says must be true." The narrator explains her situation with an extended metaphor derived from a conventional romantic one: "Mr. Linden...was...a shining mark for the arrows of all my young lady friends. I, whose quiver was empty, whose bow was unbent, by some mysterious sleight of hand, a mystery to me even to this day, shot home a keen-tipped shaft, and left it quivering in the man's heart." Of the town's most eligible bachelor's marriage proposal, the protagonist comments, "...and if I gave him all he asked for—my hand (poor little sallow digit!) what more was required. Hearts were not trumps in our game of matrimony; mine beat snugly under my crimson Zouave jacket for my birds, my flowers, my books, my relative friends, and my own precious self. Mr. Linden had a place in my head—not the shadow of a corner in my heart." As well as many metaphors, the story is characterized by many witty asides.

Setting, while little described, is significant. The glowing beauty of the sunset fades as the protagonist agrees to marry the man she does not love. As her lack of feeling for him becomes increasingly evident, she notes, "How dark it is getting." In the later parallel scene, in which she recognizes that the man with whom she has unwittingly fallen in love does not love her, the sun is again setting and the blazing sky darkening, while the songs and the story she and this young man are reading illuminate the situation. Seemingly casual conversation reflects the protagonist's own position; her companion observes of women's attitude to marriage, "For one woman who marries for love, one thousand daily marry for money. They are bought and sold—precious little creatures! as regularly as they are in Circassia." With "My Folly," Fleming demonstrates her ability to write an astringent, realistic, albeit witty and humorous, story—no happy ending, no second best marriage to the wealthy and likeable fiancé, no desperate turn to streetwalking.

∽

Suggested Reading:

Fleming, May Agnes. *Lost for a Woman*. New York: Street and Smith, 1880.
McMullen, Lorraine. "May Agnes Fleming: 'I Did Nothing but Write.'" In *Silenced Sextet*. Montreal: McGill-Queen's University Press, 1993.

THE PHILOPENA

May Agnes Fleming ("Cousin May Carleton")

O
f all the inveterate flirts it ever was my good fortune
to come across, my friend Hessie Dorset was the
worst. From morning, till night that girl did nothing
but flirt, flirt, flirt—breaking hearts with as much ease as I
broke the point out of my pen just this minute. All was fish
that came to her net, and never was there such an invincible
"fisher of men" since the world began as was she. And it was
not that she was so wonderfully handsome, either, being
only a tall, dark-eyed, dark-haired, bright faced girl; but
there was a sort of witchery about her that no one could
withstand—a witchery that made women her slaves as well
as men, when she chose to "try it on," to use her own
expression, which, with the former, she seldom thought it
worth the trouble of doing. I dare say, my dear friend and
reader, you have come across people before now who possessed this sort of charm, subtle, but irresistible. Where it
lay, or what it consisted of, I know not; but, certain it is, she
charmed all she chose, myself among the number; and
though I cannot say I exactly approved of her conduct at all
times, yet we were fast friends, and I had the most
unbounded sort of admiration for her. Hessie, on her part,
had a careless, laughing-liking for me, and used to listen
with the best possible grace to the lectures I thought it my
duty to read to her when she became too outrageous, on the
enormity of her conduct and the beauty of behaving prettily;
but as she generally fell asleep before I got properly started,

I cannot say that these lectures [had any effect. A few years ago] Hessie and I went up to Canada to visit a mutual friend, and spend a few weeks in the charming little village of Sancta Inda. Very good times we had, sleighing, and skating, and snow-balling, and attending parties, and a good many adventures we met with that eventful winter of '58, one among others in which a lot of hungry wolves came pretty near finishing me; but wolves were an every-day story in Sancta Inda, so nobody minded that much.

Our friend Irene had a brother, delightfully handsome, as most brothers are; and, of course, before Hessie got off her things, the first evening, she made a dead set at him, and succeeded, as usual, in completely bewildering the poor fellow. Then, having finished him, she began in due rotation with each gentleman she got acquainted with; and, alas! for all the broken hearts in Sancta Inda! The French Canadian demoiselles were going distracted, and no wonder—every one of their lovers were wheedled away from their allegiance by the wicked, dark-eyed sprite, whose radiant smiles and dark, witching glances did such killing execution among her majesty's subjects. It was really shameful, her conduct, and I felt properly indignant; so one night, when we were alone together in the room we occupied in common, I took it upon myself to administer a dose of severely-moral advice, which I had got by heart, hearing my mother lecture me.

"Now, Hessie, you know your conduct is abominable," said I, as I sat down to put my hair in curl papers before going to bed, "to be coquetting with three gentlemen at once—scandalous! I wonder you ain't ashamed—I am! Why the mischief don't you go and fall in love with one of them, and have done with such sinful goings on at once?"

"Yaw-w-w," said Hessie, who was stretched on a lounge, looking up with a yawn; "that's very pretty, dear, won't you say it again?"

"Disgracing yourself!" pursued I, tearing the comb frantically through my hair; "to say nothing of me, your friend—a young lady who, as everybody knows, is most frightfully proper in her conduct! Where do you expect to go to, Hessie Dorset, if you keep on like this, say?"

"To Heaven—oh, yaw-w-w! how sleepy I am. Don't bother me now, like a dear good girl, but let me get to sleep," said Hessie, turning over.

"Sleep! I wonder how you can sleep with such a guilty conscience! It's wonderful the amount of crime some people can rest easy under! How dare you go and take Lota What's-her-name De Brisay's beau away from her this evening, and leave her weeping all alone in the corner, like an old Shanghai hen with the distemper?"

"Oh, well you know I was tired of all the rest, and I wanted him for a change; and then that little Monsieur Landrey did talk so much that he loved me to death, and Miss Lota's beau looked most delightfully stupid, so I took him for a safety-valve all the rest of the evening. I don't want him, I'm sure—she's welcome to him again as fast as ever she likes."

"Yes, that's all very fine; but the fellow's been fool enough to fall in love with your wretched self, and how are you going to cure him of that?"

"Really, now! has he? I did not give him credit for so much good taste as that. Well, a little dignified letting alone will cure him, I daresay, as it has done others. I don't think his love is more than skin deep and won't seriously injure him. Now don't scold, there's a darling, and I will tell you something ever so nice. The greatest secret—O my!"

"You may keep your secrets, Hessie Dorset, I don't want to hear them. I'm real angry with you—I am so!"

"Oh, now don't get so awfully serious, like a dear little duck! I would kiss you to make up friends, only it's too much trouble to get up now and go all the way over there to do it. Fancy I have given you a chaste salute, and let us smoke the pipe of peace for this night at least. I won't tell you the secret unless you promise, for I positively can't stand any more scolding to-night. I'll be bursting into tears, or falling insensible, or committing some other atrocity, if you don't leave me alone!"

"Well, you know it's all for your good, and you need it badly enough," said I, severely, yet in a mollified tone, too;

for, to tell the true reason, I did want to know the secret. "You ought to be thankful to me for keeping you from flying off the handle altogether, instead of being ungrateful and disagreeable, as you are."

"Well, there! You're a good little thing, and mean well, and would make your mark in the Scalpem-all Indian mission; but I'll imagine all you would say, and so spare you the trouble. And now for the secret. Irene has sent for her cousin—that handsome one you heard her speak of—and he will be here to night; think of that."

"Well, and what of it? A great secret that is, I must say! Handsome men are not such wonderfully scarce articles as all that. There is corn in Egypt without his coming, Miss Dorset."

"Oh, yes, I know; but all the other ears must bow to this. He's as handsome as an angel, and handsomer. Oh, he is splendid—something sublime, you know!"

"Really! Pray, what vision revealed that to you? You never saw him."

"Well, I won't die and be so. And though I have not seen him, I have his likeness; I stole it from Irene. Look here."

She handed me an ambrotype in an elegant case, and I took it to the light to look. Such a face of perfect manly beauty as I beheld—such waves of clustering, curling hair— such splendid eyes, that seemed looking at me with a gaze so full of wicked, sly amusement, that I laughed as I handed it back.

"Isn't he beautiful—isn't he charming?" exclaimed Hessie, enthusiastically.

"Yes, so much so that I am ready to wager your flinty heart will go like a whiff of down, the moment you meet this Canadian Apollo. Heaven grant it may, and that he may jilt you."

"You malicious sinner! go to bed," said Hessie, jumping up and blowing out the light. "I shan't submit to such unchristian treatment. Me fall in love, indeed! I scorn the insinuation. I'm invulnerable—quite invulnerable to the tender passion!"

MAY AGNES FLEMING

"Don't be too sure," said I. "Remember what happened the queen of the fairies:

'When with that moment, so it come to pass,
Titania waked, and straightway loved an—ass.'

And so that her fate may be yours, I most devoutly pray. All handsome men are stupid, so—"

Before I could finish my spiteful little speech, the door was unceremoniously opened, and some one came in. Both Hessie and I looked up in astonishment, for no one entered our room but Irene and the housemaid, and neither of them without knocking. But our astonishment increased when we perceived, even in the darkness, that it was the tall figure of a man, who, in the coolest and most *nonchalant* manner, advanced, and flung himself into a chair, elevated his continuations on the back of another, thrust his hands in the pockets of that dreadful garment all men wear, but which is so atrocious that no name can be given to it in any language, tipped back his chair, and made himself completely at home.

For a moment, Hessie and I were astounded, and then the truth burst simultaneously on us at once. This must be Irene's handsome cousin, who had mistaken his room, and entered ours, as it was next to the one he was to occupy with her brother. In the darkness, he could not see me, as I was up in a corner, but turning his head, he caught the outline of Hessie's form, as she lay on the lounge, under the window.

"Oh, you're there, Phil, are you?" said he, in a clear, French-accented voice. "I was looking for you before I came up. What a pity I came too late to see this fascinating, bewitching, bewildering man-killer of yours, eh? Wasn't it?"

Hessie's reply was a loud yawn.

"Never mind, though—'better late than never.' I'll behold this incomparable vision of beauty to-morrow. Irene tells me I'm in danger; but, by Jove! if I don't let this Queen of Hearts see that two can play at that game, it won't be for want of trying. How do you think I'll succeed?"

"Don't know," replied Hessie, who was a capital mimic, imitating Phil's tone to the life. "You are handsome enough to succeed. No girl could resist you."

"Bother!" said the young gentleman, courteously, as he pulled out a cigar. "Such stuff! But I'll try, anyhow, and if I fail—"

"For the inimitable Alf Rowe there is no such word as fail."

"Why, Phil, what the dickens!—you haven't been drinking, have you?" said Mr. Rowe, wheeling round.

"No, of course I haven't," said Hessie, while I stuffed my handkerchief in my mouth in an uncontrollable fit of laughter.

"Because," said Mr. Rowe, "I can't stand too much of that sort of thing, you know; it's like spumtic soup—a very little goes a long way; and the manner in which I'm blushing [is...] appalling. How long is this Miss—Miss Corset—Dorset—what's her name?—going to stay?"

"That depends on you, a good deal."

"On me? Get out!"

"I'd rather be excused, this cold night. It does depend on you. She's going to fall in love with you, you know."

"I wish her the joy of it! Very sensible it will be of her, I must say."

"Will you return the compliment?"

"Most decidedly; do you think I would be impolite enough to refuse so slight a favor to any young lady who might desire it? Love her? You'd better believe it; and as that young woman in 'The Two Gentlemen of Verona' says:

"'We'll seal the bargain with a holy kiss.'"

"Very kind of you, indeed," said Hessie, in a voice that was slightly tremulous, while I shook so with inward laughter, that I was in danger every minute of tumbling off my seat; "but perhaps the young lady may not approve of such summary proceedings. Young ladies do not, as a general thing, I am given to understand."

"Don't you believe it—all a slander; most obliging little creatures in the world when properly managed. Why don't you have a light here?—how is a fellow to get to bed in the dark?"

118

"The lamp went out," said Hessie, in a voice which still shook a little in her efforts to be serious; "don't need one, though, when we have the light of your eyes."

"Ugh!" said Mr. Rowe, in a tone of disgust; "that's enough—I can't stand any more of that at any price. And now to dream of my future enslaver; so here goes to turn in," said the young gentleman, getting leisurely up.

I could keep in no longer, but rolled off my seat in a perfect convulsion of laughter, and finally screamed.

"Eh," said Mr. Rowe, turning sharply round; "why, what the—"

"Hush; don't mention the name of your patron saint to ears polite, my dear sis," said Hessie, composedly getting up; "it means you have made a slight mistake, and entered the room of Miss Corset—Dorset What's-her-name, instead of your cousin Phil's. Now, if you are agreeable, we will dispense with your society for the present; and both myself and my young friend there, whose profane and indecorous laughter I beg you will excuse, will have great pleasure of renewing our acquaintance in the morning. Good night, Mr. Rowe."

I am rather shocked by profanity as a general thing; but the tone of unutterable horror in which Mr. Rowe exclaimed, under his breath, "Oh, ginger!" set me off worse than before, and I fairly shouted with laughter. Even Hessie had to laugh; but the next moment she was composed again.

"I think I said good-night, sis. Allow me to repeat it—good-night, Mr. Rowe."

"Oh, thunder!" ejaculated the astounded Mr. Rowe.

And, like an arrow from a bow, off he shot without another word.

Hessie flung herself on the sofa, and laughed and laughed, and laughed again, until I began seriously to fear she would rupture an artery at last.

"Oh, dear! If that is not too good," said Hessie, at last, as soon as she could speak for laughter. "What an opening to an acquaintance. Oh, I'll certainly kill myself laughing."

"You certainly will, if you keep on," said I, drying my own eyes and getting up. "Oh, when will I forget his tone of horror when he discovered who it was?"

And overcome by the ludicrous recollections, we both fell into another paroxysm, that lasted fully half an hour.

Both Hessie and I took unusual pains with our toilet the next morning, Hessie particularly, being bound for conquest at all hazards. As we entered the breakfast parlor, Irene met us with sparkling eyes.

"Oh, girls, guess whose come?" she exclaimed.

"Our cousin Alf Rowe, of course," said Hessie, composedly.

"Yes—that very same identical Christian gentleman. Look out for your heart, Hessie, while he's here, for I honestly tell you he is irresistible."

"That's so," said an unexpected voice.

And Mr. Alf Rowe, himself handsome and elegant, and unexceptionably dressed, lounged in with the coolest air imaginable.

"Eavesdropping," said Irene, holding up her finger reprovingly, while Hessie's color perceptibly rose under the gaze of his dark, handsome eyes.

Of his last night's *contretemps* not the faintest trace remained. There he was, bowing gallantly when presented, and looking as cool and self-possessed as though he and Hessie had never exchanged a word in their lives, or enjoyed a nocturnal *tête à tête* in a chamber. I wanted to laugh, and did, if I don't mistake, while he and Hessie, sitting side by side at table, were soon deep in the mysteries of a most splendid flirtation.

From that day, matters progressed beautifully. Morning, noon, and night, those two were together; but still nothing came of it—that was the only drawback to Hessie's perfect felicity. I saw she had got deeper entangled than in all her flirtations she had ever done before. She really liked him with all her heart; but Master Alf seemed quite unconscious of it, and apparently flirted just for the love of flirting. The tables were turning on Hessie with a vengeance; and if the truth must be told, my private conviction was, that it served her just exactly right.

"Well, Hessie, our visit ends the day after to-morrow, and you have not yet subdued our fascinating friend, Alf Rowe, as far as I can see. How is it, Hess? It will never do for so experienced a general to lose the field at last," said I, one night.

Hessie colored, and turned impatiently away.

"What was that you and he were up to in that corner, just before we came away?"

"Nothing much, *ma belle*. We were eating almonds, and he found a twin nut, and challenged me for a philopena the next time we met—that's all."

"Oh! I thought perhaps he was proposing."

"No, that's the worst of it—he won't propose, and I can't make him, all I can do. Heigho! what a charming fellow he is!" And she turned her laughing eyes on me, and sang:

"I've sung him love-sonnets by dozens,
    I've worked him both slippers and hose,
And we've walked out by moonlight together,
    Yet he never attempts to propose.
You really must ask his intentions,
    Or some other beau I must find;
For indeed I won't tarry much longer
    For one who can't make up his mind."

"Would you marry him, if he were to propose, Hessie?" said I, looking at her thoughtfully.

"Me marry!—the notion!" said Hessie, laughing, yet with a crimsoning cheek.

"Oh, I see! What a thing retribution is, Hess! Here you are, after breaking Heaven knows how many hearts, caught at last by one who wouldn't give a snap for you. Well, well, the ways of Providence are inscrutable!"

"Mabel, you're a goose! hold your tongue!" said Hessie, angrily, as she turned away. "Oh, there's Mr. Rowe himself. Now, keep cool, and I'll go behind him and sing out 'philopena.'"

But Hessie was rather late. Mr. Rowe suddenly turned away, and entered the hall before she could reach him; and Irene called to her to come and look at some fragrant white chrysanthemums, at the same moment. As Hessie, with her back to the door, bent over them, Mr. Rowe re-entered; and coming up behind her suddenly, whispered the magic word —"*Philopena!*"

"Now, if that's not too bad!" said Hessie, springing back in her disappointment. "I was so sure of getting it, and making you give me something pretty; and now, to think I've lost it!"

"What did you expect me to give you?"

"Oh, anything nice—I didn't much care what."

"A wide margin. And now, what does your ladyship intend to give me?"

"Really, I haven't the slightest idea, unless you'll take a stick of candy."

"No, I'd rather be excused. Candy is all very well in its way; but my ambition soars higher, just now. I want something else."

"Well, you will want it, I guess; for I've nothing to give you."

"Allow me to contradict you, Miss Hessie—you have!"

"Indeed! What is it?"

"Yourself!"

Hessie's face flushed, and her eyes fell. One of Mr. Rowe's arms got inextricably entangled around her waist, and he bent his handsome head till it touched hers, and softly whispered:

"Come, Hessie, say you will redeem your philopena. I love the gift I ask so well, that if you refuse, I have fully made up my mind to be wretched for life. *Dear* Hessie—"

But there, I guess that's enough, reader. There was a wedding in Sancta Inda, not long after that, and the Yankee girl Hessie has since been a subject of her most gracious majesty, and has never flirted with anybody since.

And so you see what came of a philopena.

༅

New York *Sunday Mercury* (7 October 1860), 2.

MY FOLLY

May Agnes Fleming ("Cousin May Carleton")

verybody said it was an excellent match, and you know
what everybody says must be true. I wasn't so sure
about the matter myself, but then Mr. Linden—I never
got beyond calling him Mr. Linden—was young, not bad-
looking, rich, clever, courted, and a shining mark for the
arrows of all my young lady friends. I, whose quiver was
empty, whose bow was unbent, by some mysterious sleight
of hand, a mystery to me even to this day, shot home a keen-
tipped shaft, and left it quivering in the man's heart. He told
me so one evening when I was standing in the parlor window, watching the shadows of sunset come and go on the
velvet sward of the lawn, and the dying day passing forever
in a cloud of purple and crimson glory, and I opened my
eyes very wide in amaze:

"I love you, Marian. Will you be my wife?"

Frank, honest-hearted, plain-spoken Felix Linden.
What know he of romantic phraseology or flowery speech! I
am sure I did not blush. I know I felt white, startled, but a
little elate and triumphant. He had said the same words
twice, and yet I had not answered. How very still the room
was! I could hear the ticking of my watch at my girdle—the
beating of my heart. I could see the golden lances of the
sunset shooting in and out through the green gloom of the
chestnut trees; see the billowy clouds of snow, and gold, and
azure ebbing and flowing in the summer sky, but my voice
was for once completely startled away. The deep tones of

Mr. Linden, towering beside me like a modern Hercules, sounded in my ear for the third time.

"Marian—Miss Everton, will you not speak? One word, if nothing else—yes, or no?"

"Yes."

I had said it. I knew I did. Loving him not one whit—but then I had reached the mature age of twenty-one without loving anybody, and had been told a thousand times by my gushing young lady friends that I was heartless—I had, nevertheless, promised to be his wife. True, he had not asked me for love. The man wanted a wife; and of all women in the world, had taken it into his head to raise me to that honor; and if I gave him all he asked for—my hand (poor little sallow digit!) what more was required. Hearts were not trumps in our game of matrimony; mine beat snugly under my crimson Zouave jacket for my birds, my flowers, my books, my relative friends, and my own precious self. Mr. Linden had a place in my head—not the shadow of a corner in my heart. I knew I should never again, in all likelihood, have half so good an offer; and did there ever exist a girl in this world who, at the age of one-and-twenty, did not want to be married? Visions of white satin, Honiton lace, bridal veils, white gloves, kisses, orange blossoms, and bride cake floated deliciously before my mind's eyes, blotting out the radiant sky, the waving trees, the shadows lying long and dark on the grass, and splendidly in the background rose a brown-stone mansion, rosewood furniture, velvet carpets, lovely china, and silver, a barouche, and even a French maid, perhaps. O! it was charming; and when Mr. Linden caught my hand—the price of all this magnificence—and raised it to his lips, I made not the slightest effort to draw it away. I even looked at him from under my drooping lashes, and thought him almost handsome—certainly gentlemanly and distinguished-looking.

"Dear little hand!" said he, still holding it fast. "Dear Marian, you have made me the happiest of men."

"Do they all say that, I wonder?" thought I. "Is it part of the formula? or is he in earnest? If so, how very easily made happy some people are!" But aloud I only said, quietly —for my first disturbance was calmly passing away: "This is all very sudden, Mr. Linden, and very unexpected. I am sure I never dreamt of such a thing in my life!"

A smile, half-amused, half-mischievous, came over his sunburned face.

"I think it is to that very thing you owe it! All the other girls made—not to put too fine a point on it—love to me, knowing I wanted a wife. I did want a wife; but I wanted to make the love too; so the young lady who stood aloof, eyed me with cool indifference, and let the world slide, I found was just the girl for me. Dear Marian, I love you very much, and the whole business of my life will be to make you happy. Are you sure you love me?"

This was a poser. I was very sure I did not love him in the least; but it would never do to say so to the best match in the town; so I cleared my throat, and feeling dreadfully guilty and hypocritical, murmured: "Yes!"

Once more my hand was kissed. I did not mind that; but I quivered and shrank at the idea of any closer caress. I might have spared myself the trouble. Felix Linden was no impulsive, headlong, demonstrative lover; he took to love-making as coolly as he did to money-making, and was about as enthusiastic over one as the other. I drew my hand quietly away, and we both stood silent for a long time, looking out of the window. Sunset burned itself; twilight, gray, mystic, and solemn, rose up, crowned with the evening star; the breeze rustled the leaves of the chestnuts, and the grass lay all in dark shadow alike.

At last.

"Does papa know?" I asked.

"He does—I spoke to him first."

I bit my lip, and tapped the carpet impatiently with my foot. After all, though, what did it matter, first, or last? It was all the same in Greek, and Mr. Linden spoke as if he took it to be quite a matter of course.

"You have his sanction then, I suppose?"

"Most undoubtedly; and that of your poor mother, too."

A slight pause; then Mr. Linden spoke again: "Shakespeare was wrong for once—our course of true love is going to run smooth, Marian!"

"Dreadfully smooth, I am afraid; and I like romance so much! What will all the girls say?"

"What, indeed! I fancy you will take the town by surprise!"

"You will postpone your journey to the country now, I suppose? Your mother tells me you intended starting next week."

"Yes; and why should I postpone it?"

"How can you ask such a question after what has just passed?"

"Very easily; a month, more or less, is not much in a lifetime, and when I make up my mind to go anywhere, I hate to be disappointed!"

Even Mr. Linden's admirable *sang froid* could not prevent him looking a little disconcerted at this cool speech; but, like the sensible man he was, feeling quite sure of his prize, he recovered his composure instantly.

"Well, if it will afford you any pleasure, of course, I shall not say a word to oppose it. As you say, a month more or less will make no great difference, and we can write to each other very often. How soon will you start?"

"Next week, as I intended, my friend. Mrs. Gordon expects me on Thursday."

"And you will write to me as soon as you get there?"

"O, of course!"

"Meantime, I shall be very busy preparing for our marriage. What do you say to its taking place in September?"

"June, July, August, September," said I, counting on my fingers; "four months. Well, if papa and mamma are willing, I think I can get ready by that time. How dark it is getting! I think we had better go down to the sitting room. The rest are there."

So we went down together to the lighted family-room, where the curtains were drawn, the lamp lighted, and the family conclave gathered; and then mamma kissed me, and papa smiled blandly, and my sisters and brothers followed the paternal example, and Mr. Linden drew an engagement-ring out of his vest-pocket, and slipped it on my finger.

"Until I replace [it] with a plain gold one," he whispered. And I looked down at it, wondering if that glittering circlet bound me to this man—almost a stranger to me—for life.

That night I sat at my window, trying to read that unreadable riddle, a woman's heart. Though the heart in question was my own, I failed most signally. I had heard of love, I had read of love, I had dreamt, as all girls do; but, except fleeting fancies, short-lived as rainbows in an April sky, I knew nothing of it. "Yes," I said to the heart that puzzled me, as I laid my cheek on the pillow, "I will marry Mr. Linden, and try and be as good all the rest of my life as I know how. Love is very pretty to read about in stories and poems, but people must have sense, and—." I dropped asleep, and never woke till morning.

Monday came, and I was off. Mr. Linden attended me to the cars, shook hands with me as the last bell rang, told me to be sure and write soon, and then I was flying through the air on the wings of steam, absorbed in "No Name," and never casting one backward thought. All day long I sat and read; and just as the twilight was growing gray in the west, and I was following the fortunes of Magdalen, in the old house on the marsh, the train reached its terminus, and I was at my journey's end.

Of course, my old school-friend, Nettie, Mrs. Gordon, was waiting for me; and, of course, the usual amount of kissing and questioning was gone through, and then we were driving along the pleasant country-road, and I was listening to the birds singing, and inhaling the odor of the lilac trees that skirted it, and telling her all about my new engagement. Nettie was delighted, and told me, in return, how happy she was with her Edward, and what a perfect angel baby was, and what a number of strangers had lately visited the village, and how one gentleman, a friend of Edward's, was stopping with them for the summer.

"Such a handsome fellow, too, Marian!" Nettie said, gayly; "it is well for you you are engaged, or you would not have the faintest symptom of a heart ten minutes after seeing him. All the girls here are dying for him, and he plays Grand Mogul, and treats them with the greatest indifference. I warn you to take care!"

"Forewarned is forearmed. Besides, you know, my heart is lost and won already."

"That is the only reason why I risk the responsibility of having you both under my roof. He is a desperate flirt, Ed says, and will be sure to make love to you."

"Will he—very kind of him, really ! What is his name?"

"Richard Carstone. O, here we are at home, and there's Ed, I declare, nursing the baby. Bless its little heart!"

After Ed had been shaken hands with, and baby duly kissed and admired, Nettie and I went upstairs to the parlor. Two doors were at the opposite extremity, one of which she threw open.

"This is your room, Marian dear; the other is Mr. Carstone's *sanctum sanctorum*. Do take a peep at it; he has it fitted up with his own things; and it is more like a lady's boudoir than a gentleman's chamber."

I glanced over Kitty's shoulder rather curiously, for the character of the occupant is sure to look out in the look of the room they occupy most. Pictures, mirrors, inlaid tables, mother-of-pearl dressing-cases, cashmere dressing-gowns, velvet smoking-caps, fancy watch-pockets, pen-wipers, lovely portfolios, cigar-cases, wonderful meer-schaums, piles of books in radiant binding, papers, magazines, and even flower-pots, filled with roses and geraniums, and so on, *ad infinitum*.

"Is he a Sybarite, to sleep on rose-leaves and dine on nectar and ambrosia; or can he really eat beefsteak, and drink the coffee of common humanity?"

"My dear, these pretty nick-nacks are all presents, trophies of triumph, spoils of his victims, which he displays here in much the same spirit as a young Indian chieftain decorates his wigwam with the scalps of his enemies. O, there never was such a conqueror as our handsome Richard."

Of course, you all know how curious I was to see him; and, of course, I took more than ordinary pains with my toilet before going down to tea. I might have spared myself the trouble—he did not appear at all. "Mr. Carstone won't be here this evening, Nettie," Edward said; "he has gone to the sociable over the river."

"That's always the way," said Nettie, with an impatient shrug; "they pester his life out with invitations, one-half of which he never accepts. He might have declined this one, I think; I wanted so much to introduce him to Marian."

"All in good time, good wife. Is your heart iron clad, Miss Marian? If not, beware!"

It was late that night when I retired to my room, and I sat en sac-de-nuit long afterward, watching the starlit sky, and thinking how pleasant it was to be away from home sometimes, and how happy I meant to be while here. As I thought, the parlor-door opened, a step quick, light, firm, crossed the floor; the door of the next chamber opened, and the same quick, light tread, sounded within. Somebody was whistling, too, clear and sweet, a favorite waltz-tune of mine. Mr. Carstone, the Great Irresistible, had returned from the party, and was preparing to seek the balcony. I smiled to myself as I listened, and he changed from whistling to singing, "Rally Round the Flag, Boys," and wondered if he knew he was serenading a young lady.

"You may be very fascinating, my dear Sir," thought I, as I rose from my star-gazing and closed the curtains, "but I am not afraid. I have never been in love yet, in my life; and on the eve of matrimony, it is not likely the catastrophe will happen. What is Mr. Linden about, I wonder?" And so I fell asleep.

Next morning, at some dismally early hour, the peculiar step, and the singing and whistling, were renewed. It pleased me to listen, and I drew a fancy-picture of my next-door neighbor. Judging from his walk he must be quick and energetic; from his musical propensities, his heart must be as light as his tread. Then I heard him go out, run down stairs; and then I got up, dressed, and went down too. Nettie was just coming to call me to breakfast, and I found the table laid for two.

"Eat breakfast at seven every morning—business-hours, you know—and Mr. Carstone does the same. Tea, or coffee? Help yourself to muffins, and try that ham."

"Mr. Carstone is an early bird. He was up with the lark this morning."

"He always is, and scours the country on horseback until breakfast-hour, to the great improvement of his spirits and appetite. I told him you were here, and he was very much alarmed lest he had disturbed you by singing in his room—a fashion he always has."

"He need not fret. I am fond of music, and he sings extremely well."

"He does everything well," Nettie said. And then we rose to prepare for a shopping and sight-seeing excursion through the town.

Just before dinner we returned, and I was sitting up in the parlor, with baby in my lap, talking and laughing to the little crowing thing, when the same fleet step I heard last night ran up the stairs, three at a time, and Mr. Carstone, youthful, handsome, and stylishly dressed, stood before me. I looked up. He looked over, and doffed the Wide-Awake worn jauntily on the side of his head.

"Beg your pardon!" he said, easily. "I was not aware this room was occupied, and I was on my way to my room."

I bowed in silence, and he disappeared in his own apartment. A moment after, the parlor was vacant, and I was down stairs giving baby to her mamma, and informing that lady that I had seen the "irresistible."

"And how do you like him?" Nettie asked.

"Exceedingly. We complimented each other for fully a minute."

"What did you think of him?"

"That he is very handsome, and knows it. I hate vain men. What are you laughing at?"

For Nettie, looking at the door behind, had broke out laughing suddenly, and following her eye, I saw the object of my criticism standing there, listening coolly to every word.

"My friend, Miss Everton, Mr. Carstone," Nettie said, still laughing. "Eavesdroppers never hear any good of themselves, so you are properly punished for entering the room without making a noise. Excuse me a moment. I must go and see after Jane, and to dinner."

So Mrs. Nettie made her exit, and there I was shaking hands with Mr. Carstone, whose black eyes were laughing wickedly, and feeling dreadfully uncomfortable, as I had every right to do, after making such a speech. Very cold and dignified I tried to be at first; but no one could be that long with this Magnus Apollo of Nature! Something in his frank laugh; in his gay, boyish manner; in his bright, handsome face; in the dark splendor of his ever-laughing eyes, in the thousand and one graceful little ways he had of making himself agreeable in his tact choosing subjects, made him in reality what I had called him in sport—irresistible. Before ten minutes, we were chatting away like old friends, laughing and talking as if we had known each other ten years. And as Nettie came in, I found myself promising to drive with him through the town that afternoon, if Nettie would come, too. Of course, Nettie would come; should like it of all things, she said; and then we all went in to dinner, and I wondered no longer that his room was filled with souvenirs of his numberless conquests. A male flirt is a despicable creature! But how can a young man be blamed for being divinely handsome and irresistibly fascinating? And if girls will make love to them, what are they to do? St. Kevin threw Kathleen over the rocks, I know, and drowned her; poor thing! But the saint deserved hanging for it, and Richard Carstone had a heart like a woman. A little spoiled by flattery and petting, he was, you could see; but, then, it was as impossible to know and not like and pet him, as it would be to see a Bird of Paradise and not admire it. Well, we had our drive that afternoon, and enjoyed it; had many more drives, and enjoyed them all. There never was an acquaintance ripened as ours did; we were friends the first hour—something more than friends before we parted that night. Neither of us had anything to do; it was down in the country among green fields, waving trees, singing-birds, trout-streams, and shady lanes. There were long, lonely walks, rambles after berries, excursions for fish, sails on the river, horseback rides in the morning, moonlight walks in the evening; and always Richard and I were together, and Nettie was—in the moon, for all we knew. Mr. Linden was a sensible man—a fearfully sensible man—but he never did a more foolish thing in his life than letting his betrothed wife to the country. I had written him half a dozen brief lines, beginning: "Dear Mr. Linden," and ending, "Yours, truly," and had received quite a long and lover-like reply in return—wonderful to relate, on pink-tinted paper. It came one evening as I lay in the darkened parlor on the sofa, suffering with a nervous headache, and Richard sat beside me, reading Harper. "Katy Reitt" was the story, I remember, and he stopped as Nettie came in with the letter.

"I have brought you something to cure your headache, Marian!" she said, "here's a love-letter for you!"

She went out again, not knowing how near the truth she had stumbled, and I tore off the envelope.

"Dear Marian!" it began, in a strange hand, and I turned hastily to the signature, "Felix Linden." That was enough. Impossible to read it, then and there, with those powerful black eyes upon me; and I crumpled it up and thrust it into my pocket, and turned my face, burning now with something more than my feverish headache, down among the pillows.

"Will you not read your letter?" he said, still searching my face with his keen eyes. "I will retire!"

"No, no! it is nothing—it can wait. Go on with the story."

He half laughed.

"Then, it is not a love-letter, after all; else it would not be dismissed so carelessly. Or, perhaps you are keeping it, as I used to keep peaches at school, thinking it too good to devour at once."

"What nonsense! Do go on—I want to know whom Katie married."

"How do you know she married at all?"

"Ridiculous! Fancy the heroine of a story not marrying some one!"

"What makes women want to marry so badly, I wonder? I never knew a girl yet who did not want to be married before she was thirteen years old. Men are not so; for my part, I intend to be an old bachelor."

"Very likely! You have the look of a crusty old bachelor incipient! Will you go on with the story?"

He laughed and finished it; I was sorry when he ceased, it was so pleasant lying there and listening to his clear, low voice; for he possessed the rare accomplishment of being a good reader.

"How do you like it?" he asked.

"I am sorry Katy did not marry the author. Why did she take that rich man—I am sure she liked the other best?"

"My dear girl, for one woman who marries for love, one thousand daily marry for money. They are bought and sold—precious little creatures! as regularly as they are in Circassia. When I purchase, I think I shall go there—they have a better and more business-like way of doing it there than here in America."

"You will never need to buy a wife!" I said, the words coming involuntary from my heart. "You will find enough to love you without."

He laughed—a laugh sharp and cynical, peculiar to him when women and love were the subjects, and that I hated to hear. He threw down the magazine and began pacing up and down the floor.

"And you, Marian"—it had come quite natural to us to say Richard and Marian from the first—"for what will you marry?"

"I shall never marry!" I said, turning my hot face from him, and trying to laugh. "You will be an old bachelor, and I will be an old maid!"

"Ah—and who then is this Mr. Linden, Nettie drops hints about sometimes?"

"Who is taking Nettie's name in vain?" cried that lady putting in her head, "come down to tea, good folks, and be quick, if you please, for Ed is here, and as hungry as a bear!"

How glad I was of the respite, it did not last long, however, for as Nettie handed me my tea, she asked:

"And how did you like your love-letter, pray?"

"I have not read it."

"O, what a shame! but then I don't believe a word of it!"

"It is quite true, nevertheless," said Richard. "I saw her look at the name, then crumple it up, and put it affectionately in her pocket."

"Perhaps Miss Marian found the conversation so pleasant," began Edward, slyly; but as she saw the guilty red blood rise to my face, his wife gave him a matrimonial signal with her foot, and he stopped.

In my room after tea I read my letter. It was long; it was kind—he missed me, but he was busy preparing our new home, and happy in the knowledge of my love and truth, and anticipations of a blissful future. A step, only too well-known, too often listened for, crossed the rooms as I read— he was in his own room, humming to himself as usual, and I heard the words:

"It was with doubt and trembling
    I whispered in her ear,
O take the answer bonny bird
    That all the world may hear.

"Sing it, sing it, silver throat,
    Upon the wayside tree,
How good she is, how true she is,
    And how she loveth me!"

As I listened, I laid my head down on the table, trying to shut out all thought of him, the sound of his step, of his voice, of his presence so near, that it was thrilling through every vein and nerve of my body. In vain, in vain! every pulse in my weak heart throbbed with the truth that I loved him, loved him unsought, unasked, unloved in return. How I hated, how I despised myself! how unworthy I felt ever to look in the honest truthful face of the man I had promised to marry again.

> "How good she is, how true she is,
>   And how she loveth me."

I heard him walking up and down the parlor, humming the refrain to himself, and waiting for me to join him, according to custom. But no; I wouldn't go again, never would. I was a fool and he knew it—no need to make a greater fool of myself than I was at present. I would not lift my head, I lay there—the letter that had fully opened my eyes crushed in my hot hand, while the sunset blazed itself out in the sky, and the gloaming stole gray, solemn, and mystic into my lovely little room. At last, I heard the door open, heard him run down stairs, heard him walk down the gravel path outside, and with strange miserable inconsistency I hurried to the outer room to catch a glimpse of him as he walked away. I had my reward—a lovely young girl tripped after him, joined him a few yards off, and I saw them pass from view together, laughing and talking as if there were no one in the world but themselves. The door opened and Nettie came in.

"All alone—where is Mr. Carstone?"

"Gone out, I think!" How thankful I was it was too dark for her to see my face.

"Edward and I are going to run up to his mother's for a while—will you come?"

"I think not; my head aches a little, and I feel like staying home!"

"You are sure you won't be lonesome, though?"

"Quite sure!" And then I kissed her, and turned her out of the room, and sat down by the open window, and looked out at the flowing river, and the moon rising round and full over the distant tree-tops, and learned the lesson of life—the sad, sad, lesson of loving to my heart's content. It was nothing new, I suppose, to love one man and marry another, but my whole soul was up in revolt that night. Everything outside was holy, peaceful, and calm, within my burning heart a war was waging. I feared myself—I had trusted in my strength, and had fallen; there was nothing for it but a "masterly retreat." (O convenient phrase!) I would go home, I would be married, I would go through the world like a decent woman, and sneer at love all the rest of my life. Every one does that who is crossed in love, as the house-maids call it; why should I differ from the rest?

"Marian!"

Two hands were on my shoulders, some one had entered unheard, and was standing beside me. No need to look up; the blood that rushed to my face, the thrill that shook me, the quivering heart that responded to the voice, all told me who was there.

"Well," I said, trying to steady my mutinous voice.

"Of what are you thinking so intently?"

"Of going home!"

"Nonsense! You surely do not dream of such a thing."

"I have been here a month—the time allotted—I leave the day after to-morrow!"

Something in my voice must have convinced him I was desperately in earnest, for dead silence fell. I wanted him to go away, he must have heard and felt the loud beating of my heart. Then—

"And when is it to be?" he slowly asked.

"When is what to be?"

"Your marriage, of course!"

"Mr. Carstone!"

"It used to be Richard; no matter though, since we part the day after to-morrow. I suppose I shall receive wedding-cards, Marian. Mr. Linden is a lucky man."

"Who has been talking to you?" I cried out, half frantic with inward pain.

"A little bird—listen to that."

A serenading party were out on the river, singing as they skimmed along in the moonlight. I had heard without comprehending, but I listened now.

> "Love may come, and love may go,
>   And fly like a bird from tree to tree,
> But I will love no more no more,
>   Till Ellen Adair comes back to me."

"My Ellen Adair is leaving me," said the low voice behind, "and I shall love no more until she returns."

I knew he meant nothing by the words, but my rebellious heart would speak out.

"I shall never return!" I cried out, passionately; "I wish I had been dead before I came here at all!"

"You will go home and be married," he said, quietly, "and you do not love this man?"

What right had he to judge? I knew it well yet I asked:

"Will you despise me if I do?"

"Yes!" he said, clearly and calmly.

"Then I never shall marry him."

He took my hand and held it between both his own for a moment, then dropped it and said, softly and very kindly: "You are right, Marian!" and was gone.

I sought my room—pen and ink were there, and with a steady hand wrote:

"I have deceived you, I do not love you, I never have, and I can't be your wife! I am coming home, but I do not wish to see you—nothing can alter this decision. Inclosed you will find your ring and letter, be good enough to return mine. ...YOUR FRIEND."

Richard went with me to the cars the morning I left. For the last time I looked in those dear dark eyes, as I clung to his hand at parting.

"Be a good girl, Marian," he said, smiling, "and don't you quite forget old friends. Good-bye, don't cry so—you will make yourself sick!"

So we parted, I was at home—the angry storm of remonstrance and amazement passed. I was firm, and all was over. So I had lost the man I loved, and the man who loved me—my only consolation being that I was not the first girl who had made a fool of herself for nothing, and would not be the last.

∽

New York *Sunday Mercury* (5 July 1863), 2–3.

MAY AGNES FLEMING

Mary Eliza Herbert (1829–1872)

Light in the Darkness: A Sketch from Life (1865)

Mary Eliza Herbert, like May Agnes Fleming, and the later Alice Jones and Marshall Saunders, was a Maritime woman writer whose activities have broadened our concept of the literary history of the last century in that region beyond the activities of well-known male writers such as Thomas Haliburton, Thomas McCulloch, Bliss Carman, and Charles G.D. Roberts. As Gwendolyn Davies has observed, there was in the nineteenth-century Maritimes, particularly in Nova Scotia, a "subculture of women's literature and influence," albeit one limited by the financial and social constraints which dogged women's writing at the time.

Mary Eliza Herbert, poet, editor, and novelist, was born in Halifax in 1829, the daughter of Irish immigrants, Catherine and Nicholas Michael Herbert. Her father, a shoemaker and blacking manufacturer, was a staunch Methodist. His activity in the temperance movement was a commitment his daughter would share and infuse into her writing. Mary Eliza began to write early, possibly inspired by the example of her older half-sister Sarah (1824–1846), a poet and novelist who died young. She is eulogized in Herbert's "The Faded Blossoms," one of the prose pieces in *Flowers by the Wayside* from which "Light in the Darkness" is taken.

In 1851 Herbert founded *The Mayflower*, a periodical directed to women that invited contributions by local writers and promised its readers "the flowery fields of romance" yoked to a devotion to Methodism and temperance. *The Mayflower* struggled to survive in a literary climate not yet viable for such an enterprise, while its editor contributed much of its material herself under such pseudonyms as "M.E.H.," "M.," "H.," and "Marion," but it ceased publication in February 1852. Herbert also produced *Belinda*

Dalton; or, Scenes in the Life of a Halifax Belle (1859) and
two other novels, as well as *The Aeolian Harp* (1857), a
volume of poetry. Her life, like her sister's, was cut short by
tuberculosis in 1872. She died at "Belle Aire," her father's
home, on 15 July 1872.

In 1865, Herbert published privately—as she did
most of her work—*Flowers by the Wayside: A Miscellany of
Prose and Verse*. The underlying theme of the volume is an
admonition to "suffer and be strong": much of the work in
the volumes chronicles the struggles of women against
bereavement, drink, suffering, or death. The imagery
of flowers and of the wayside runs through much of the
work: her heroines are variously "fading flowers" or "faded
blossoms" struggling in the wayside of obscurity or on the
"alien shore" of Earth as they await their heavenly surcease.

The plot of "Light in the Darkness" draws on a
situation Herbert knew well—the woman writer's struggle
for publication and recompense. Here a valiant young girl
finds not only a publisher but a husband, and the story
passes from the realities of Herbert's life to the flowery ending of romance. Blanche is a "tender and delicate plant" who
combines intellect and domestic virtue to successfully escape
the wayside of poverty. Like "At the Harbour's Mouth," the
story in *New Women* written by Halifax writer Alice Jones
some forty years later, "Light in the Darkness" portrays the
historical reality of Maritimers seeking economic sustenance
in New England. In terms of career, the female protagonist
is psychologically freed to become the provider by the death
and illness of the males in the family, and her self-expression
and striving are buttressed by her desire to sustain the
domestic hearth, thereby welding her creative strivings to
traditional female values. This rationale is typical of the
fiction of nineteenth-century American women writers as
literary historian Mary Kelley has observed. The story is
also realistic in that access to publication in nineteenth-
century North America was usually in male hands. Ironically
the story's conclusion leaves the reader in no doubt about

Blanche's role as daughter and wife, but is ambiguous about
the continuance of her writing.

~

Suggested Reading:

Davies, Gwendolyn. "'Dearer than Her Dog': Literary
    Women in Pre-Confederation Nova Scotia." In
    Gynocritics/Gynocritiques, edited by Barbara Godard,
    111–129. Toronto: ECW Press, 1987.

Herbert, Mary Eliza. *Belinda Dalton; or, Scenes in the Life of a
    Halifax Belle*. Halifax, 1859.

Kelley, Mary. *Private Woman, Public Stage: Literary
    Domesticity in Nineteenth-Century America*.
    New York: Oxford, 1984.

Light in the Darkness: A Sketch from Life

Mary Eliza Herbert

"Watcher look up where the day-star is dawning,
   Hope in thy heart let its promise awake;
And fearless and tireless wait for the morning,
   Never a night but its morning shall break!"

"To suffer and be strong." The words almost involuntarily escaped from the lips of a pale and pensive girl who stood beside a narrow casement, watching the dusky light of the planet Mars.

A clear, cold night in autumn, very still, even here in this busy New England city, for the dwelling was situated in an obscure street in its suburbs, where the sound of rattling wheels and the bustle of more important thoroughfares seldom intruded.

The room was neatly yet far from lavishly furnished; certainly not the abode of wealth and ease, yet not wanting in appliances of comfort, as the chintz-covered couch and easy chairs seemed to testify.

A lamp stood in the centre of a crimson-covered table, still unlit, but the fire gleamed cheerfully through the room, and shone on the face of the watcher by the window, who, turning away with a sigh, drew the curtains closer together, and proceeded to arrange the table for the evening meal.

She had just finished her task when the door opened, and an elderly lady entered the apartment.

"How is Edward now, mamma?"

"He seems a little better and inclined to sleep, so I ventured to leave him for a few moments, and have come to learn what success your efforts have met with."

"Ah! dear mamma, had I met with any encouragement, I should have soon apprised you of it; but I felt so crushed, so dispirited, on my return, that I had not the heart to tell you."

"Well, dear Blanche," said the mother, cheeringly, as she marked the depression which stole over her daughter's countenance, and the tears that unbidden filled her eyes, "you must not forget our favourite motto, 'Hope on, hope ever!'"

"I know it, dear mother, but to-night hope itself seems to have taken flight. I feel so totally discouraged, so utterly helpless. I went forward this morning with such a trusting, buoyant heart, for I had carefully selected what I considered my best manuscripts, and fully anticipated meeting with some little success; but all the publishers of the periodicals to whom I applied, informed me that they had already as large a list of contributors as they required, or as their means would warrant them in securing; and so, with many courteous apologies, politely bowed me out. It is of no use, dear mamma, I plainly see I must relinquish my hopes of securing a livelihood through literature, and betake myself to a more humble sphere; but the question still remains, 'What can I do?' Tolerably expert as I am with my needle, I could scarcely hope to earn more than a precarious subsistence by it, if, indeed, I could do as much; and in every department of human industry there are so many toilers, that I fear, sometimes, there is no place for me. But I will try. To-morrow I shall endeavour to go forth again, and laying aside my foolish and too sensitive feelings, strive to find something to do, in this busy city, this great hive of human industry."

There was touching resignation as well as earnest resolve depicted on Blanche's face, as she raised her eyes and glanced at her mother.

"Dear mamma, you look pale to night. Sit down in the arm-chair by the fire, and let me make you comfortable."

Mrs. Dormer quietly acquiesced in her daughter's wishes, and sat down in the chair drawn up to the hearth, but said nothing, for her thoughts went back to the past.

Blanche, meanwhile, had seated herself on an ottoman at her feet, and almost unconsciously the mother's hand smoothed the soft shining hair of the youthful head that reclined so tenderly against her.

But her daughter's voice again broke the stillness.

"Dear mamma, how selfish I have been; my dejection I fear is contagious, for you, so generally hopeful, look desponding and unnerved."

"No, dear, do not blame yourself. My thoughts wandered for a moment to the past, but it is over now; we must brace up all our energies for present exertion. For a willing heart and willing hands there surely will something be found to do, and yet——"

Pausing she glanced at Blanche, who sat in a thoughtful attitude at her feet, gazing abstractedly into the glowing embers.

A slight almost fragile form, a pale intellectual countenance, large eyes, whose dreamy depths were radiant with tenderness and emotion—a noble head and well developed brow that spoke of lofty intellect; but the soft flashing eye, the small, pensive mouth and tremulous lips were expressive of all loving and tender feelings; a nature heroic and steadfast in adversity, but one which perhaps the sunshine of prosperity alone could ripen into perfect loveliness: such was Blanche Dormer.

Mrs. Dormer was the daughter of an intellectual and aristocratic family; but having married against their will, an inferior in position and circumstances, not in mind, one of "nature's noblemen," she had been utterly cast off by her relatives. True to her woman's nature, she but clung the more closely to him for whom she had forsaken all; and though much of privation characterized her married life, never had she cause to regret the step she had taken, for

MARY ELIZA HERBERT

love, the truest, the most devoted, was her portion, an abundant recompense, as she well knew, for every other loss sustained; and truly their quiet, humble cottage, illuminated by mutual affection, was to them an earthly Paradise.

But Death had entered their abode, and now, "a widow indeed and desolate," she had accompanied her only children, Blanche and her son Edward, to a large and wealthy city of New England, believing that here their talents might find appropriate spheres of usefulness, denied them in their native land.

But Edward had fallen ill. A slow fever wasted his strength day by day, until even the physician looked doubtful, and hinted his fears of its termination in a rapid decline.

Edward had been, since the death of his father, the support and comfort of his mother and sister; but now, stricken down by disease, to what source could they look for help?

"What could they do?" and day after day Blanche and her mother discussed, with a fainting heart, that vexing question of "ways and means," which has puzzled so many an able financier; but unhappily in their case, with little satisfactory result.

Blanche's intellect was of no mean order. From her earliest childhood she had been distinguished by an ardent love for knowledge, and her naturally fine literary taste, judiciously cultivated by parental care, had evinced itself in productions of very superior merit.

These had been penned chiefly for the gratification of her friends; but a few days since she had resolved on endeavouring to turn them to some account, and having obtained the address of the publishers of some of the principal literary periodicals, she had gone forth on the afternoon of the evening in which our sketch commences, with a tremulous heart, yet hopeful of success, to return, as our readers have already learned, dispirited and disappointed.

No wonder, then, that the mother, as she glanced at that sensitive and refined countenance, felt, sadly felt, how unfitted was so tender and delicate a plant to encounter the rude storms of life.

But quickly checking such thoughts, and remembering Him who has promised to be a "Father to the fatherless," and a "Husband to the widow," she tenderly strove to cheer and encourage Blanche, reminding her of many a gracious promise made to those who seek aright the blessing of Heaven on their earnest endeavors, until Faith and Hope sprang up afresh in each desponding heart, and striving to obey the injunction "Take no thought for the morrow," they thankfully partook of their evening's repast, and speedily resumed their watching by the couch of the beloved and patient sufferer.

∾

"Frederick," said a portly-looking, elderly gentleman, as alighting from his carriage, he entered the office of the principal proprietor and editor of —— Magazine, one which has obtained a world-wide renown.

"What now, father?" said the young man, good-humouredly, as the former presented him a roll of manuscript.

"Why, I have brought you, if I mistake not, some gems of literature, and, remember, I expect to be largely recompensed."

"Well done father! so you have turned writer at last, notwithstanding your opposition to your son engaging in so precarious a profession?"

"Not so fast, young man; not so fast. Use your eyesight a little, and tell me if that elegant penmanship resembles at all my cramped chirography. No, I assure you I have no intention of relinquishing my saddle-bags and golden fees for the pains and pleasures of authorship, for I much fear the former would far outweigh the latter."

"But where then did you obtain these?" inquired the young man, giving another glance at the roll of papers he held in his hand.

"Never mind, I will wait till I hear your opinion of them; and then, perhaps, may inform you as to their authorship; though," he added, with a quizzical smile, "I shall hardly venture to enlighten you as to the locality of her abode, lest you find it convenient very often to turn your steps in that direction."

"I must go now, for patients will be clamorous for their morning's visit, but will call again in the course of the day and learn what you think of my literary taste, and remember, I shall demand a large remuneration for bringing to light hidden genius."

The young man laughed as he bade his father "Good morning," and turned with some curiosity to peruse the manuscript so highly eulogized.

∽

"Dear Blanche, I have good news for you," said Edward, one morning, just after the Doctor's departure, as his sister entered his chamber.

"The best news, Edward, is that you are getting so much better," said Blanche, affectionately, as she handed him a refreshing beverage she had just prepared.

"Really this is delicious, Blanche. I think you would make an excellent cook. Suppose you apply," he said, with a mischievous smile, "for cooks are always in great demand, while authors are of small account."

"I am afraid it is your partiality that heightens the flavor of the draught, but to other lips it might prove less palatable. But what is this 'good news' you are so anxious to impart to me?"

"Sit down here beside me then, for I require your most patient attention. Do you remember those writings you left on the table a few mornings since?"

"Perfectly; when I came back I missed them, and would have inquired of you, but you appeared to be asleep, so I would not disturb you, and concluding that mamma had laid them aside in the desk, dismissed the matter from my mind; indeed I had forgotten all about it until now you remind me of them."

"Well, the Doctor came in a little while after you left the room that morning, and after various inquiries respecting my health, &c.,—for you know how pleasant and chatty he is,—his eye—always a sharp one—happened to light on those papers.

"I hope you have not been trying to write," he said.

"Oh no, Doctor, nothing of the kind, I assure you. Those writings are my sister's compositions, and were accidentally left on the table."

"Would you permit me to look at them?"

I gladly assented, and he glanced over several pages.

"These seem of no ordinary merit, he remarked; but I should like to peruse them at my leisure. My eldest son is the publisher of a flourishing periodical, and it is quite probable would be anxious to secure your sister's services as contributor to its columns."

"You may be sure I gladly consented to his taking the manuscript, though I resolved to say nothing to you about it, fearing to excite hopes which might be unfounded; but this morning he told me that his son, having, as he anticipated, been much delighted with the articles, intends to wait on you to-day, and engage your services, if you are willing, as a contributor to the pages of his magazine."

True to his promise, Frederick Templeman came, and satisfactory terms for both parties were arranged; but, as his father afterwards laughingly averred, he must have been endowed, at least for once in his life, with a prophet's ken, for, judging from the young man's frequent visits, an unwonted attraction drew him in that direction; nor did it cease until as his wife, transplanted to a sumptuous abode, Blanche Dormer bade adieu to the adversities which had chequered her earliest youth.

Yet were these not forgotten; they but enabled her more fully to sympathise in the sorrows of others; encouraging them, as she is wont to do, to hope on, while she points them to a higher source of trust, and, reverting to her own experience, often exclaims,—

"The light of smiles again shall fill
    The lids that overflow with tears;
And weary hours of woe and pain
    Are promises of happier years."

∽

Flowers by the Wayside: A Miscellany of Prose and Verse, 60–68.
Halifax: Citizen Office, 1865.

Rosanna Mullins Leprohon (1829–1879)

Alice Sydenham's First Ball (1849)
My Visit to Fairview Villa (1870)

A remarkable woman in many ways, Rosanna Mullins
Leprohon, daughter of anglophone parents and married
into a French Canadian family, was at home in both of
Canada's two founding cultures. Born in Montreal on
12 January 1829, she was the second of six children of
Rosanna Connolly, daughter of a Montreal school teacher
and Francis Mullins, an Irish immigrant. Rosanna began
her writing career at the age of seventeen, first publishing
poems in the *Literary Garland*, and later publishing serialized courtship stories set in upper-class English society.
Following her marriage in 1851 to Jean-Lukin Leprohon,
of an old French Canadian family, she shifted her focus to
Quebec, writing three important novels of French Canadian
life. Leprohon then turned to English Canadian life for
subject matter. She must have had a compelling desire to
write, for she was the wife of a public-spirited doctor who
took on many social responsibilities and she bore thirteen
children, of whom eight survived to adulthood.

Leprohon's first novel of French Canada, *The
Manor House of De Villerai. A Tale of Canada under the French
Dominion*, published in the *Family Herald* (1859–1860), is
set in Quebec at the time of the British conquest of New
France, and is told from a French Canadian perspective.
Leprohon alters the romance plot as her protagonist first
refuses to marry the young man to whom her parents had
engaged her in childhood unless she comes to love him. She
later rejects him completely with the words, "I hope, Gustave,
you do not share the vulgar error, that an unmarried woman
must necessarily be unhappy . . . though I may eventually
marry, if I chance to meet one of your sex whom I may learn
to love and respect, I certainly will never marry to please

them, and to escape the dreaded appelation of old maid."
Four years later, in 1864, Leprohon published *Antoinette
de Mirecourt; or, Secret Marrying and Secret Sorrowing*. Set
in Quebec immediately after the Conquest, a period of
reconciliation and adjustment, this novel concerns English-
French relations. Its preface indicates Leprohon's intention
to contribute to a specifically Canadian literature. "Canadians
should not be discouraged from endeavoring to form and
foster a literature of their own," she writes, noting in the
apologetic tone not uncommon among women writers, "If
Antoinette de Mirecourt possesses no other merit, it will, at
least, be found to have that of being essentially Canadian."
Leprohon's third novel of French Canada, *Armand Durand;
or, A Promise Fulfilled* (1868), is a study of marital relations
through two generations in rural and urban Quebec.

Throughout her work, Leprohon is concerned
with exploring human nature and problems of relationships,
as well as entertaining her readers. Her courtship stories
deal often with the maturation of young women. Her three
novels of French Canada, which bring the Quebec past to
life effectively, contribute to "an essentially Canadian literature" well before Confederation. Translated immediately
into French and at least as popular in French translation as
in English, these Quebec novels precede by a considerable
time William Kirby's *Golden Dog* and George Parker's
Seats of the Mighty.

When "Alice Sydenham's First Ball" appeared in
the *Literary Garland* in 1849, the author, then twenty years
of age, had already published two serialized novels and a
number of poems. The story shows development of two
technical devices already introduced in the early novels and
which Leprohon continued to use in later ones, the mirror
image and the overheard conversation. Touches of social
realism in the ballroom scene demonstrate the pettiness and
competitiveness of a young woman's world. The author
does not suggest real evil, but rather thoughtlessness, in the
behaviour of the social elite of Alice's world; indeed, Alice
happily accepts the possibility of entering the fray once

more. The surprising plot twist for the happy ending was typical of short stories at this time.

The plot of "My Visit to Fairview Villa," written more than twenty years later—once again hinges upon the favourite Leprohon ploy, inadvertent overhearing. "Men are such selfish, grasping, egotistical creatures!" are the words heard by the young male narrator in the first of three instances of inadvertent overhearing in the story, as he joins a group of young people holidaying at a country villa. Although increasingly attracted to Geraldine (the witty and vivacious young woman who has made this remark, and who provides him with numerous hints that she, too, is attracted to him), the young narrator manages to rebuff all overtures.

The voice is doubly ironic. The central tension lies between the narrator's actions in response to Geraldine and his thoughts and emotions, revealed to the reader. A second area of irony resides between his interpretation of Geraldine's overtures toward him, which he views as a flirtatious attempt to add another scalp to her "girdle of feminine triumphs," and the reader's appreciation that it is his determinedly defensive attitude that blinds him to her genuine attraction to him. There is a third ironic dimension: the young man twice interrupts his narrative to confess his temptation to deviate from the truth in order to embellish his story with exaggeratedly romantic accounts of his behaviour in specific situations; in fact, his supposedly truthful report of his encounters with Geraldine are inter-pretatively untrue.

The reader is entertained by witty dialogue, amusing incidents, and a surprisingly light tone with which the author gently parodies the traditional romantic plot. Although set just outside Quebec City, the activities in this comedy of manners recall traditional English stories of partying at country estates.

Suggested Reading:

Leprohon, Rosanna. *The Manor House of De Villerai*. 1859.
     Reprint. *Journal of Canadian Fiction* 34 (1982).
     _____. *Antoinette de Mirecourt; or, Secret Marrying and
     Sweet Sorrowing*. Toronto: McClelland and Stewart,
     NCL edition, 1973.
Gerson, Carole. "Three Writers of Victorian Canada." In
     Canadian Writers and their Works, vol. 1. Toronto:
     ECW Press, 1983.
McMullen, Lorraine and Elizabeth Waterston. "Rosanna
     Leprohon: At Home in Many Worlds." In *Silenced
     Sextet*. Montreal: McGill-Queen's University Press,
     1993.

Alice Sydenham's First Ball

Rosanna Mullins Leprohon

"Fill the bright goblet, spread the festive board,
Summon the gay, the noble and the fair;
Through the loud hall, in joyous concert pour'd,
Let mirth and music sound the dirge of care—
But ask not thou if happiness be there."

[Sir Walter] Scott

"Mamma, dear mama, may I not go to Mrs. Belmont's party, to-morrow night?" exclaimed Alice Sydenham, awakening from the revery, in which she had been absorbed for the previous half hour.

The lady, at whose feet she sat, laid down the book which had engrossed her attention, and replied with gentle earnestness:

"My dear child, wherefore should you wish to go? The Belmonts are people entirely out of our present sphere, and though Mrs. Belmont herself, remembering your early school girl friendship, may have extended you this invitation, her memory refreshed, as it has lately been, by meeting you some few weeks since, on your return from the country; believe me, she has no serious intention of keeping up your revived acquaintance. She knows our circumstances perfectly well; knows, that whatever our condition may at one time have been, at present we have barely the means of subsistence, and she doubtless supposes you will regard the card you have received in the same light as that in which it was sent, an unmeaning compliment. Where would a poor, portionless girl, like you, find means for procuring the splendid dress, necessary to your appearing in her fashionable and gorgeous drawing rooms?"

A long pause followed, broken at length by her young companion, who exclaimed, whilst a very perceptible cloud passed over her countenance:

"And to think, mamma,—to think, that you have a rich uncle, who is surrounded by all the luxuries of life; an uncle who possesses no other living relative, save yourself."

"True, Alice, but by his own patient, unremitting industry alone, has he amassed his wealth, and it is but just, he should dispose of it as best pleases him. I never was a favorite with him. How could I be? Brought up from earliest childhood, at a boarding school, miles from home, I never saw him but three times in my life."

"Did you ever see him after your marriage?"

"Never; your father brought me immediately to my new home, in a distant part of England, and thus effectually precluded all further intercourse. However, about a month after your poor father's death, I received a letter from him, enclosing the sum of twenty pounds, which he has regularly transmitted to us, every new year, till the last. He must be either ill, or abroad; but doubtless we will speedily receive the usual sum, for surely he cannot be so cruel as to deprive us so suddenly, without any plausible pretext, of what has for years proved our chief, I may say, our only support."

"And has he never written to you but once, mamma?"

"Never—the letter enclosing his earliest remittance was his first and last. It was a cold, formal missive, indeed, informing me, in measured terms, that he had heard of Mr. Sydenham's decease, and of my destitution, a natural consequence of wedding a young gentleman whose only possessions were a graceful address, and high lineage; concluding, by assuring me, the annuity should be continued as long as I remained deserving of it, and peremptorily forbidding my seeking further intercourse with him, either in person, or by letter."

"Well! we will talk of him no more, mamma; I am sure 'tis anything but a pleasant topic. I will sing some lively ballad, to chase away any sad thoughts which the remembrance of this open-hearted uncle of ours may have excited."

And she advanced towards the piano forte, but notwithstanding the seeming cheerfulness of her tones, there was a slight quivering of the lip, and an almost imperceptible shade of sadness in the full, soft eye, which the observant mother at once detected.

"Come here, Alice," she said, pointing to the stool her daughter had quitted.

The latter silently obeyed.

"You cannot deceive me, my child. You feel this deprivation more acutely than you are willing to avow; but Alice, Alice—this is childish," she continued, as her daughter, whose assumed fortitude suddenly deserted her, burst into tears. "You are sixteen years of age, and to weep thus, like a child, for so trivial a disappointment."

There was a kind smile, however, hovering round the mother's lips, which contradicted the seeming reproof her words conveyed.

"But 'tis my first ball," sobbed the young girl; "and you know how long and earnestly I have desired to go to one. You remember, in the winter evenings, how I have listened to you for hours, describing those at which you assisted in your youth, and the first years of your marriage; scarcely daring to indulge a hope, that I might ever have the happiness of witnessing such a scene of brilliancy; and, now, when I have the opportunity, 'tis too hard to be disappointed."

"You shall not be disappointed, my child, for you shall go; but dry up those tears. Really I would scold, only 'tis so very seldom you indulge in them. Ah! sunshine is restored," she added, as, with a radiant smile, Alice looked up into her mother's face. "Now tell me, dearest, what are the pleasures you expect at this ball? Let me see if their loss is worth weeping for."

The young girl's cheek flushed.

"Why, dear mother, novelty, gaiety, and—and—"

"Admiration," subjoined her mother, quietly.

"And admiration too," was the low-toned reply.

A pause succeeded, when Alice, suddenly raising her dark, lustrous eyes to her mother's face, exclaimed:

"And why not admiration, mamma? I have been always told I am a graceful dancer, and am I not handsome?"

"Yes, you *are* handsome," replied Mrs. Sydenham gravely, and for a moment her glance rested with earnestness on the brilliant complexion and raven tresses of her beautiful daughter. "You are handsome and graceful; yet, Alice, possessing both these qualifications, as I have often told you, you may find yourself greatly neglected, and feel very miserable at a ball."

"Let me make the experiment, mamma, dear," was the girlish rejoinder.

"You shall, dear Alice," smilingly returned Mrs. Sydenham, who, as she looked on the sparkling eyes, and sweet smile, dimpling the rose-bud mouth of her companion, felt how improbable it was, that her forebodings would be realized. "And may it prove satisfactory—but away and prepare your gay attire. You have not much time."

With the sparkling delight of a child, the young girl bounded from the room to enter on her task; and a difficult task it was indeed, for poor Alice's wardrobe contained, not one single one of the many articles indispensable to that of any ball-going young lady. However, Mrs. Sydenham ventured on the unusual extravagance of purchasing a white tarlatane dress, whilst Alice expended the little hoard, she had been for months accumulating for the purchase of new books and music, in the absolute requisites of kid gloves, shoes, flowers, &c. The important night at length arrived, and long before any of the fashionables invited had thought of entering on the duties of the toilet, Alice, her preparations nearly completed, sat in her mother's room, awaiting her new dress, which had not yet arrived—half reclining in an easy chair, her dreamy gaze fixed on the carpet, as if absorbed in contemplating its dull, faded pattern; for one long hour she sat, without proffering a word. Suddenly Mrs. Sydenham, who had been regarding her some time in silence, exclaimed:

"Why, Alice, you are unusually, wonderfully pre-occupied. What are you thinking of?"

A flood of vivid carnation instantly dyed her cheek and brow, as, after a second's hesitation, she murmured:

"Of to-night and its pleasures, dear mamma."

Ah, Alice! Alice! That answer, though partly true, was not what it should have been. The ball indeed, occupied those thoughts, but only as connected with a still more engrossing subject. It was of Henry St. John, the handsome and elegant brother of Mrs. Belmont, a being she had never met but once, and that only for a few minutes in the company of his sister; but whose high-bred politeness, and evident admiration of herself, had left a deep and durable impression on her mind. 'Twere hard to say how many aerial castles she had constructed during the hour she had sat wrapped in silent revery; but however wild or improbable they may have been, she ever finished the construction of each, by the sober, natural thought:

"I shall at least see him, for he will be there, and surely he will ask me *once* to dance."

But her mother's address dispelled, at least for the moment, her fleeting visions, and after replying to her question, she suddenly remembered that her dress, that dress whose vast importance she alone could thoroughly appreciate, had not yet come home. Looking at the timepiece, however, she saw it was still early, and after reviewing again, every article, to see that all was complete, she sat down to her instrument, to wile away the time, and practise a few songs and pieces, in case she should be called on to play; but hour after hour passed on, and still the priestess of fashion, with her priceless treasure, the dress, came not. Poor Alice, who had long previously abandoned her instrument, and endeavoured to dispel her nervous impatience by pacing the room with rapid steps, felt her hopefulness gradually ebbing, and at length, when ten o'clock struck, her fortitude completely overcome, she flung herself on the sofa in a paroxysm of tears. Mrs. Sydenham, really sympathizing with her natural distress, kindly endeavoured to soothe her, reminding her it was not yet too late for fashionable hours, and that Mrs. Graham, the lady who had undertaken to *chaperone* her, being an ultra-fashionable, would not probably call for some time to come.

"Dry your tears, my own Alice," she said, raising carefully the rich tresses of her daughter, which the latter in her emotion had entirely forgotten. "See, your curls are already commencing to droop; they are positively damp, and your eyes, my dear child, will be quite red."

"'Tis useless! mother, useless!" was the sobbing reply; "and there is Mrs. Graham's ring," she added, starting, as the hall bell pealed violently, from the sofa, on which she however immediately threw herself again with a fresh burst of grief. "Go, and tell her 'tis impossible for me to go."

With a slow step Mrs. Sydenham left the room, but she almost immediately returned, and, with a beaming countenance, exclaimed:

"'Tis not Mrs. Graham, Alice, but the girl with your dress. Quick, quick, here it is!"

Her daughter sprang to her feet with a bright smile, though the tears yet hung on her long lashes, and proceeded to try on the dress. But alas! fresh disappointments! slight, graceful as Alice's figure was, the milliner had thought fit to improve on it, and accordingly had made the dress so tight that, when strained to the utmost, the lower hooks were still nearly an inch apart.

"Positively, this is too provoking!" exclaimed Mrs. Sydenham, almost as much annoyed as her daughter. "Why, it would not fit an infant. 'Tis no use," she added as the girl, after another superhuman effort, fell on a chair in sheer exhaustion, her face scarlet with her exertions. "Take it off again," said Alice quietly, seating herself with the calmness of despair. A solemn pause succeeded during which the spectators looked at each other in funereal silence, when suddenly a bright idea entered the head of Alice's humble tirewoman:

"Sure, Miss, you can hide it with your sash." The suggestion was like the plank to the drowning mariner, the wellspring in the desert, and was promptly, eagerly acted upon; but many a crease, and ungraceful fold, was the sad consequence. This, however, was of minor importance, as the milliner, who was anything but a proficient in her art— poor Alice could not afford to procure the services of a better—had left so many proofs of her skill in the shape of numberless awkward discrepancies and creases, that those formed by the subterfuge of the sash, passed undistinguished, if not unobserved. The dress, however, was at length adjusted; and, now, the gloves had to be tried, but they were certainly many removes from French kid, for with the first effort made to draw them on, one finger tore from top to bottom. Poor Alice was by this time, however, inured to misfortune, and the only additional evidence of annoyance perceptible was in the deepening of her former faint flush, into intense scarlet. The glove, however, was at length mended, the white rose placed in the dark hair, and the last act of the drama, the large cloak thrown over her, when a furious peal at the bell announced the arrival of her *chaperone*.

With a hasty kiss from her mother, Alice, without a parting look at her mirror, hurried down stairs, sprang into Mrs. Graham's carriage, and, secure in the consciousness that all her dreams, her hopes, were now on the point of fulfilment, sank back with a sigh of relief on its cushioned seat. Mrs. Graham happened to be in a very ill temper, and it was not therefore in the most amiable of tones, she exclaimed: "I hope you will excuse me, Miss Sydenham, for being so late; but I have only just returned from the Opera, and I scarcely waited to change an article of dress. Indeed, had it not been for my promise to Mrs. Sydenham and yourself, I should have dismissed all thought of appearing in Mrs. Belmont's rooms to-night."

Her young companion, who felt greatly disconcerted by this communication, murmured some inarticulate words about gratitude, thanks, and a long pause followed. Suddenly, Mrs. Graham asked, "if she were acquainted with any of the expected guests."

"I know none but Mrs. Belmont herself—and Mr. St. John," she added, after a moment's hesitation.

"Both passable people in their way," rejoined the lady in a careless tone; "but Mrs. Belmont is one of the most capricious, uncertain women I know of, and Henry St. John is—but what do you think of him?"

It was well for Alice that the darkness hid from Mrs. Graham's penetrating eye the vivid flush that overspread her cheek. The consciousness, however, that her companion could not read her countenance enabled her to reply with the most perfect calmness.

"Indeed, I am scarcely competent to pass any opinion on Mr. St. John, as I have never spent more than a half hour altogether in his society."

"Well! I will give you his character, and in a few words too, for I *pique* myself on my brevity and clearness, at least in describing the weaknesses of my friends. Henry St. John is a young gentleman, strikingly like most of his class, very handsome, very elegant, and very conceited. Passing rich, and well-born too, he thinks so many qualifications exempt him from the necessity of ever troubling himself in the slightest degree about any body, or even stooping to be polite to any one, unless he have some peculiar end in view. Then he can render himself almost irresistible."

Alice remembered at the moment with gratitude, and it must be confessed a light tincture of vanity, that this well-born, handsome, haughty individual had thought it worth while to be not only polite, but particularly attentive to herself. She did not however reply, and Mrs. Graham, after a few additional remarks of the same charitable nature, suddenly awoke to the consciousness that she was wasting her powers of satire and comment on one of the *uninitiated*, an individual who, being out of her sphere, could not appreciate them. She therefore relapsed into silence, which remained unbroken till they stopped before Mrs. Belmont's elegant mansion. The brilliantly illuminated windows, before which light indistinct figures were perpetually passing and repassing, the rich strains of music, the confused

sounds of voices and laughter, betokened that mirth and fes-
tivity were in full flow.

"We are very late!" was Mrs. Graham's exclamation, as,
after ascending the wide staircase, she threw herself on a
couch in the elegant but deserted dressing room. "However,
we shall have the mirrors entirely to ourselves. That is some
consolation. Really," she added, as the waiting maid divested
her of her cloaks and shawls, "I never felt less disposed for
gaiety. Carelessly dressed, looking so shockingly ill," and she
cast anything but a pleasant glance at her figure, which a
superb mirror, opposite, reflected at full length. Alice turned,
and that toilette, so slightingly spoken of, fairly dazzled
her—a light gossamer fabric of delicate pink, over rich white
satin, looped up with bows of delicate beauty; and then the
exquisite wreath encircling the plain, glossy hair, the splendid bracelets and rings. The heart of poor Alice sank within
her; and as the reflection: "Perhaps they are all dressed like
her, even more elegantly," presented itself, she was conscious
for the first time of an almost involuntary wish that she could
transport herself at once to her mother's quiet happy room;
but she had little time to indulge in aspirations of any sort,
for Mrs. Graham, who had just despatched the maid on some
commission, turned, exclaiming:

"And, now, Miss Sydenham, let me examine you; but,
my heavens!" she added, as a rapid change came over her
countenance; "is that the dress you intend to wear? Who on
earth could have made such a thing? Such a waist! and such
fitting sleeves!" Poor Alice bowed her head, but spoke not.
"And do inform me," she added, in a still sharper tone, for
her ill humour had completely gained the ascendancy over
her politeness, "do inform me, what this heavy band on your
arm is intended for? Surely not a bracelet?"

As her companion made no reply, she had no answer
to cavil at, and she impatiently exclaimed:

"In pity to yourself, take it off, and here, clasp this on."
As she spoke, she presented the jewel which she had just
taken from her own arm, and Alice, fearing to remonstrate,
silently obeyed. It was an ornament indeed of excessive

beauty—a rare and magnificent opal, surrounded by splendid rubies.

"And now," added Mrs. Graham, giving a last impatient twist to her sash; "I can do no more for you. We will go—but, are you ill?" she asked, perceiving that Alice trembled from head to foot.

"'Tis nothing," was the murmured reply. "I feel a little faint."

Mrs. Graham signed the servant, who had just entered, to hand a glass of water, and the young girl, fearing to put her companion's patience to any further trial, hastily swallowed it, and rose to follow her. With the first glance at the large and glittering saloon they were entering, her self-possession, her very sense of perception, seemed to desert her, and when at length she recovered, she found herself seated in a corner, near a large table, covered with magazines and engravings. Almost opposite her was a young and pretty lady, leaning on the arm of a gentleman, and both were attentively regarding her. The lady stooped and whispered something, with a smile, to her companion, who replied by a light laugh; but, observing that they had attracted the attention of their victim, they turned away. With a strange feeling of loneliness, mortification and fear, she surveyed the brilliant scene before her. All seemed happy, cared for, but her. Those who were not dancing, conversed in groups, partook of refreshments, or promenaded, in couples, the lofty apartments. How painfully, too, did the contrast between herself and the other, faultlessly attired girls, who flitted before her, with their graceful draperies and delicate ornaments, strike upon her heart. Suddenly, while glancing from group to group, with a feeling of sickly despair, her eye fell on the elegant figure of Henry St. John, who was dancing with a haughty-looking, but fashionable, girl. Entirely engrossed by his partner, he of course saw not Alice, who was almost concealed by the heavy draperies of the window on one side, and, on the other, by the shadow of a large lamp on the table beside her. From that moment, however, things appeared in a new, a roseate light. There was, at least, one person present who knew her, and who would surely ask her once to dance. That person would introduce others, and —in fine, Alice had already arrived at the second story of one of her aerial edifices, when Mrs. Belmont passed her with a rapid step. She would not have perceived Alice, but her *bouquet* happened to fall at the feet of the latter, who immediately bent to raise it.

"What! you, my dear Miss Sydenham—not dancing! but I must get you a partner."

She turned and beckoned apparently to someone in the crowd, whilst her young companion, ready to sink with shame at the idea of being thus forced in a manner on a partner, cast down her eyes in speechless confusion. She raised them, however, as a light step approached, and saw Henry St. John before her.

"I have reserved a partner for you, Henry," said Mrs. Belmont, in her soft voice.

"Miss Sydenham!" exclaimed the young man, springing forward with much *empressement*. "This is, indeed, an unexpected pleasure; but how is it I have not seen you before?"

"We arrived very late," rejoined Alice, crimsoning to her temples.

"And you were dancing in the next apartment, nearly all the time, Henry!" quickly interposed Mrs. Belmont, who, with ready tact, at once divined that her guest, failing a partner, had not left as yet the quiet corner in which she had sought refuge on her entrance. After a few additional words of silvery courtesy, the hostess gracefully turned away, whilst Alice, leaning on the arm of her handsome and distinguished partner, her heart beating with mingled fear and delight, joined the quadrille now forming, inwardly congratulating herself that she was now, indeed, participating in the pleasures of a ball. For a few moments, Henry St. John was all gaiety and devotion, but gradually his tones grew colder, his mirthful sallies and compliments became fewer and fewer, and, before the end of the third figure, had entirely ceased. Poor Alice, who had replied to him heretofore only by smiles and blushes, instantaneously perceived the desolating change, and for the first time, raised her eyes from the ground, to discover, if possible, the cause. As she did so, the whispered words:

"*Ciel! quelle tournure!*" and then, in a still lower tone: "What on earth could have induced Henry St. John to select such a partner?" fell on her ear. With what volumes of horror were those short sentences fraught! For a moment she actually gasped for breath, but her positive terror enabled her quickly to subdue her emotions, and she cast a stolen glance from beneath her long lashes, at her partner. He was looking studiously in a distant direction of the room, but his deepened colour, and a certain nameless air of embarrassment pervading his whole figure, told that he too had heard the comments which had just been uttered. Involuntarily she turned her glance on one of the large mirrors lining the sides of the apartment, and she almost started at the figure it reflected. True, it gave back many figures, all light and graceful, all faultlessly attired, but *one* stood out pre-eminent to the horrified gaze of Alice. One ill-dressed, flushed, awkward-looking girl, with long, black hair, hanging in immense uncurled masses around her neck and shoulders. Oh! how fearful seemed to her, her vast inferiority to all around her, and the consciousness of that inferiority was accompanied by a pang so bitter, that the colour which had hitherto equally dyed cheek and brow retreated, leaving her pale as a statue, and with a haggard, worn-out look, which certainly appertained not to a girl of sixteen. Her confusion was further increased, by the contemptuous scrutiny with which the lady opposite (the same with whom St. John had been dancing when she had first perceived him) regarded her. Though fully twelve or thirteen years older than Alice, with a dark, colourless complexion, and haughty, irregular features, yet her air of dignity, of fashionable repose, combined with an elegant and faultless toilette, gave her a strange and wonderful advantage over the latter, with all her youth and beauty. What an hour of torture was that quadrille to Alice; and when her now silent and inanimate

ROSANNA MULLINS LEPROHON

partner, after leading her to her seat, and uttering a few words of cold, common-place civility, left her, she felt too unhappy, too disheartened, to wish for his return. Nor did he return. The film which had invested, even for a few moments, the poor and portionless girl with winning charms, had fallen from his eyes, and he saw again, with his usual faultless clear-sightedness. The young and beautiful creature, with the aristocratic name and graceful address— for Alice was then at her ease, who had attracted his admiration when he had first met her in the company of his sister,—was a very different being from the unfashionable, neglected, unknown girl, whom he had been entrapped into dancing with. Inwardly vowing it would be his last folly of the like nature, and muttering, we will charitably suppose, only a doubtful sort of benediction on his sister's officiousness, which had led to such a result, Henry St. John, the hero of the ball-room, immediately sought out the lady with the faultless toilette, and engaged her hand for the ensuing dance, endeavouring, by increased devotion and graceful flattery, to obliterate any evil impressions his late ill-directed choice of a partner might have left on her mind. The lady was placable, and to Henry St. John's great delight, for Miss Aberton was a wealthy heiress, he succeeded. Meanwhile, poor Alice was nearly half dead with agitation and inanition, for she had as yet taken no refreshment whatever, save one jelly, which a tall, grave-looking gentleman with a bald head had presented, chancing to observe her glance at the tray which he was setting down on the table beside her. This abstinence was the more acutely felt, as she had not tasted food that day; her excitement and the bright hopes and anticipations which had thronged upon her, effectually precluding such a thing. It had been with the greatest difficulty Mrs. Sydenham had prevailed upon her to take a cup of tea an hour or two before leaving. What would she not have given now for that, or any other refreshment. She looked around in despair; no one knew, noticed, or saw her, and she was too young and timid to think of asking.

At length, beginning to feel really ill, she formed the desperate determination of seeking Mrs. Graham, and begging her to send her home immediately. Twice she rose to cross the brilliantly lighted room, and twice her courage failed her; but finally taking advantage of the confusion of a rapid *galop*, she succeeded in gliding unobserved into the next apartment. It was a small sitting room, opening on the conservatory, and was empty at the time, but, ere she had half crossed it, the sound of laughter and voices approaching, filled her with dismay. Hastily raising the purple draperies which hung before a recess at the other end, she sprang behind them, and had hardly time to readjust their folds, when the party entered.

"Do let us rest here a moment," exclaimed a fashionable, and not unmusical voice. "I am completely exhausted! The heat is *so* oppressive in that dancing room."

"Permit me, then, to bring you some refreshments," rejoined the clear, yet soft accents of Henry St. John. "I will not be absent a moment."

Alice glanced through a small opening in the fold of the curtain, which commanded a full view of the room. Thrown negligently but gracefully on a crimson couch was her disagreeable *vis-à-vis*, the object of Henry St. John's devotion; whilst two or three young ladies were sitting or standing round; St. John himself, and the other gentlemen of the party, had gone in quest of refreshments.

"My ringlets are all out," exclaimed the youngest and prettiest of the group; as she twined a glossy auburn tress round her white fingers. "They are positively straight."

"Yes, something like the abundant locks of Henry St. John's partner," was the laughing rejoinder. "Where on earth did he contrive to find her? He may certainly pride himself, on having had a partner who, if she possessed no other attraction, had at least the rare one of being *unique* of her kind. But, seriously, Miss Aberton," she continued, addressing the lady on the couch, "do you know who she is? I would never have noticed her, nor I dare say would any of us, but for the circumstances of the usually exclusive and over-fastidious Henry St. John, having chosen her for a partner. Who can she be?"

"I for one, know nothing about the girl," returned Miss Aberton, closing her haughty eyelids: "but I rather suspect she came with Mrs. Graham. Perhaps some country cousin."

"Who is paying the usual penalty of the absent now?" gaily interrupted St. John, who entered at the moment. "I hope I am not the hapless one."

"Not exactly," returned the former speaker, with a mischievous smile. "Still, there is no material difference—for 'tis your whilom partner. Pardon me, but as I really feel a friendly solicitude regarding your peace of mind, I must inquire her name," and she raised her sparkling eyes with a pretty air of gravity to his face. St. John's brow instantly became scarlet, and he bit his lip as if to restrain his impatience.

"Surely, Mr. St. John, *sur ce chapitre on peut se rapporter à vous*," said Miss Aberton, with a somewhat sarcastic smile, curling her lip. "A guest of your sister's, and a partner of your own choice."

"Her name is Sydenham," rejoined the young man with ill-dissembled annoyance. "That is all I know of her, beyond exchanging a few words, when introduced to her by Mrs. Belmont."

"Oh! fie, fie, Mr. St. John," interrupted his former tormentor, the Honorable Miss Templeton. "Do you count for nothing all the flattering smiles and compliments you showered upon her, during that short but blissful dance? A dance, too, of your seeking, for 'tis to be presumed, the lady did not solicit your hand."

"Not exactly, Miss Templeton," was the cool reply; "but when my sister, who was a schoolfellow of Miss Sydenham's, gave her to me as a partner, I could scarcely, even to win Miss Templeton's priceless approbation," here he bowed low, "be sufficiently ungallant to inform the young lady I had no particular desire for the honour."

"Dear Mrs. Belmont has so warm a heart," sweetly lisped the Lady Helena Stratton. "How few of us are so faithful to those delightful things, school-girl friendships."

"Sydenham is a good name, though," said another, in a more matter of fact tone; "and Miss Aberton says she came with Mrs. Graham."

"I said, I supposed so, from the circumstances of perceiving on her arm, a rare and magnificent bracelet, the only passable thing the young girl had on her person, which I am convinced belongs to Mrs. Graham."

"An opal set in rubies," exclaimed Lady Helena. "I have seen it on her several times, and 'tis a very rare ornament. I also saw Mrs. Graham address a few words to her at the beginning of the evening."

"But Mrs. Graham has not troubled herself much about her since," rejoined Miss Templeton.

"How could she? Mrs. Graham, ethereal soul! being, as she herself says, poetically, a creature whose whole being is devoted to sweet sounds. I really believe she has been in the music room all night, and hush! I hear her full tones at the present moment."

"She certainly has a beautiful voice," said St. John, sincerely delighted with the change the conversation had taken. "We can distinguish the words partly from here, 'I'll hang my harp on a willow tree.'"

"I sincerely wish she would 'hang her harp on a willow tree,' for I am heartily sick of its strains," said Miss Aberton, as she rose from the couch; "but, come, let us leave Mrs. Graham, and her charming *protégée*, to their fate. The subject is worn out."

"Nay, do not let us leave this sweet spot so soon," returned Miss Templeton. "I really shall change the hangings of my morning room, and adopt this beautiful shade. And what a charmingly mysterious recess! Do you remember the words of the old song,

'I'm weary of dancing now, she cried,
Here tarry a moment, I'll hide, I'll hide.'

"Shall I follow her example?" and with the graceful *étourderie* of a child, she sprang forward, and grasped the purple draperies in her small hand. What a moment of fearful, of breathless agony, must that have been for the trembling being they screened! For a second, Miss Templeton held the curtains, and then with a gay laugh, she turned away, exclaiming: "No! I had better not be too rash. Who knows but yonder draperies conceal some solemn mysteries? There never was such a thing heard of in a romance, as a recess without its grisly skeleton, or mysterious portrait, making awful descents from its frame, and taking short pedestrian excursions through the halls and passages. Really, I appeal to you, Miss Aberton, does it not look like the nooks we read of in old fashioned novels? Dark, rich folds, hanging from the lofty ceiling!"

"It looks like a nook marvellously well adapted to play the eaves-dropper in," drily returned Miss Aberton, who concealed with difficulty, the disgust which the *enfantillage* of her friend excited.

"Nay, do not check Miss Templeton's delightful enthusiasm," said Henry St. John, in a tone whose double refined politeness savoured strongly of sarcasm. "Really, such freshness, such *naïve* eagerness, is a charming deviation from our customary monotonous insipidity."

Miss Templeton saw at once that Mr. St. John was "paying her off" for her former unwelcome jests at his expense, and resolving not to leave him "victor of the field," she rejoined:

"You are too complimentary, Mr. St. John. I am not the only one who does occasionally display traits of a better nature. What greater example could we require of unworldly enthusiasm, of heroic indifference to the world's opinion, than that with which you edified us to-night in your selection of the being to whom you doubtless offered your heart as well as hand. Ah! she indeed is a bright specimen of that sweet, silent sensibility, that fascinating, rural timidity, so highly eulogized by boarding school teachers and middle aged people, and so signally distinguished by Mr. St. John."

"But, really, St. John," said a tall, affected looking young gentleman, who rejoiced in the appellation of Viscount Howard. "Really, you, whom the lady promoted to the dignity of her *preux chevalier*, are bound by all the laws of chivalry and knighthood to go in search of her. She is doubtless at the present moment, making signals of distress for an ice, or calling on you to rescue her from some remote corner, where no other partner can penetrate."

"Had you not better make the experiment yourself, my lord? As your fancy is so very lively in conjuring up scenes of distress, probably your generosity is equally prompt in relieving them."

There was a very perceptible tone of sarcasm in the words, and a slight contraction of the high brow of the speaker, which told that further jesting on the subject would prove anything but conducive to mirth or friendship, and Lord Howard, taking the hint, drew the fair Lady Helena's arm in his own, and passed on to the adjoining saloon. The others followed in like order—Miss Aberton and St. John last. The latter had lingered to gather a blossom from a superb Indian jasmine that stood in the conservatory, which he presented, repeating in a tone half playful, half serious, the sentiment it imaged: "I attach myself to thee." It was graciously accepted, and the delicate compliments, the words of homage he whispered, as they slowly followed their companions, proved that Henry St. John was a proficient in the science of flattery.

Meanwhile, what were the feelings of the young and sensitive girl, who, an unsuspected listener to that long dialogue, with all its bitter contemptuousness, its heartless egotism, had thus received her first terrible lesson in the world's ways. For an hour, a long hour after the thoughtless revellers had passed out, she stood leaning against the tapestried wall, her eyes closed, her small hand pressed on her heart as if to still its wild, convulsive throbbing. At length a feeling of strange bewildering weakness crept over her, and, conscious that she was on the point of fainting, she left the recess, and, with some difficulty, reached the table on which

ROSANNA MULLINS LEPROHON

fortunately stood a vase of water, a glass of which somewhat revived her, and a few moments rest on the couch on which Miss Aberton had late reclined in all the pride of wealth and rank, comparatively restored her. But, with returning force returned her old fear, that some gay party, if not the same one that had lately passed, might enter and see her sitting there, so lone, so neglected. That would have been indeed the last drop in her cup of bitterness; but what was she to do? There was no alternative save to seek Mrs. Graham, and entreat her to return; but where was she to be found, and how could Alice summon courage to approach her before a crowded room, and importune her, perhaps at a time where she might be totally engrossed by some other subject.

"Oh! that I might go home myself," murmured Alice, clasping her hands. "How willingly would I set out on foot in damp and darkness. Yet alas! I have no resource save patience. But I must seek my former place of refuge. There at least I may remain unobserved, unseen—how happy I shall feel if I can but reach it without meeting any of those heartless fashionables. I will not be tempted to leave it again."

With a beating heart and timid step she reentered the ball-room, and was quietly and unobservedly gliding back to her former seat, when directly in her path, advancing towards her, was Henry St. John, Miss Aberton leaning on his arm. Alice stood transfixed with positive terror; but she was at least spared that mortification, for without having perceived her, they turned off in another direction. With renewed hope she continued to advance, when something soft, crushing beneath her foot, caused her to stoop. It was the white rose, now soiled and discoloured, which her fond mother had placed with such maternal pride, some hours before, amid her dark tresses. The sight brought back in all their vivid bitterness, the mortifications, the humiliations, which had been her portion that night. What a contrast to the roseate visions, the soft hopes, that had flitted before her, when that rose, white and lovely, had been placed amid her hair. The hot tears of acute mental suffering gushed to

her eyes; spite of her efforts, they fell faster and faster. Half
blinded by them, she hurried on. At length her haven was all
but won, when suddenly—how closely is the sublime
blended with the ridiculous, the mournful with the mirthful,
in this changing world of ours—in her feverish haste, she
stepped on the outstretched foot of an old gentleman, with
venerable white hair and rather choleric face, who was
reclining in solitary dignity, on a couch adjoining her former seat. The injured individual instantly sprang to his feet
with a muttered apostrophe, in which the name of a certain
sovereign, whose dominions are not on the earth, nor yet
above the earth, was distinctly audible. But the soft, entreating voice, the pale, tearful face of the young girl, as she
earnestly apologized, calmed his ire, and he fell back in his
former position, murmuring:

"Never mind, ma'am! Accidents will happen to the
best-intentioned persons."

With a heart full to bursting, Alice glided past him,
and sank on her chair. Secure in the grateful shade of the
lamp, she covered her face with her hands, and gave free
vent to the passionate emotion she could no longer control
or restrain. Suddenly a slight noise caused her to look up.
The old gentleman was standing before her, and regarding
her with a very benevolent expression of countenance.

"Forgive the meddling impertinence of an old man,"
he kindly said; "but you seem unhappy, my dear young lady;
surely, you are too young for that."

"Oh! I am very, very miserable," sobbed poor Alice,
feeling it was useless to attempt controlling her grief.

"No! That can scarcely be at your age; 'tis but a summer shower, heavy while it lasts, but of short duration. The
sunshine will be brighter after. But, you look very pale! Let
me get you some refreshments?" She gratefully bowed, and
he hastened off on his kind mission. Ere many minutes had
lapsed, he returned with a cup of fragrant coffee, and some
cold chicken,—we beseech our romantic readers to close
their eyes to this passage, for 'twill shock every sentiment of
their exquisitely refined natures—which our heroine not

only accepted, but heartily partook of. Thankful for the old man's kindness, and greatly refreshed, she endeavoured effectually to calm her still excited feelings, and in answer to his question: "If she felt better," replied, with an effort at cheerfulness: "Yes; a great deal. Thanks to your double kindness."

"You are a good girl," he returned, "and more sensible than I expected; but if you do not think it too great a liberty for an old man like me to take, may I ask the cause of your sorrow?"

A pause followed, during which the rich colour mounted to her very temples, and, at length, she replied with downcast eyes:

"Wounded vanity, and self-love. I came here expecting gaiety, attention, admiration; and I have met nothing but contempt and neglect."

"Just so, my child," said her companion; "you expected too much, and you must not repine that your expectations have been disappointed."

"But, surely, I have not deserved the entire, the bitter contempt I have met with. I am neither old nor ugly."

"You are indeed neither, but beautiful, very beautiful," he rejoined as he gazed earnestly on the deep truthful eyes now raised to his: "but you have yet to learn that beauty and grace, when ill dressed or obscure, will meet with nothing but neglect in a ball-room. And now, tell me your name as frankly as you have told me the rest of your story."

"Alice Sydenham."

"Sydenham!" he repeated reflectively. "A high name."

"'Tis all is left us of former grandeur," said Alice sadly. "Poor, unpretending, as we are, how wrong, how foolish of me to thrust myself into a scene so utterly removed from our present sphere; but I acted contrary to mamma's wishes, her earnest remonstrances, and I have been justly punished."

"Your mother—is she here?" said the old man quickly. "And neglect you thus!"

"No, no! she is at home. I came with a Mrs. Graham."

"A lady very youthfully dressed with a parterre of roses scattered about her robes? She has been screaming Italian *canzonets* in the music room all night."

"The same," said Alice, the first smile that had illumined her pale features that night, stealing over them.

"Hem!" coughed her companion; "but who have we here?"

This exclamation was called forth by the approach of the lady Helena Stratton, leaning on the arm of the Viscount Howard, both of whom Alice had seen with Miss Aberton's party in the ante-room. Deeply engrossed in conversation, they slowly advanced towards the table, as if to examine the engravings upon it.

"Hollo!" suddenly exclaimed a loud voice. "Look where you're going to, young lady!"

Lady Helena, who was unconscious of the sofa's having an occupant, had nearly deposited her delicate satin shoe on the irritable toes of the old gentleman, who seemed as if in very malice to keep them extended in the way. The lady thus cavalierly addressed, sprang round with a violent start, widely different from her usual languid movements, whilst her partner angrily said:

"I think, Sir, you might show a little more regard for the young lady's nerves."

"Let the young lady then shew a little more regard for other people's toes," was the unceremonious rejoinder.

The young viscount turned fiercely upon him, but there was something so very irascible in his venerable antagonist's face, whose hue had now deepened to a fiery red, that he thought it wiser to forbear. A duel with a man sufficiently old to be his father, would be anything but creditable, and, whispering something to his fair partner, who replied by smilingly elevating her shoulders, they turned away.

"We have disposed of them at last," he said, turning with his former benevolent smile to Alice, who was actually trembling to find herself in such close proximity with so very fiery a neighbour. "What! you are afraid of me," he continued in a kind tone. "Why, you little simpleton, that scene was half got up to give yon supercilious young lady, with her foppish companion, a lesson, and to deliver us from their company. And now, preparatory to returning to our former topic, I must inform you of my name, as freely as you gave me yours. 'Tis Hammersly, a plain name, but one never sullied, I believe, by falsehood or dishonesty. Now, my dear child, tell me, have you no brother or cousin, whose attentions would shield you from the slights you have experienced to-night?"

"No; I had three brothers, but they all died in infancy. The only living relative I possess is an uncle of mamma's, but he lives in a distant part of England."

"What county?"

"Cumberland."

"What name?"

"Weston—James Weston, I think—but to tell you the truth, I know very little about him."

"And care still less," said the old man, interpreting aright an almost imperceptible smile that curved the rosy lips of his companion. "But, have you ever seen him?"

"Never, in person—but I have seen his miniatures; a stern, grave-looking man, with raven hair and black eyes. Mamma says I strongly resemble him."

"That were paying him indeed a compliment; but if I am not mistaken, I know this same Mr. Weston, and without further preamble, a more egotistical, churlish being, never existed."

"Oh! shame! shame!" exclaimed Alice, really indignant at hearing her relative thus unceremoniously condemned by a stranger.

"Pardon me! I speak truth; but, however, I can also say, he has a good heart, though its better qualities are nearly choked up by selfishness. You need not speak, young lady," he continued, raising his hand to silence the warm remonstrance hovering on Alice's lips. "Were he not selfish, he would not have left you and your mother—Pardon me! —in the comparative destitution you are in, whilst he, himself, is surrounded by all earth's luxuries, rolling in wealth."

"That is his own affair," was the somewhat cold reply; "and, notwithstanding we have no real claims upon him, since the death of my father, he has regularly transmitted to us, every year, a considerable sum."

"Well, that is something; however, the generosity of the act depends greatly on the extent of the gift. But, I think, my dear child," he added, glancing at his gold repeater, as the strains of the band suddenly ceased, preparatory to commencing some new dance; "I think you had better prepare for leaving. You look very pale, indeed worn out."

"But not with pleasure," said poor Alice, the cheerful smile which had lately animated her features, fading away, as the recollection arose that the night to which she had so eagerly looked forward, which was to have witnessed her first essay in the brilliant gaieties of the world, had come and passed away, leaving nought but bitter remembrances behind.

"Wait, I will bring you a glass of wine first," said her kind companion. "Remain here a moment."

He soon returned and in compliance with his entreaties, she tasted the refreshments he offered.

"And now," he exclaimed; "take my arm, and we will go in quest of your very attentive and thoughtful *chaperone*."

With a feeling of comparative ease and confidence, to which she had as yet been a stranger, Alice obeyed, and they proceeded together to the music room. The crowd near the door was so great, they were forced to stand aside for a moment, and during the time, she noticed many polite bows and smiles directed to her companion, whilst as many scrutinizing, impertinently inquisitive glances were bent on herself. To the courtesies showered upon him, Mr. Hammersly replied only by an abrupt nod or careless smile; and when Miss Aberton, in sweeping past, accidentally dropped her handkerchief at his very feet, he never bent himself, and by pressing Alice's arm, restrained her first involuntary impulse to raise it. The haughty girl glanced at him with a look of indignant surprise, which he returned by one of the most provoking unconsciousness; but fortunately for her, a gentleman standing in the crowd perceived her embarrassment, and springing forward to the rescue, gracefully presented it. That gentleman was Henry St. John.

Courteously saluting Alice's companion, he turned to him, as if to address a few words, but the latter, with a stiff bow, passed out. Mr. St. John was equally unsuccessful in an effort which he made to attract the glance of Alice, which was instantly averted from him. In the adjoining apartment they encountered Mrs. Graham, who, at the centre of a small *coterie*, was vehemently discussing the merits and demerits of the last new Opera.

"Why, where have you been all this time, Miss Sydenham?" immediately exclaimed the lady, on the entrance of her charge. "I have been searching for you in every direction."

"Either your researches did not extend beyond the music room, or you will soon require spectacles, madam, for Miss Sydenham has never left the adjoining room, the whole night."

Mrs. Graham drew herself up, with a lightning glance, but the hostess, who at the moment joined the group, foreseeing the impending storm, instantly interposed.

"Ah! my sweet young friend!" addressing Alice, after bestowing a beaming smile on her companion, "I hope you have enjoyed yourself."

"Vastly, madam; I can vouch for the truth of that," drily rejoined the old man, who seemed to have taken on himself the task of answering for Alice on all occasions. "Complete neglect, entire isolation, is so delightful, not to speak of the facility thus afforded, of indulging in philosophical meditations, undisturbed by such vanities as dancing or attention. Oh! 'twas all doubtless charming for a girl of sixteen."

Mrs. Belmont would not see the very palpable cut thus given her, but continued to chat pleasantly with him, whilst Alice glided after Mrs. Graham to the dressing room. It was crowded with ladies, all eagerly conversing together, discussing the pleasures of the night, or planning future amusements. A group of these immediately surrounded Mrs. Graham, and Alice was again left, as she had been the greater part of the evening, entirely alone. She was soon cloaked and veiled, and leaning against the large mirror, at the deserted end of the apartment, where she had attired herself, she gazed sadly, upon the pale, haggard face it reflected. But her thoughts dwelt not long there; they wandered soon back to the bitter events of the night, the slights, the humiliations showered on one whose birth was equal to the proudest there, whose only inferiority was in the paltriest of earth's distinctions, wealth. Suddenly the voice of Mrs. Graham sharply exclaimed.

"Miss Sydenham, are you ready yet?"

Conscious that her pre-occupation had been observed, the latter quickly turned, but as she did so, she heard Miss Aberton whisper to her neighbour.

"'Tis cruel of Mrs. Graham to disturb so blissful a revery. We are all fond of meditating on our conquests."

Alice, irritated beyond expression, fixed her eyes upon the speaker, with a glance of such profound, unutterable contempt, that the lady, to the secret delight of her companions, with whom she was no favorite, turned away her head, in silent embarrassment. Arrived at the landing place, Mrs. Graham stopped to exchange a few parting words with a friend, whilst her young companion shrank timidly behind her. Sometime after, her *chaperone*'s carriage was announced, when Mr. St. John, who had been leaning listlessly over the staircase, sprang forward, and with his most fascinating smile, "begged the honour of handing Miss Sydenham in."

Alice raised her eyes in wondering astonishment at this unaccountable change, when she suddenly encountered the glance of her kind friend of the evening. Instantly comprehending his quick, but meaning look, she coldly thanked Mr. St. John for the intended favour, and with a stiff bow, turned away.

To fill the measure of the latter's mortification, the old man unceremoniously pushed past him, exclaiming:

"'Tis rather late to renew your acquaintance with Miss Sydenham now," and presenting his arm to Alice, they moved off, leaving him biting his lips with vexation.

"St. John, do tell us who that old bear is?" asked a fashionable looking young man who had witnessed the whole scene, with very lively demonstrations of satisfaction.

"Some rich old Hottentot whom my sister made acquaintance with, during her travels. She says he is worth thousands. In payment alone of some kind of forfeit, or jesting bet, he presented her with a brooch worth at the least eighty guineas."

"Well! he is a fiery old gentleman, and I suspected it was something of that sort when I witnessed the lamb-like gentleness with which you suffered his onset. St. John, St. John, gold is then thy god."

"A god whom we all worship, you among the rest," rejoined the other, peevishly, as he turned away. Meanwhile Alice and her friend had reached the carriage, in which Mrs. Graham was already seated. Warmly pressing her hand, he assisted her in, and then turning to her *chaperone*, he exclaimed:

"I resign your charge, madam, but before doing so, allow me to congratulate you on the tender solicitude, the scrupulous fidelity, with which you have discharged your trust."

Ere the lady addressed had time to recover from the breathless astonishment in which his audacity had thrown her, he had disappeared.

"Upon my word!" she exclaimed, "this is something novel," and she again relapsed into silence; but suddenly she resumed, in a much louder key: "Will you have the goodness, Miss Sydenham, to inform me, who this new and singular acquaintance of yours, is?"

"I—I really forget," stammered poor Alice, who had but little heeded the information which the stranger had imparted to her concerning himself.

"Forget his name!" was the indignant rejoinder. "Really, Miss Sydenham, you surprise me. Forget his name!

and, yet, you took his arm, conversed with him, treated him with all the familiarity of an old acquaintance."

"Because he was the only being who seemed to possess one spark of kindness, or feeling for me," vehemently replied Alice, to whom the remembrance of her wrongs imparted a sudden and unusual courage.

"That has no connexion with the subject, whatever, Miss Sydenham. I allude to the strange and unaccountable error you have committed in thus receiving, and encouraging the attentions of a nameless individual; I am certain, were Mrs. Sydenham to know it, she would feel deeply pained. How did you know, but your acquaintance may be some old tradesman? or—or," she continued, evidently seeking for some term of suitable degradation—"a pickpocket!"

"In that case, he would scarcely be admitted into Mrs. Belmont's saloons," said her companion, gently.

"I am not so sure of that," rejoined Mrs. Graham, with increased asperity. "Mrs. Belmont is not so remarkably select. We meet many persons in her circles whom we would not dream of finding there."

Oh! how deeply Alice felt the ungenerous, the unkind insinuation, but she made no retort. She was reflecting that this was but her first essay in the bitter path of dependence, and she vowed, in her inmost heart, that as far as lay in her power, it should be her last. At the moment, her handkerchief fell, and as she bent forward to raise it, the light of the lamps shone full upon her figure. Whiter than marble instantly became her cheek, and clasping her hands, she murmured in accents of horror: "Good God!"

"How! what is the matter?" quickly exclaimed Mrs. Graham, springing from her seat. But she heard her not. Gazing with an air of total stupefaction upon her small white arms, she ejaculated in the same thrilling tone, "*the bracelet!*" Yes! the opal bracelet, the rare, costly jewel, which had called forth the admiration of even the supercilious children of wealth, was gone. Her companion understood at once the meaning conveyed in Alice's one exclamation, and she rapidly repeated, sinking back on the cushions:

"What! my bracelet? You do not mean to say, Miss Sydenham, that you have lost it?"

"Yes! I have been indeed so utterly unfortunate," murmured poor Alice, who, overwhelmed with agonized shame and regret, would have gladly welcomed death at the moment to deliver her from this last climax of misery.

"Did you lose it in Mrs. Belmont's rooms?" was the sudden and eager query.

"Alas! no. I must have lost it in getting into the carriage. 'Tis by this time broken to atoms, or appropriated by some foot passenger."

"Unless your new acquaintance anticipated them, and performed that duty himself," exclaimed Mrs. Graham, who, even in the midst of her trouble, could not resist the temptation of launching a sarcasm at the head of the audacious meddler, who had presumed to question so insolently her conduct. But her satire fell unmarked. Alice was too wretched to heed it, and the lady might, with equal impunity, have styled the old gentleman a robber, or a murderer. An ominous pause followed, broken by the young girl's saying in a low tone:

"And it was so very valuable, too?"

"It only cost three hundred guineas," rejoined Mrs. Graham, sarcastically.

"But you value it for its own sake, only," said Alice eagerly, a ray of joy lighting up her haggard face, which already bore the marks of care, the first that had ever rested there. "'Tis no *souvenir*, no cherished remembrance! Oh! there is yet hope!" And already in fancy, she had rapidly pictured to herself the sacrifices she would make, the unwearying diligence with which she would toil night and day, denying herself every comfort, even necessary, till she had discharged her fearful obligation. Her companion, who instantly comprehended the meaning conveyed in her hurried words, exclaimed in a cold, stiff tone:

"I hope, Miss Sydenham, you do not intend insulting me by ever talking about restitution. It was entirely an accident. You are in no manner accountable, and you will oblige me by waiving the subject for ever."

Even had she possessed the strength and voice, what could Alice say? In total silence they arrived at her humble home: in total silence, the footman let down the steps, pulled the bell, and then, Mrs. Graham frigidly exclaiming: "Good night," the carriage drove off. It was Mrs. Sydenham who answered the summons, her one domestic having hours before retired to rest, and an exclamation of horror escaped her, as the pale, suffering face of her daughter met her view.

"Alice! Alice! You look dreadfully pale. What is the matter?"

"Oh! mamma, I am so wretched," sobbed the young girl, as she threw herself in a paroxysm of tears into the fond arms so eagerly opened to receive her. "I have been tried beyond my strength."

Mrs. Sydenham, seeing the inutility of attempting to restrain her emotion, permitted her daughter to indulge freely in it, her only token of sympathy, a gentle pressure of her hand; but after a time, the violence of her sorrow began to subside, and the mother softly whispered.

"Then, my own Alice, your bright expectations have not been fulfilled."

"Alas! no!" she rejoined, raising her streaming eyes. "Would that I had never gone! Would that, by the sacrifice of half my existence, I could blot out from my happy life, this last night of bitterness, of suffering, of agony."

"Hush! my child! this wild sorrow is sinful in the eyes of your Creator. He has not afflicted you so heavily as to call forth such vehement grief. Be patient, and bear as a Christian should this your first trial. Alas! my darling! you will through life, be that life ever so fortunate, have many such. Retire to rest now, and to-morrow you will tell me all."

"Oh! no, mother! let me tell you now. It will relieve my heart, which seems almost breaking."

"Well, as you will, my child! but throw off that foolish dress, and set yourself near the fire, whilst I get you some hot coffee, which you sadly need."

When Mrs. Sydenham returned, she found poor Alice seated in an easy chair, in her dressing gown, gazing on the bright coals in the grate, whilst she silently wiped away the burning tears which, notwithstanding her late outburst of emotion, continued to fall like rain. But loving tones and cheerful words are efficient aids in dispelling sorrow, and the young girl was soon able to relate, with tolerable calmness, the many bitter events of the night. Nothing did she omit, nothing did she equivocate, even to the episode of Henry St. John, and the vain fancies she had wasted on him. We will pass over the gentle, yet forcible, counsels imparted by Mrs. Sydenham to her daughter—the moral she drew from the bitter lessons she had received; suffice it to say, they sank into her heart, and in after life, bore noble fruit.

The following day, after a sleepless, tearful night, Alice was seated in the sitting-room, despoiling her festal robe, which she inwardly vowed never to wear again, of the ribands adorning it, which she intended converting to some more useful purpose; but though the white fingers moved with strange rapidity, they often desisted to dash aside the glittering drops that fell upon them. The door unclosed, but she heard it not; a step approached, and the next moment Alice was clasped in the arms of the old gentleman, her friend of the preceding night.

Ere she could disengage herself from his warm, heartfelt embrace, the voice of Mrs. Sydenham, who had entered at the moment, exclaimed, in tones of startled surprise:

"Good Heavens! Uncle Weston! Is it possible!"

It was indeed the wealthy but eccentric James Weston, her indifferent, cold hearted relative.

"Well! my own little Alice!" said the old man, drawing tenderly towards him the young girl, whose changing colour betokened her astonishment. "Tell me, are you willing to acknowledge the relationship?"

"But—but,"—she at length stammered; "how can you be my uncle? You are not like the miniature. You have neither raven hair nor dark eyes?"

"Not now, but I had twenty years ago," he returned, bursting into a merry laugh. "You do not imagine I was to have remained always in the same state of preservation I happened to be in, when I sat for the portrait in your mother's possession."

"And you told me your name was—was—" Alice paused, for though she felt assured it was not Weston, yet she could not recall the appellation he had given.

"Yes, I told you my name was Hammersly, and that was no great departure from truth, for I was christened James Hammersly Weston."

Her doubts all dispelled, with a confused though happy smile, she threw herself in his arms, murmuring:

"My dear, good uncle! How different are you to the stern, unkind being my traitorous imagination had painted."

"And whose cause you nevertheless so warmly, so nobly defended. Oh! how grateful should I feel! I, the solitary, isolated old man; thus suddenly enriched, by the gift of two beloved children, blessed by the certainty that I may end my days among you. Truly, Alice, may it be said, that out of seeming evil springeth good, and but for that ball, painful, trying as it has proved, I would have never have known or loved you half as well as you deserve. Had I come here to you, formally announced, as I had intended, suspicious as I am by nature, I might have mistaken your sweetness, your girlish frankness, for the refinement of art; a plan to secure the good will of an old man, tolerated only for his riches."

"But, tell me, uncle, did you know from the first I was your own Alice?"

"No, dear, but I had strong suspicions. In truth, from the moment I saw your gentle face, its wonderful resemblance to your mother, struck me. You were just what she was at your age, when I beheld her, on her return from school. When I left you a moment, in quest of refreshments, I carelessly asked Mrs. Belmont, who you were. Supposing it was merely an old man's curiosity, she instantly informed me. Wishing to obtain a further insight into your character, I dissembled my secret, resolving to keep the explanation for to-day. You may judge, Alice, whether I was pleased or not with your appearance, when I assure you, that even, had I found you were in no manner related to me, I would have still found you out, and in as delicate a manner as I could, bestowed on you many, and substantial proofs of my good will."

We will not weary the reader with further details. Better than we can portray them, can they imagine the heartfelt gratitude of Mrs. Sydenham, the delight of Alice, and the perfect happiness of Mr. Weston. The latter immediately procured an elegant mansion, in one of the most fashionable localities, purchased a splendid carriage, and superb horses, engaged a retinue of servants, whilst he daily showered money, jewels, the costliest gifts on Alice, who retained in prosperity the sweet gentleness which characterized her in cloudier days, and which justly rendered her, the idol of her old uncle's heart. The first care of Mr. Weston, to whom she had soon recounted the mishap of the bracelet, was to set out for the jeweller's. He returned, after some delay, and handing a casket to Alice, exclaimed:

"There, Mrs. Graham's bracelet cost three hundred guineas—that cost nearly double the sum."

It was a magnificent jewel, surpassing far in beauty, the one she had lost—the opal being replaced by a diamond. Mr. Weston proposed enclosing it, in a sheet of paper, with the words: "In discharge of Miss Sydenham's debt to Mrs. Graham," but yielding to the entreaties of Alice, he consented to abandon his first project. Taking another sheet, he wrote: "From Mr. Weston, to Mrs. Graham, as a token of his deep gratitude for the care and attention she has displayed towards his niece, Miss Sydenham."

"There! Alice," said the old man smiling, "if that does not bring a blush to her cheek, I do not know what will."

The gift was duly received, and the intelligence of Miss Sydenham's sudden change of fortune, circulated with lightning rapidity. The invitations and the cards hourly heaped upon the table, almost bewildered Alice. First among these was that of Henry St. John, who immediately decided on abandoning Miss Aberton, who possessed neither the beauty nor brilliant prospects of her rival, and laying close siege to the niece, and professed heiress of the individual he had classically designated as "an old Hottentot." To Henry St. John, however, for a long period, Alice was never "at home," and when at length, constrained to receive him by the frequency of his visits, and the affectionate attentions of his sister, Mrs. Belmont, the cold civility with which she ever treated him, shewed that she had profited of her first bitter lesson. That lesson proved indeed a blessing, doubly precious, preceding as it did, her sudden elevation to a sphere where she was the object of unceasing homage and adulation. It taught her to value according to their proper worth, the flatterers who immediately surrounded her, and when listening to the praises of her grace, her beauty, so often now poured into her ear, she ever found an antidote against the vanity the silvery words might have excited, in the remembrance of the trials and humiliations of her FIRST BALL.

↪

Literary Garland (January 1849), 1–14. Reprinted in *Nineteenth-Century Canadian Stories*, edited by David Arnason (Toronto: Macmillan, 1976), 96–127. The story is published here as it first appeared in the *Literary Garland*.

ROSANNA MULLINS LEPROHON

MY VISIT TO FAIRVIEW VILLA

Rosanna Mullins Leprohon

"LOVE! PSHAW! I don't believe in it, and I really think I shall live and die an old maid, lest I should be wooed and married for my money. Men are such selfish, grasping, egotistical creatures!"

Such was the uncompromising judgment I heard pronounced on my sex as I entered the pleasant shady drawing-room of my friend, Stephen Merton, in compliance with a pressing invitation lately received, to spend a few weeks of the hot, dusty summer months at his pleasant residence, Fairview Villa, situated on the beautiful Saint Foy Road, some short distance from picturesque old Quebec.

The moment of my arrival was rather unpropitious, and I think I would have retreated had not my hostess caught sight of my rather embarrassed countenance. Instantly rising, she came forward and kindly welcomed me, introducing me afterwards to her two daughters, Fanny and Charlotte Merton, her niece, Miss Gray, and a young lady guest, Miss Otway.

"Hem!" thought I, when fairly seated, and replying with tolerable composure to the liberally gay small talk addressed me on all sides: "Which of these fair ladies has just proclaimed so unequivocally her contempt for mankind?" and my glance here travelled round the fair circle. "Oh, that is the one," I pronounced, as my gaze rested on Miss Geraldine Otway, who stood haughtily erect beside the mantlepiece, twisting a piece of honey-suckle round her taper fingers. The scorn was yet lingering in the dark eyes that met mine so fearlessly—in the rosy lip so contemptuously curved, and a yet more femininely beautiful being I had rarely met. Features of childish delicacy, a varying, transparent complexion, and a figure of the most fragile, though graceful proportions, were hers; all forming a striking contrast to the words and manner of this determined hater of mankind.

"Pray, Mr. Saville, did you overhear any part of the discussion we were engaged in when you opportunely entered to prevent its animation degenerating into animosity?" enquired Miss Gray, with a mischievous glance towards Miss Otway.

"Only the concluding sentences," I replied.

"If Mr. Saville wishes, I am ready to repeat what I have already said, and to defend it," exclaimed the lovely occupant of the hearth-rug, nibbling with superb indifference at the spray of honey-suckle in her hand.

"No, Miss Otway," I rejoined with a low bow, "that would be unnecessary, for I acknowledge the justice of your remarks. More than that, I will say you were not half severe enough."

I had flattered myself that my ironical acquiescence in her stern views would have slightly disconcerted this fair Amazon with the tender bloom of eighteen summers still fresh on her cheek, but so far from that, she merely averted her long fringed azure eyes contemptuously from me, as if judging me unworthy of further notice.

"Why, Mr. Saville," interposed little Charlotte Merton, "you should blush for subscribing so unreservedly to such a sweeping, odious accusation against your sex!"

"I beg pardon, Miss Merton, but since you take me up so seriously, I must say that I assent only in part to Miss Otway's opinions."

"And pray what part does Mr. Saville judge fit to dispute?" questioned my fair enemy, pursuing her fragrant repast without deigning to cast a glance in my direction.

The overwhelming contempt for my humble self and judgment, conveyed in the clear cold tones and averted eyes, was something really wonderful in its way, and would have utterly annihilated a more sensitive individual than myself. I contrived, however, with tolerable composure, to rejoin:

"As to the selfishness and rapacity of men, we will leave it an open question; but with regard to Miss Otway's intention of living and dying in single blessedness, holding as she does, so poor an opinion of our sex, I highly applaud her wisdom."

"Oh!" thought I, inwardly elated, "what a magnificent thrust! She'll scarcely get over it!"

Slowly she brought her full clear eyes to bear on mine, and having steadily stared at my hapless countenance a full moment, quietly said:

"It is barely possible I may yet be induced to change my present opinion of the lords of creation for a more favourable one; to commit the egregious folly of trusting in them; but I do not think," and here she came to a pause expressive of the most unutterable scorn; "I do not think that Mr. Saville, or any person at all resembling him, will be the one who shall succeed in making me do so."

I was vanquished, for I could not descend to vulgar retort and tell her she might rest assured that Mr. Saville would never seek her capricious favour, so making her a low bow I retired from the lists, intercepting as I did so a deprecating look from dove-eyed Fanny Merton towards Miss Otway, which that young lady answered by a slight toss of her graceful head. My gentle hostess here compassionately hastened to my assistance, and became suddenly interested in the health of my married sister and her olive branches, till the entrance of Mr. Merton, his two sons, and a couple of gentlemen guests, completely restored my equanimity.

Smarting as I still was under the unsparing onslaught Miss Otway had just made on me, I found my gaze involuntarily following and I fear admiring her every movement, so full of careless grace, of easy elegance. Of course she was surrounded, flattered, courted, for she was an heiress as well as a beauty, not to speak of her being a matchless and most capricious coquette. How bewitchingly she would smile one moment on the suitor from whom she would scornfully turn the next!—how she would overwhelm with contemptuous raillery this hour the unlucky being to whose whispered flatteries she had perhaps silently listened a short time before!

Beautiful, wonderfully beautiful she was, and changeable in her loveliness as an April day; now all smiles, sparkling epigram and repartee, then full of quiet, graceful dignity, a creature formed surely to bewilder, fascinate, utterly bewitch a man, do anything but make him happy. Such were my reflections, despite all efforts to the contrary, as I sat beside pretty, gentle Miss Merton, vainly endeavouring to concentrate my attention on herself. My folly, however, went no farther and I never joined the group paying Miss Otway such assiduous court. I felt instinctively that my nature was capable of conceiving a deep and lasting attachment, one which, if unhappy, would cloud a great part perhaps of my future life, and I knew that Geraldine Otway was one formed to inspire such a feeling, and after winning her aim, to laugh at the sufferings of her victim. Warned in time, I resolved to be prudent, and to keep without the charmed circle surrounding this modern Circe.

After the lapse of a few days, during the course of which we had barely exchanged a few words of commonplace civility, she seemed to become gradually aware of my existence, and then came my fiery ordeal. When she would ask with her bewildering smile, "Mr. Saville, please turn my music for me?" how could I say no, and then, when I would make a feeble effort to get away from her side, from the witchery of her sparkling eyes, and she would softly say, "What, tired so soon?" I would struggle like a bird in the grasp of the fowler, and for the time submit. I began to fear it was my destiny to love this beautiful, wayward siren, and well I knew what my reward would be if I weakly allowed myself to do so. I never deceived myself by indulging any illusory hopes. I knew that I was passably good-looking, young, and not a dunce. My family was as good as her own.

My income, though likely to appear small in the eyes of an heiress, was a comfortable one, but these advantages never induced me to hope even for one moment that I would have any chance with her. I knew that she had spent a winter in Quebec and another in Montreal, during both of which she had been a reigning *belle*, had discarded men far superior to myself in wealth and position, and would probably yield up her freedom only to some great magnet whose social standing would elevate him, at least in her estimation, above the greater part of his fellow-men.

Life would have been very pleasant to me during my visit at Fairview Villa had it not been for the constant struggle between judgment and inclination. Could I have blindly yielded myself up to her fascinations, living only for the present, careless—oblivious of the future, all would have been sunshine; but I knew that an awakening from the intoxicating trance, bringing with it an hour of reckoning for me, not for her, would come, when she would say "good-bye for ever," and go on her way careless and smiling, leaving me to the misery of shattered hopes and an aching heart. I repeated inwardly, over and over again, that it should never come to this—that I would turn a deaf ear to her soft words, be marble to her wiles. We shall see with what success.

Pic-nics, boating and riding parties; walks by moonlight, sunlight, starlight; croquet on the lawn; billiards in the parlour; music in the drawing-room, succeeded each other with bewildering rapidity, and through all, Geraldine Otway shone, and glittered, and queened it, till I sometimes feared my only chance of safety lay in instant flight. Prudence whispered it would be my surest protection, but weak will found many excuses for avoiding the step. My sudden departure might offend Mrs. Merton; I wanted change of air; I was conscious of danger, and therefore able to take care of myself, and—in short, I stayed.

Pic-nics were a favourite pastime with us, and we often resorted to the beautiful woods that lay about a mile from Fairview Villa, and spent a pleasant time with green foliage and sunbeams overhead, and soft moss and wild flowers beneath our feet.

On one occasion that our wandering had extended into the green depths of the wood farther than usual, a sudden and violent rainstorm set in. I happened to be somewhat behind my companions, intent on gathering a bouquet of wild flowers for Charlotte Merton, a duty she had laughingly charged me with, when the deluge came down, and finding myself in a comparatively open clearing, where my choice summer suit was receiving more than a fair share of the shower, I quickened my steps to a run. On reaching a dense part of the wood I slackened my pace, and casting a glance of satisfaction at the thick roof of verdure overhead, suddenly perceived Miss Otway standing drenched and draggled (no other word for it, dear reader) under the shelter of a huge maple.

"Why, you are all wet, Miss Otway," I hastily said. "And alone, too!"

"Yes, that stupid Willy Merton worried me into standing here whilst he should go back to the carriages in search of an umbrella and shawls," was her petulant answer. "I do not think I will wait, though. I will try a race through the shower."

I held up my finger warningly as the rain suddenly poured down with renewed violence, whilst a vivid flash of lightning rent the sky, and was succeeded by a sullen peal of thunder.

She turned pale as death, murmuring:

"I do not fear many things, but I certainly stand in awe of lightning and thunder."

What was to be done? The rain pouring down with added force was penetrating the thick foliage, literally drenching my delicate companion. After a moment I removed my light over-coat and, with considerable hesitation, asked might I wrap it around her. She was generally so haughty and independent I made the offer timidly, fearing perhaps a sharp rebuff, but instead, she gratefully thanked me, and nestled her little cheek inside the collar with a child-like satisfaction at the additional shelter it afforded. Wrenching off the little dainty fabric of tulle and rosebuds that had done duty as a bonnet a few minutes before, but which was now a shapeless, gaudy pulp, she flung it away, saying:

"Now, I have an excuse for getting a new one to-morrow. It shall be illusion, trimmed with honeysuckle."

"But you must not let the rain pour down on your uncovered head in this way," I remonstrated.

"Oh, it will do no harm. There are no false tresses embellishing it."

How very lovely she was! Disordered, drenched, still the face looked out so calmly beautiful from amid the shining wet masses of hair on either side. I felt the spell of her rare loveliness stealing over me, and I knew I must strengthen myself against its dangerous influence, doubly insidious in the soft, feminine mood that ruled her at the moment.

Another vivid flash with accompanying sullen rumble, and again the colour left her cheek, and a look of terror crept over her face.

"What are we to do?" she piteously asked, turning to me.

She was so touching, so winning in her girlish tremors and helplessness that a wild impulse to tell her there and then how loveable, how fascinating she was, took possession of me, and afraid of myself, of my own want of self-control, I stood silent at her side. Another flash, another peal, and she convulsively clutched my arm, bowing her head on it to shut out the lightning from her sight. She was trembling in every limb, her very lips white with terror, and I, weak fool, was as unnerved as herself, though from a very different cause. Ah, my fears, my presentiments had all pointed to the truth, and I had learned to love her in spite of prudence, judgment, and common sense. Yes, I had fallen into the snare I had so firmly resolved on avoiding, but she, at least, should never know my folly, never have an opportunity of curling her lip in scorn at my audacity—of trampling on feelings that to me, alas! were only too earnest. Was I not tried—tried almost beyond my strength with her clinging, trembling and helpless to my arm in the recesses of that dim wood? Surely I would betray myself. Ability to act or speak with outward calmness was fast deserting me. Again another terrible flash. The very elements were leagued against me. Closer she clung, whispering:

"Lawrence, Mr. Saville, I shall die with terror."

The sound of my Christian name, which seemed to have escaped her lips involuntarily, the close, but soft pressure of her little fingers as they closed so imploringly on my arm, the graceful head bowed almost on my shoulder, all combined to rout completely my presence of mind—the calmness so necessary to me then, and I felt that unless I made a mighty and immediate effort, my doom was sealed.

"Miss Otway," I quietly said, "there is really no danger. Pray be calm, and allow me to seat you here, under the tree, where you will be more sheltered from the rain."

Whether owing to the struggle going on within me, my voice had assumed a degree of coldness I had not intended it should, or that the words in themselves, containing a sort of implied wish to rid myself of the duty of supporting her, incensed her proud spirit, she instantly raised her head from my arm, and with the look and bearing of an offended queen, flung my coat from her and walked forth in the midst of the deluge coming down still with undiminished violence.

"Miss Otway," I besought, I urged, "for heaven's sake wait a few moments longer. This heavy rain will soon be over!"

She made no reply beyond slightly contracting her dark eyebrows, and pursued her course. It was distressing beyond measure to see that delicate frail creature exposed to such a storm, and I renewed my entreaties for her to return to the shelter of the wood, but received no reply, nothing but contemptuous silence. Again a vivid flash of lightning, a crashing peal of thunder overhead. "Ah, poor girl, she will stop now," thought I. But I was mistaken. Her indomitable pride triumphed over every feeling, and though her cheek became if possible of a still more deathly whiteness, she steadily kept on her way. I came closer to her, proffering my arm, my coat, which were both mutely but disdainfully rejected. Thus, I following her in an ignominious, valet style of companionship, we plashed on through rain and mire till we at length reached our party, the men of which had constructed a temporary shelter for the ladies by drawing the carriages together.

"Why, you are in a shocking plight, Miss Otway. I hope friend Saville has taken good care of you," said Mr. Merton.

"Oh yes," she rejoined with stinging sarcasm; "he is such a very prudent young gentleman."

"Come, Geraldine, don't be cross because your pretty bonnet is among the things that were," interrupted Miss Merton, who always kindly came to my rescue.

"But did you not meet Willy and the shawls?" questioned our host. "He set off some time ago with a sufficient quantity to construct a wigwam if you had desired it, not to mention two umbrellas and a parasol."

"We did not meet him, Mr. Merton. I suppose he has been seeking for a short cut through the wood, which instead has proved a long one."

"Geraldine, quick, step into the carriage. We have plenty of place for you," called out Miss Gray.

"Yes, if you are not afraid of getting your dresses wet or spoiled, or of my fatiguing you otherwise," she replied, darting another withering look towards my hapless self.

"What an unlucky fellow I am," I mournfully thought when, fairly started some time later on our homeward route, I wondered over the events of the day. "I have made myself fairly odious to her; and heavens! what a fire-brand she is!" But, alas, I vainly sought to fortify myself by the latter uncharitable reflection, and I was no sooner in my own room, whither I had instantly retired on arriving at the house, to change my wet clothes, than I found myself kissing like a verdant school boy the silk lining of my coat collar against which her soft cheek had so prettily nestled a short while ago.

"Fool! idiot! mad-man!" I groaned, as the full meaning of this act of folly rose suddenly upon me, revealing that love for this peerless creature had indeed, spite of all my resolutions and efforts, crept into my heart. "All I can do now is to hide my madness from every eye, but from hers above all other. She hates, scorns me now, but, so help me heaven, she shall never laugh at me!"

On entering the drawing-room, there was Miss Otway in a fresh, delicate tinted robe, showing no signs of the late great fatigue and exposure she had undergone beyond a brighter flush on her cheek and a greater brilliancy in her dark eyes. She never noticed me all the evening beyond launching at my devoted head, on one or two occasions, some sarcasms as cutting as they were wholly unprovoked, and from which I sought refuge in the society of Miss Merton. The companionship of the latter really pretty, amiable girl was always agreeable to me, principally for two reasons. First, she was quite in love, I well knew, with the gallant Captain Graham, of the ——th, a handsome young officer who had lately joined our party, (and who by the way was hopelessly in love himself with Miss Otway) so I saw no risk of my attentions being misinterpreted; secondly, she was an intimate, or as young ladies call it, a bosom friend of the wilful mistress of my heart, and often chose her for the theme of our long chats together, recounting so many instances of the generosity, kindness and better nature of the latter that my chains after each such dangerous dialogue were more closely riveted than if I had been in company with Miss Otway herself. The conduct of that young lady continued the same for a few days as it had been on the evening of the luckless pic-nic, I, all the time, even whilst smarting under her petulant injustice, finding a gloomy satisfaction in the thought that my secret was safe. Then again her mood changed, and she became friendly and conciliating even to the point of making advances which I certainly did not meet more than half way, even if I went that far.

One beautiful afternoon that several of us had gone on an exploring expedition on horseback to some fine view in

RosannA Mullins Leprohon

the neighbourhood, I found myself by her side with Capt. Graham as we were turning our horses' heads homewards. Suddenly she discovered that "she had forgotten her lace handkerchief, and hoped that Captain Graham would have gallantry enough to go for it." The directions, to say the least, were rather vague, and the accomplished son of Mars departed on his mission, smiles on his lips and weary disgust in his heart. Turning towards me she said with her softest smile:

"Spur up, Mr. Saville. We can ride two abreast here."

Ah! merciless coquette! arch traitress! she was determined on leading me into a confession. How could I resist her? Would that she had been a serf—a peasant girl, anything that I might have hoped to have room for my own, but instead she was the petted heiress, the merciless flirt, and I a miserable captive with nothing to console me under the weight of my chains save the certainty that none knew I wore them. Very calmly I accepted her invitation to ride beside her, and we journeyed on, the golden sunlight quivering through the green branches overhead, the soft summer winds caressing our foreheads, and yet our talk was as dull and prosaic as if we had been a couple of elderly respectable people with the cares of the state, or of a family, on our shoulders. Suddenly she turned full towards me, saying with a charming smile:

"Now for a race, Mr. Saville. If you win, you may name your reward."

With a look of laughing defiance that wonderfully heightened her exquisite beauty, she glanced archly at me and then set off at full speed. Easily I could have overtaken her and she must have known that well, for few horses excelled in speed my own good steed kindly accommodated with a comfortable stall in the stables at Fairview Villa, but I had no intention of jeopardizing my secret which this girl seemed bent on wringing from me, and at a very moderate rate of speed I followed in her wake. After a time she looked sharply round, and either angered by the slowness of my pace, or by my preoccupied look, she struck her spirited little mare angrily across the ears, and the latter catching the fiery mood of her mistress, gave a bound forward and set off at break-neck speed. Anxious beyond measure, I spurred forward, dreading every moment some accident to the frail girlish creature I saw flying before me through the interstices of the wood with such reckless disregard of caution. Now, had I not firmly determined when commencing this humble recital, that it should possess the merit of being at least veracious, even at the expense of dullness, I should here enliven it by a rapid, brilliant account of some deadly peril which would suddenly menace Miss Otway, say for instance, her horse rearing on the brink of a precipice, from which strait she would be delivered entirely by my strength of arm and presence of mind; but resisting manfully the temptation, doubly strong in the present case, as I feel convinced I could make a graphic, indeed splendid sketch of the thing, I will honestly confess that she at length drew rein, safe though flushed and panting, at Fairview Villa.

I hastily dismounted so as to assist her to alight, but without waiting for my help, she sprang to the ground at the risk of a sprained ankle if not of more serious injury, and as I pressed towards her, uttered the one word, "Laggard!" with a look and voice of indignant contempt, striking at the same time her horse another light but angry blow over its neck. From her expression as she swept by me, I knew she would much rather have applied the whip to my own shoulders, but had she done so, I would not only have borne it, but spaniel-like have caressed the hand that struck me, for alas! my desperate struggles were but rivetting my chains the more securely, and I felt I was beginning to love Geraldine Otway with a love almost terrible in its intensity. Surely, surely, I was foolish—mad—to remain longer exposed to the fascinations of this temptress. I must leave without delay, leave before yielding to the impulse of some moment of passion, I should utter words of love which would be answered by smiles of ridicule; before laying bare feelings too sacred and secret to be made the jest of a hollow-hearted coquette and her friends.

ROSANNA MULLINS LEPROHON

How she persecuted, lashed, taunted me that evening! More than once I retorted, sharply if not rudely, for my own character was beginning to suffer from the peculiar irritation engendered by mental suffering. Really this girl was trying me in every way beyond my strength! On my pillow, that night, I made up my mind that the next day should be my last at Fairview Villa and that I should tear myself away from the fascinations of this Eden, the memories of which would embitter many a long hour in the dreary future.

With the sunshine of the following morning, Miss Otway's smiles had returned, and as the day was bright but pleasantly cool, Miss Gray proposed a botanizing excursion to the woods, indignantly protesting against baskets of refreshments which would give our expedition the air of a vulgar, every day pic-nic, instead of a scientific exploration. "Papa" Merton quietly smiled at this, and in despite of the warning, some hampers containing the *materiel* of a very dainty lunch, were slipped into the carriage, proving I may as well say before hand, as welcome to Miss Gray as to the rest of our hungry party when luncheon hour came round.

The members of the coming expedition were already standing in groups on the verandah when I joined them, and Miss Otway, radiant in fresh loveliness, and in the coolest and most becoming of morning toilettes, was standing chatting to Miss Gray who, armed with a basket and some tiny garden implement for transplanting, looked as if she intended business.

"Who knows anything about plants, their classes, orders and genera?" inquired Miss Otway.

As she fixed her eyes on me at the conclusion of the sentence, I muttered something about having forgotten Botany since I had left college. The other gentlemen of the party murmured a similar confession.

"Well, as I do not intend that Miss Gray, who is really well versed in it, shall have all the glory of the expedition to herself, I propose we make it a sort of generally scientific thing. Each member shall pursue the study for which he or she has most aptitude, be it geology, mineralogy, botany, so that all may return learned-looking and triumphant. What do you think Mr. Saville?"

"I have forgotten them all," I pleaded. A general and significant cough of acquiescence, each on his own count, again ran round the gentlemen of the circle, when Miss Otway reported:

"I see Mr. Saville is bent on demoralizing our scientific forces, so to punish his indolence and keep him out of mischief, I shall condemn him to hold my specimens. He will at least be able to do that."

Thus enlisted in her train, and only too happy, if the truth be told, for the circumstance, I approached her side, inwardly thinking that as it was my last day (for her smiles and charms had but strengthened my resolve of leaving her) I might take one more sip of the intoxicating happiness I found in her society ere I renounced it for ever.

Started on our way, she turned to me, saying, "Now, every little weed or wild flower you see, gather it so that in such a number we may chance on getting some verdant treasure with which to astonish and delight the real botanists of the party."

Oh, what a walk that was! Loitering among sunshine and flowers—stooping sometimes to gather plant or fern.

"It is fortunate for me," thought I, "that this is the last day of temptation, or otherwise I should surely make a fool of myself."

"Come, show me the fruits or rather flowers of your industry, Mr. Saville. What! common clover—dandelion—catnip—why, what are you thinking of? If this is a specimen of your abilities, I fear I will never be able to teach you even the little botany I know myself."

I looked steadily, earnestly at her as she stood beside me, smiling up in my face, and then suddenly said, it seemed in spite of myself:

"You have taught me one lesson too many already—one which I only hope I may be able to speedily forget."

I was unprepared for the crimson tide that so abruptly rushed to her face, flushing even the tiny shell-shaped ears showing so daintily from under her little hat, and I was equally unprepared for the suddenness with which her eyes, abashed and half frightened-looking, sought the ground. A long silence followed, I inwardly ruminating on my rashness and resolving on more circumspection; when at length raising her eyes, but still looking away from me, she hesitatingly said in a low tone, very unlike her usual clear ringing accents,

"Explain your words, Mr. Saville."

Ah, Siren! She had brought me to the very verge of a declaration—another moment and I would have been at her feet, almost kissing the hem of her garments, but summoning all my self-command, my manhood's pride to my aid, I replied with a tone of gay politeness that cost me a mighty effort, for I had to bite my lip till the blood almost started.

"You have taught me, Miss Otway, how charming, how irresistible a pretty woman can render herself."

Her face flushed again, but this time angrily and proudly.

"Good!" thought I, finding even in the midst of my own secret suffering, a satisfaction in the pang I had just inflicted on her vanity.

"Diamond cut diamond, wily coquette! You have robbed me of happiness and hope, but not of self-respect. You shall have one *scalp* the less to hang on to your girdle of feminine triumphs."

Another pause, during which I assiduously commenced gathering another handful of the first weeds that came within reach, to replace the former specimens which she had thrown away. As usual, she first broke silence by carelessly asking,

"Are you going to row for Mrs. Merton's silver arrow in the boat race coming off this week?"

"I won't be here, Miss Otway. I am obliged to leave."

"Yes—when?" she calmly asked, as she carefully shook off a little insect resting on a pretty fern, forming part of her collection.

"To-morrow," was my brief rejoinder.

If I had unconsciously calculated on the sudden announcement of my approaching departure producing an impression on her flinty heart, I had good cause to feel woefully disappointed. There was no regret, no emotion exhibited, not even as much interest as she displayed in getting rid of the tiny beetle on which her eyes were fixed. Chatting freely on different topics, expressing much interest in the forthcoming race in which Captain Graham was to ply an oar, accompanied by a carelessly polite regret that I should miss it, as well as a moonlight drive and some other pleasures in contemplation, we hastened our steps and soon rejoined the party, finding Miss Gray severely lecturing some of its members on the nature of the botanical collections they had made.

"The charity-school children might have known better than to have gathered such trash," she indignantly exclaimed, tossing aside bundles of what she sarcastically suggested might be useful to the cook at Fairview Villa as "greens." Lunch was immediately produced, however, and in the welcome prospect thus afforded to all, Miss Gray's denunciations were borne with considerable philosophy. Our return home was very cheerful, the mineralogists of the party amusing themselves by firing their specimens at each other, or at a given mark.

Miss Otway was in excellent spirits, brilliant, witty, playful, a strong contrast to my own self, wrapped up in moody taciturnity, brooding over the woeful thought that on the morrow I should be far away from the enchantress who, despite prudence, reticence, resolve, had called to life so strong a passion in my aching heart.

After our return the ladies sought their rooms to dress for dinner. She (what other woman than Geraldine Otway did I give a thought to now) came down soon in one of the light, transparent, soft-tinted toilets that became her delicate beauty so well, and looking so childishly lighthearted as she fondled and teazed a pretty King Charles given her by Captain Graham, that I was divided between a wish to strangle the dog on one hand, and on the other to curse the day on which I had first met its radiant mistress. After a time Mr. Merton came in with some papers and letters, one of which he handed to Miss Otway. She opened it and then retired into the embrasure of the window to read it at her leisure behind the lace curtains. Restless and wretched, I strolled out on the lawn. Capt. Graham accosted me—I turned shortly from him. Then Miss Merton, but for once she failed to please. Next I encountered my hostess to whom I had not as yet spoken of my intended departure, but I wanted energy to meet and resist the kind entreaties which I knew would be forthcoming to induce me to change my intention.

After a listless half-hour I re-entered the drawing-room, like the moth returning to the flame that had already singed my heart, I suppose I must say, instead of wings. No one was there except Miss Otway, who was still standing near the window, looking absently from it, and mechanically twisting and creasing the corners of the envelope she held in her hand. Approaching her, I made some slight common-place remark which she as indifferently answered, and then suddenly, without word or warning, she burst into tears. Grieved, shocked, I ventured to hope that Miss Otway had received no painful news from her correspondents.

Springing to her feet, she exclaimed:

"Dolt! Don't you know that nine times out of ten a woman cries without cause?"

Ere I could recover from my astonishment, she was gone, whilst I remained rooted dumbly to the spot, not so much by the unprovoked epithet flung at my head with such a wrathful glance, as by the wondering surmise of what had I done to offend her, to call forth such an exhibition of anger.

What a termagant she was, and yet what would I not have given for the privilege of taking that termagant to my heart for life.

I saw no more of her till evening, when returning from a short stroll with my host, in which I had declared my resolve of starting, not-withstanding his hospitable entreaties, the following morning, I noted Geraldine's slight figure step forth on the verandah. Anxious for a kindly farewell word, for I knew my departure would take place the following morning ere she should have left her couch, I broke off a sprig of ivy twining round one of the pillars of the porch, and approached her.

"May I offer this as a species of olive branch, Miss Otway? I leave tomorrow."

"But we have not quarrelled," she coldly said, drawing back from me.

"Because I would not quarrel with you," I retorted, with considerable bitterness, for the thought of all she was making me suffer in the present, as well as what I would suffer in the future, awoke angry feelings within me. "Provocation on your part was certainly not wanting. Accept, however, my token, and our parting will at least be friendly. Ignorant as I am of botany, I know this leaf signifies friendship. Pray take it?"

"Why should I?" she asked. "It would be even more utterly worthless than the vegetable phenomena which Miss Gray suggested this morning might answer for greens," and with a scornful look she flung my offering away and turned back into the house. Ah, she had had the best of our singular duel, and she was still heart-free, unfettered, able to heap scorn on me which burned like fire into my very soul. Cruel, merciless flirt! Why had destiny ever permitted us to meet?

But we learn to dissemble through life, and as I sauntered round the grounds later that evening, for the glorious beauty of the moonlight tempted us all into the open air, no one would have suspected from my calm cheerful look and easy playful retorts to friendly witticisms, that I had already entered on what I feared would be to me a life-long, absorbing sorrow. Still I yearned for solitude, for quiet, and on seeing Miss Merton step forth from the library on the lawn, I quietly fell back into the shade of the trees to avoid her. My heart was too sore for even her gentle companionship then; and as soon as chance favoured me, I stole up into the room she had just left. It was as I expected, quite deserted, and lit only by the arrowy beams of moonlight that streamed through the half-drawn curtains. It was a welcome haven, and peering about through the semi-obscurity, I saw a small sofa, deep in shadow, on which I seated myself, and which probably had just been vacated by Miss Merton, for her handkerchief, recognizable by her favourite perfume, Mignionette, lay yet upon it. I took it up and inhaled the fragrance its folds gave forth, thinking all the while how feminine was the gentle owner, how different to the mocking Circe on whom I had so idly lavished the treasured love of an honest heart.

Suddenly a light figure entered from the garden and approached my obscure sofa. "Ah! here comes Miss Merton," I thought. "I will give her a surprise."

But the figure quietly seated itself beside me, saying, "I have kept you waiting, Fanny, dear; but I could not get away from that tiresome Graham before;" and the speaker was not Fanny Merton but Geraldine Otway.

And now had I not so exactly and fearlessly told the plain truth up to this present moment, I should feel tempted here to depart from it, and slur over matters a little, for instead of instantly rising, and saying as any honourable high principled man would have done, "Miss Otway, it is Lawrence Saville, not Miss Merton," I treacherously and silently retained my seat, still keeping the handkerchief to my face.

"I promised you, dear friend, to tell you what I was crying for before I should go to bed to-night," she said in a low, sweet tone, which, alas, was almost unknown to me, so rarely had she employed it in my presence.

"It was not the letter as you thought. No, it is because that wretch, Saville, who does not care one farthing for me, is going away tomorrow, and, God help me, Fanny! I dearly love him."

Here a little soft arm stole round my neck, and with a gasping sob she laid her head upon my breast.

Suddenly, involuntarily, I pressed her to my heart with a rapture beyond the power of words to express. Whether the fervour of my embrace awoke her suspicions; or, that her soft cheek had come in contact with my rough bearded one, she suddenly sprang from my side, and in a voice thrilling in its agonized shame and terror, gasped forth,

"For God's sake, who are you?"

In a moment I was at her feet, telling I was one who loved as no man had ever loved her yet, loved her in silence, in hopeless despair, almost from the moment we had first met.

"What! Lawrence Saville?" she whispered.

I renewed my prayers, my vows; but she recoiled from me in horror.

"False, cruel, treacherous!" she faltered. "How dare you allow me to betray myself thus?"

Almost forgetting in my sympathy with the terrible humiliation of that proud though noble nature, my own boundless joy to know myself beloved by her, I still knelt at her feet, imploring her to forgive—to listen to me.

"Begone from my sight, for ever," she passionately exclaimed.

"I believe not in this story of your new-found love, and even if it be true, I shall go down unwedded to my grave before you shall ever place a ring on my finger."

At this moment the door opened, and Mrs. Merton, bearing a waxen taper, entered. Her look of offended amazement on seeing Miss Otway's terrible agitation, and I kneeling at her feet, was indescribable.

"What is it?" she asked. "Tell me, Geraldine, at once."

"He, that man has insulted me," she answered, with death-pale face and glittering eyes.

My hostess turned majestically towards me, and I rose to my feet.

"How dare you, sir," she angrily questioned. "How dare you insult a young lady under my protection—under my roof. It is fortunate that you intend leaving without delay, or I should be under the necessity of saying to you—go. Mr. Saville, I have been terribly deceived in you. You are one of the very last I would have suspected capable of such conduct!"

I listened in silence to all this, for a firm resolution was taken by me in that moment to never give to man or woman explanation of the present scene; and if she chose to leave me open to obloquy and blame, was it not a cheap price to pay for the knowledge that the priceless treasure of her love was mine?

"Leave me, sir, and never let me see you again under my roof," continued Mrs. Merton, waving me imperiously from the room, whilst Miss Otway, turning to still more marble whiteness, leaned against her for support.

Resolving to make my preparations for departure without delay, I proceeded to my own room, but 'ere I had been long there, a slight tap sounded at my door, and opening it, I found it was Captain Graham.

"Mr. Saville," he said. "We are both men of the world, so a few words will suffice. I happened to be in the hall when Miss Otway made her indignant complaint to Mrs. Merton that you had insulted her. Though having no legal right to defend that young lady, she is very dear to me and without waiting for further formalities, I ask at your hands reparation for the insult she alleges having received from you?"

"At your time and hour, Captain Graham," I stiffly replied.

"Well, if I mistake not, you intend leaving for town, early to-morrow, and I will run down the day after. We can then settle everything, as well as invent a cause for our quarrel, for the young lady's name must not be mixed up in it."

I handed him my card with place of residence on it, inwardly thinking he was a manly and spirited, if not successful wooer, and with a formal interchange of bows, we parted.

Then I sat down to think for my brain was almost giddy. I who had never yet been engaged in a duel, even as a second, was now pledged to one with an adversary who was a practical hand; then again, I, a most peaceful, unoffending man by disposition, found myself lying under the grave charge of having grossly insulted a young lady in a house where I was a guest. But what mattered it all? I was beloved by her whom I had so blindly worshipped in secret, and even though she might never consent to look on me again (a thing possible with that wayward, proud spirit) the blissful consciousness that her love was mine, was amply worth all I had suffered or might suffer.

When my parting arrangements were completed, I sat down and wrote to Geraldine Otway a letter such as a man on the brink of parting from life might write to her who was the chief link that bound him to it. There was no mocking smile to dread now, no scornful taunt to fear; and I poured out my whole soul in the letter I was writing. All was earnest between her and I now. I told her, my proud, beautiful darling, how, from the first, I had struggled against loving her, how when affection for her, despite my efforts had crept into my heart, I had striven to tear it thence, never daring to dream it could be returned, but had been foiled, worsted in the combat, succeeding only in hiding my secret, and finding the only sure means of doing that—flight. I went over it all; my struggle with self in the wood the day of the storm; during our ride; our botanical excursions; and then, when my letter was finished, I sealed, pressed it to my lips for her sake, and rose to my feet.

Day was dawning cold and chill; and I resolved to hasten down to the stables and get out my horse myself, but the bridle was not to be found, and the servants were still in bed. Action was necessary to me, and finding the keen sharp air of early morning welcome to my hot cheek and temples, I decided on a stroll down the road. On my return I saw a sleepy stable boy lounging near the gate, and I gave him the requisite directions. Whilst he was attending to them, I scribbled a line to my host containing farewell thanks and excuses for my early departure, mentioning I should send for my luggage the ensuing day. This note I left on the hall table, then with one long yearning look towards the closely curtained window of Miss Otway's room, one wild agonized wish that we might yet meet again, were it only for a moment, I descended the stairs and took my solitary way.

It was hard, too, loving and loved, to part thus, but earth gives only a certain portion of happiness to each of her children, and I had had probably my share, surely an ample one, when leaning her head on my breast she had avowed her love. Would she ever relent later? Well, it did not matter much, for though no coward, I was also no shot, Graham a sure one, so in all probability, my heart so restless and full of throbbing emotions now, would soon be quiet enough. Suddenly, who should confront me emerging from a side alley but Miss Otway herself. Despite the great agitation of the moment, I noticed she looked very ill, and her eyes were swollen as if with weeping.

Almost as much embarrassed as herself, I was silent for a moment and then entreatingly said:

"Miss Otway, dare I hope that your hand will touch mine in friendly greeting before we part? I am leaving now."

"Ah, so you and that tiresome Captain Graham are really running to town to have a quiet shot at each other. What redoubtable Don Quixotes you both are!"

This was said with a very wretched attempt at her usual careless sarcasm, and then suddenly bursting into tears, she covered her face with her hands, whispering:

"Forgive me, Lawrence, forgive me! Your noble letter (I have already stolen and mean to always keep it) has softened at last my icy, selfish heart, and I can bring myself not only to confess to my follies, but also to plead for your pardon."

My darling! Surely the rapture of that moment was worth a life's ransom. Then we walked to a garden seat near us, and with the soft twittering of birds overhead and the glorious hues of sunrise rolling up in the east, bringing morning's pure fragrant breath to us, she entered on her short tale. I have never witnessed a summer sunrise since that memorable morning without recalling with gratitude to the Giver of all Good the happiness its soft dawning once brought me.

"Well, Lawrence, for so I will henceforth call you," she faltered, her charming colour and frequent pauses betraying an agitation that rendered her so feminine, so doubly dear to me, "after you left us last night, I went at once to my room, and throwing myself on a sofa, sobbed and raved alternately at myself and you, till I was almost exhausted. It was so inexpressibly mortifying to have betrayed myself so utterly to you, who had always recoiled from my advances; as to your avowal of love, I looked on it as a fiction, invented at the moment to meet that which I had so openly declared to yourself. After a time reason regained some little sway, and then Mrs. Merton knocked at my door and entered, full of wrath against you and compassion for myself. Oh, Lawrence, it was decreed that you should be an instrument in cruelly humbling my overweening pride, for there, sitting at her feet, my burning face bowed on her motherly lap, I had to do you justice and tell my tale clearly and plainly. Once finished she gently stroked my head and said: "Noble young man, how generously he bore for your sake unmerited obloquy and reproach!" Whilst Mrs. Merton was yet speaking, her quick ear caught the sound of cautious footsteps in the passage. She carefully peered out and saw Capt. Graham enter your room. The circumstance was unusual, for all the household had retired to rest, and divining some mischief, she lay in wait for him, and on his return pounced on and dragged him into the small sitting-room where we often sew and chat on rainy mornings. When smilingly but abruptly interrogated as to his business with yourself, he hesitated and stammered, upon which Mrs. Merton, who immediately began to suspect the true state of things, subjected him to a most searching cross-examination. He was yet blundering through a confused, equivocating reply, through which, however, a portion of truth penetrated, when she called my trembling self in. Again, Lawrence, you were avenged for all I had made you suffer, as I stammered forth a declaration that not only were you entirely guiltless of having insulted me in any manner, but that, I know not how it came out, you were anything but an object of dislike to me. I found some consolation for my own overwhelming mortification in the knowledge of the pang I inflicted at the same time on my luckless admirer whose officiousness had rendered the explanation necessary.

"This hard task over, Mrs. Merton brought me back to my room, and insisted on my lying down, as all danger of a duel between yourself and Captain Graham was now over. But I could not rest. I still feared some rashness on your part, some treachery on his, and I resolved to have an explanation with yourself in the morning before you should leave, a coldly polite one of course, containing a final farewell, something very different to this; so that anything like mischief should be entirely precluded. Worn out with watching, I fell into a doze on the sofa, a little before day-break.

"Awoke by the sound of a door closing, I sprang to the window, and saw you leaving the house. Oh, in that moment, Lawrence, I first realized how dear you were to me, and, trembling with anxiety, I hurried in the direction of your room, the door of which was open, to gather, if possible, some indication of where or for what you had gone so early. This letter (my darling pressed it to her lips as she spoke) was lying on the table. It was addressed to me, and, breaking the seal, I read it. Need I say its generous devotion touched me even to the inmost core of my wayward heart; need I tell you I sobbed and cried over it, fearing you had left me for ever. Ah, my selfish pride was utterly and completely subdued! Suddenly I heard the front gate unclose, and looking out, saw you enter the grounds. No time for delay, for hesitation now, and with a beating heart I hastened down the side staircase. A few moments of irresolution, a last short, sharp struggle with myself, as I saw you hastening away, and the end is told."

It was my turn now, and at the risk of being tedious, I went over all that I had previously said in my letter, and she listened in blushing quiet happiness. After a long, blissful hour together, my promised wife left me to dress for breakfast, and I, still almost unable to believe in my unhoped for happiness, sat on, listening in a sort of dream-like rapture to the pleasant sounds of morning.

A more prosaical turn was given to my thoughts after a time by seeing Captain Graham coming leisurely down the walk. He certainly did not look so miserable as I expected, but the latent fierceness with which he occasionally decapitated some harmless flower that grew within reach of his tiny cane proved his thoughts were not of a very pleasant character. Scarcely decided how to meet him, I silently waited his approach, but as soon as he saw me, he languidly said:

"Aw! Good morning, Saville. I'm deuced glad there's no necessity for that little affair between us coming off. 'Tis really as unpleasant to shoot at a fellow as to be shot at. Must say I was never in my life so taken aback, indeed, I may say stunned, as when Geraldine, hem! Miss Otway, I should say, informed me in one breath that I was an officious noodle, whom she hated as much as she liked yourself. You are a deuced sly fellow, Saville! Thought all along you were in love with that pretty little Merton girl."

"So I might have been at one time, only her affections were otherwise engaged," I answered, anxious to give my blue eyed friend a "lift."

"Really! To that big shouldered Chester, I suppose. Some women are so fond of giants. Yet no, she'd often cut him confoundedly short when he'd go up to talk to her. Perhaps it is that clever Canadian party who came from town last week, and wrote smart verses in French about her eyes and golden tresses. Wonder if he meant that Japanese switch, as the ladies call it, which she coils round her head?"

"The fact is, Captain Graham, Miss Merton never made me her confidant, but I have a considerable amount of sharpness, hem! where I am not concerned myself," I suddenly added, remembering my own late inveterate blindness in a case somewhat analogous, "and I have only to say that you are no coxcomb."

The significant emphasis, and significant look I favoured my companion with here must have been very eloquent indeed, for all at once opening his sleepy, hazel eyes very wide, his cheek slightly flushing at the same time, he said:

"You don't mean to say that I'm the favoured man?"

I smiled, but maintained a prudent silence.

"Well, I never dreamed of such a thing. I was so taken up with that shrewish, hem! with Miss Otway, I mean. But, say, hadn't you better try to look a little more like a man going to breakfast, and a little less like Speke, Livingston, or any of those other great travellers?"

Thanking him for the really serviceable hint, for my actual equipment was certainly not a proper, breakfast costume where ladies were expected to be present, my beard, owing to mental agitation, having remained unshorn, whilst my portmanteau lay prostrate on the ground a few paces from me, I left him, inwardly hoping that the saying about hearts being easily caught at a rebound, might hold good in his case and that of my fair ally.

Later it really did, and Fanny Merton, long since Mrs. Captain Graham, is still an intimate friend of Geraldine Saville, my well-loved wife.

In justice to the latter I must say before closing this short episode of my life, that Miss Otway showed me more temper and waywardness during the period I knew her, than Mrs. Saville has done in the course of the sixteen years that have elapsed since we joined our destinies together, a step, I may safely aver, neither of us have ever once regretted.

༄

Canadian Illustrated News (Montreal) 14, 21 and 28 May 1870; reprinted in *Literature in Canada*, vol. I, edited by Douglas Daymond and Leslie Monkman (Toronto: Gage, 1978), 200–220.

Ellen Kyle Vavasour Noel (Mrs. J. V. Noel) (1815–1873)

A Night of Peril! (1872)

If Ellen Kyle Noel's *The Abbey of Rathmore and Other Tales* (1859) is Mrs. Noel's first published work, as it appears to be, she began her writing career late in life. Born Ellen Kyle on 22 December 1815, in Ireland, she emigrated to Brockville, Upper Canada, in 1832 and married John Le Vavasseur Noel on 7 December 1833. The couple lived in Kingston for several years, and it was here that their daughter, also named Ellen, was born 14 January 1835. The family moved to Savannah, Georgia, where Noel ran a girls' school. It was on their return to Kingston about 1857 that Noel, the family name now Anglicized to Vavasour Noel, began publishing. Ireland, Canada, and the southern United States all feature in her fiction. *The Abbey of Rathmore* signals its gothicism by its title. It is a collection of three short novels—*The Abbey of Rathmore*, *Madeline Beresford; or, The Infidel's Betrothed*, and *Grace Raymond; or, The Slave's Revenge*. Of most interest is *Grace Raymond*, the story of a young Irish immigrant woman, which includes a description of the situation of black slaves on southern plantations and their relationship to their owners.

Other works by Noel appeared in *Canadian Illustrated News* (Montreal), *Canadian Illustrated News* (Hamilton), the *Canadian Monthly and National Review*, the *Saturday Reader*, and the *Family Herald*. Most were serialized novels that, like *The Abbey of Rathmore*, are characterized by involved plots, mystery, suspense, and other gothic features. "The Secret of Stanley Hall," a six-part serial that appeared in the *Saturday Reader* from 3 February 1866 to 10 March 1866, is Noel's most successful incorporation of gothic features into her story. Beginning in Montreal, then shifting to England, the story is a gothic bildungsroman that follows the young protagonist as she seeks her true identity.

Noel also published a few short stories in the same journals. "A Night of Peril!" is one such story that appeared in the *Canadian Illustrated News* (Montreal), 24 August and 31 August 1872. A note above the story's title states it was "written for the *Canadian Illustrated News*." As with several of Noel's longer fictions, "A Night of Peril!" is set on the west coast of Ireland during the Fenian rebellion. Suspense derives from a plot to kill a young Dublin lawyer who has successfully won the death penalty for rebel friends and relatives of local peasants. The young Irish woman and her grandmother who protect the lawyer at great personal risk demonstrate the courage and initiative of women who oppose violence, whether perpetrated by their own family and friends or by their enemies. Noel uses the wild, rugged, and picturesque setting in which the young man finds himself as darkness falls, to create a gothic atmosphere suitable to her story. The plot is kept to a single incident, and dialogue is used effectively to further the action.

~

Suggested Reading:
Gerson, Carole. "Mrs. J. V. Noel, Novelist," *Canadian Notes and Queries*, no. 41 (Autumn 1989), 9–11.
Noel, Mrs. J. V. "Grace Raymond; or, The Slave's Revenge." In *The Abbey of Rathmore and Other Tales*, 1859.
_____. "The Secret of Stanley Hall," *The Saturday Reader* (Montreal) February–March 1866.

A Night of Peril!

Ellen Kyle Vavasour Noel (Mrs. J. V. Noel)

The evening train from Dublin was due at the railway station near T———, an obscure town in the south-west of Ireland. A few travellers were impatiently pacing the platform and occasionally expressing their fears that some accident had caused the delay. Ere many minutes had elapsed, however, dark clouds of vapour in the distance and a rumbling sound gradually growing louder gave notice of the approach of the train. A few minutes afterwards the shriek of the engine was heard startling a thousand echoes in the neighbouring mountains, and the long line of cars rushed with fearful velocity into the station.

"Only five minutes here! Any passengers for T———!" was shouted by the guard in stentorian accents.

Only one solitary passenger obeyed the summons to alight at this wayside station. The waiting passengers and their luggage were speedily transferred from the platform to the cars, and at the expiration of the allotted five minutes the train was in motion thundering on its way to K———.

The passenger left behind was a gentleman about thirty, of pleasing appearance; the figure above the medium height, slightly formed, with a manly bearing; the face interesting; the noble brow and thoughtful eye denoting intellect of no common order. Though still young he had already attained considerable reputation in the legal profession and had lately rendered himself conspicuous at the Irish bar by his able prosecution of some Fenian prisoners, he being retained as counsel for the Crown, which prosecution had ended in their conviction of treason and consequent condemnation and imprisonment for life.

As the train moved off a railway porter approached the traveller we have been describing, and asked if he was going to stop at T———, and wished his luggage sent on to the hotel.

A curt negative was the reply.

"Is there no conveyance here from Mr. Meredith's. I hoped to find a carriage waiting to take me to the Lodge," remarked the traveller in tones of disappointment.

"Shure, yer honour wasn't expected till to-morrow!" broke in suddenly a gaunt wild-looking creature who, with other loiterers, had gathered on the railway platform to see the Dublin train come and go. He was considered half-witted, but there were some persons who declared he was more knave than fool. He made mendicancy a trade, not from inability to labour, but from the love of a vagrant life, appealing to the compassion of his fellow-creatures by the utter wretchedness of his appearance. A coat literally of many colours—owing to its various patches—fastened round the throat, hung from his shoulders, leaving the muscular arms bare, an old felt hat or caubeen battered into a grotesque shape, traheens—or stockings without feet—and tattered brogues completed his attire. His face was exceedingly repulsive from the sinister expression of the deep-set eyes which flashed their baneful light from beneath the shaggy brow which, as well as the matted locks covering the ill-shapen head, were of an ebony hue.

"Not expected! did they not get my note informing them that I should arrive this evening?" asked the traveller in tones of annoyance.

"Not a letther ever came. In coorse if it did they would be here to meet yer honour."

"And who are you who speak so confidently on the subject," and the gentleman eyed the vagrant with mingled curiosity and disgust.

"Tony *dhu*, or black Anthony, plase yer honour—
that's what they call me. And you are Counshellor Dalton
from Dublin, I'll go bail!" he added with a glance of peculiar
meaning at one of the bystanders, a dark-visaged countryman who was listening eagerly to the colloquy between the
vagrant and the traveller.

"How do you know my name? You never saw me
before."

"Shure you say you want to go to the Big House, and
didn't Mike the futman tell me yestherday you was comin'
down to visit the young lady," and Tony leered hideously at
the Counsellor.

"When did he say I was coming?"

"To-morrow, plase yer honour, and he was to come
over wid the dog-cart to dhrive yerself and the portmanty to
the Lodge."

Mr. Dalton paced the platform a few moments in
some perplexity, then turning to the porter who was still
guarding his luggage he said:

"I will leave my portmanteau in your care until to-
morrow and walk to the Lodge. It is not very far, I believe,
taking the mountain road."

"Not more than three miles, and the evening is pleasant," was the porter's observation.

"Yes, I shall no doubt enjoy the walk, and the pure
mountain breezes will be quite refreshing after being shut
up in a crowded court house, inhaling the heated atmosphere, during the last week."

Dalton was then turning quickly away about to leave
the station when he was stopped by a whining appeal from
Tony.

"The Saints bless yer honour! won't you give a shilling
to the poor beggar to dhrink yer health and success to ye at
the Big House with the purty lady. Shure isn't she the greatest beauty in the counthry. Sorra one in the barony can
hould a candle to her. And won't ye be the happy man when
ye get her. And aren't you the clever counshellor, Misther
Dalton. Didn't you do for 'the boys' in the Dublin Court

House. Bedad, by the power of yer tongue, ye brought them all in guilty, the crathurs! And isn't it yerself will have the curses showered thick and heavy on yer head—the curses of the widdy and the orphant!"

This last remark was muttered to himself as he clutched the silver coin Counsellor Dalton flung to him as he left the platform, and a malignant light shone in his eye as he watched him take the road to the mountains.

"He is come afore we looked for him, Dennis!" the vagrant added, in a low voice addressing the countryman already mentioned.

"So he is, Tony! but for all that he'll not escape us, the villyn! 'The boys' must be tould. Run for the bare life, man! don't let the grass grow undher yer feet! I'll take to the road meself, and afore long the news of his coming will spread through the counthry. He mustn't lave the mountains alive. It's well he took the road through them, for he'll loose his way and the night won't be long falling."

Dennis and his vagrant companion now hurriedly left the station, each rapidly pursuing a different way.

The evening was fine. An autumnal sunset was shedding a mellowed radiance over the wild but picturesque scenery of the mountains, glinting on their granite peaks, which rose bare and abrupt into the clear blue sky, and touching with golden light the dark green leaves of the holly and the silvery foliage of the ash, which sprung out grotesquely from the deep fissures in the cliffs. The road which Dalton pursued at first led up a precipitous ascent, then at a considerable elevation it wound through a deep defile, in some places so narrow that it seemed to be cut in the rugged cliffs that bordered it on either side rising high as the eye could reach. At the end of this gloomy pass the prospect suddenly opened, and Dalton, struck by the savage grandeur of the scene, seated himself on a moss-covered rock to contemplate it a while and indulge in the luxury of a cigar. Ranges of mountains piercing the clouds rose boldly around him, their sides showing magnificent precipices entirely destitute of herbage, with more than one silvery waterfall leaping from crag to crag. Far below was a deep secluded glen, through which a mountain torrent wound a tortuous course, rushing and foaming over its rugged bed. On the bank of this noisy stream rose the humble cottage of a peasant, the only habitation Dalton had yet seen in his brisk walk from the road-side station. Nothing could exceed the picturesque solitude of its situation, hemmed in by the towering mountains. One solitary figure was seen crossing the glen in the direction of the cottage or cabin, as it is called in Ireland. It was a young girl in the picturesque costume of the Irish peasant, her scarlet cloak—the hood of which was partly drawn over her face—contrasting brightly with the verdant turf over which she lightly sped and the sombre hue of the surrounding mountains. After a while the shades of evening gathered over the scene, and although daylight still lingered on the fantastic peaks above, in the glen below the twilight was deepening rapidly.

"By Jove! I shall be benighted in this wild place," exclaimed Dalton, flinging away his cigar and continuing his way by hastily descending the precipitous path leading to the glen, through which the road to the Lodge lay. "How foolish I was to remain so long admiring the sublimity of nature! It would not be so pleasant to have to spend the night in these deep solitudes, although they do look so grand and imposing by day."

From the glen more than one narrow defile opened a way through the mountains. One of these led in the direction of the Lodge, the residence of Owen Meredith, Esq. In the darkening twilight, Dalton was obliged to approach the cottage in order to inquire his way. As in most Irish cabins the door was open, and through it he could see the interior. There was an air of comfort, and an appearance of neatness, not always seen in the dwelling of the Irish poor. A large turf fire burned in the wide fire-place, to which a piece of bog-wood had been added, and by the ruddy light it cast around, the inmates were distinctly seen. There were two women, one old, the other in the bloom of girlhood. The older woman was sitting on a low seat on one side of the hearth, busily knitting, while she listened with eager interest to some piece of news the girl was telling, and so deeply were they engaged talking, that they heard not the footsteps of Dalton approaching the door, which, however, fell softly on the grassy paths without.

The countenance of the girl was very prepossessing, the blue eyes had a peculiar sweetness of expression, and her rich masses of auburn hair might have excited the envy of a city belle.

His own name pronounced by the girl, arrested Dalton's steps on the threshold, and made him pause to listen.

"And who tould you he was come, Aileen?" the old woman asked, dropping her knitting and looking anxiously at her young companion.

"Tony *dhu* the vagabone, and he tould some of the boys, and sent them on his thrack."

"And where did you see Tony, avourneen?"

"When I was leaving T———, afther selling the eggs this evening, he come up to me and tould me to tell Brian." He was going at full speed to carry the news to Mike Devanny. "You know granny, two of his sons was among the presoners."

"And what do 'the boys' intend to do wid the misfortunate gintleman. Shure it isn't his life they are afther."

"Meself doesn't know, granny, but Tony said as much that nothing else would satisfy them. I hope Brian won't take any part in the business. Shure it would be the manes of turning Misther Meredith and Miss Dora agin us, and aren't they the best friends we have in the counthry?"

At this moment the old woman's eye fell on the distinguished-looking stranger standing in the doorway, and at her exclamation of surprise, Aileen turned eagerly round. With a start of dismay she recognised the Counsellor, the lurid light of the fire gleaming on his now troubled face. She had seen him before more than once, during his visits to the Lodge.

"Pardon my intrusion," he said, advancing a few steps, "night has overtaken me on my way to Mr. Meredith's, and

I called to inquire in what direction is the pass leading to the Lodge."

Aileen and her grandmother exchanged glances.

"I have heard part of your conversation," he continued, "and I am aware of some danger threatening me, though I have yet to learn how I have incurred the ill-will of those who are strangers to me."

"Well then, sir, the thruth is 'the boys' have sworn to be revinged bekase ye proshecuted some of their people that was took up for Fenians, and denounced 'the cause' in yer grand speech afore the judge."

"Ah, now I understand, I was Queen's Counsel in the case," and a sense of the danger of his position impressed Dalton painfully.

"Shure it was the witnesses that swore agin them that was most to blame," remarked Aileen, "and that is what I tould Tony dhu this blessed evening, but he wouldn't listen. He said it was yer honour's clever tongue cross-examining them that ruined the crathurs intirely."

"That fellow is no fool," said Dalton half irritably, "He should be taken up for vagrancy."

"Thrue for you, sir! but beggar as he is, and fool as he purtinds to be, he is mighty useful to 'the boys,' for he goes everywhere and picks up bits of news here and there."

"The distance from this glen to the Lodge isn't more than a mile," Dalton resumed after a short pause, "If you point out the way I may yet reach it in safety."

"Don't attimpt it, Misther Dalton," put in Aileen eagerly, "The road is beset wid them that is no friends of yours."

"Perhaps I had better turn back and seek refuge in T———." There was perplexity, but no craven fear in the fine eyes looking so anxiously into the commiserating face of pretty Aileen Hanlon.

"That wouldn't save ye I'm afeard. Afther dark the mountains is no safe place for thravellers. The counthry is in a dhreadful state, sir. I wish you hadn't vintured down here now, when the feeling is so hard agin you."

"My coming unexpectedly is very unfortunate. If I had waited until to-morrow, and been met by a servant with a conveyance from the Lodge, I would have escaped this peril."

"I doubt it, sir! they would have attacked you even then. The very servints at the Lodge couldn't be depinded on."

"Is there no place where I could be secreted till morning?" Dalton asked very anxiously, for his situation was looking alarming, and even his brave spirit quailed before the danger threatening him.

Aileen turned eagerly to the old woman who had remained silent during this conversation between the counsellor and her granddaughter, and they conversed in Irish for a few moments. By their gestures and the expression of the old woman's face, Dalton conjectured that the girl was proposing something which she did not approve. In the midst of this altercation a distant whistle was heard.

"Holy Biddy!" if it isn't that vagabone Tony coming for Brian. He'll be here in no time!" exclaimed Aileen excitedly, "Granny, ye must consint! You wouldn't have him kilt at our door. Think of Miss Dora and all she done for you."

"Well, do as you like, Alannah! Shure you are right. It is his only chance."

As the giant figure of Tony *dhu* appeared in the doorway Aileen, in order to hide the trepidation his unexpected arrival caused, busied herself with some oatmeal cakes that were baking on the hearth for their evening meal.

"God save all here!" was Tony's salutation as he strode into the cabin.

There was no response of "God save you kindly," for both women were annoyed at his intrusion. He noticed the coolness of his reception, but no ways abashed he advanced towards the fire, and squatting down beside Aileen's kneeling figure, stretched out his large ill-shapen hands before the blaze, while he abruptly asked:

"Where's Brian?"

"Keep yer distance!" exclaimed Aileen fiercely, as she sprang indignantly to her feet and shrank with aversion from the vagrant.

"Won't ye let a body have an air of that fire?" he asked sullenly.

"Shure it isn't cowld ye are this fine evening," she retorted angrily, "and what brings ye here at all when ye aren't wanted."

"I'm not going to inconvanience ye long, and ye might keep a civil tongue in yer head, Aileen Hanlon, and not thrate a poor omadhawn in that way. Is them the manners ye larn't her, granny?" he added, turning indignantly to the old woman.

"Never heed her, Tony," she answered soothingly. "She is not in the best of timpers to-night, but what are ye wanting, avick?"

"Where's Brian? he is wanted out," was Tony's answer.

"Who wants him?" asked the widow sharply.

"'The boys,'" was the curt reply.

"Well, Brian isn't to the fore, as you can see. He's not back yet from T———," broke in Aileen, her eyes still flashing anger as she turned them on Tony. "So be off wid ye at onct and leave Brian alone."

"Is there any work on hand, Tony?" asked Mrs. Hanlon, anxious to find out 'the boys'' intention with regard to Dalton.

"Meself doesn't know, granny; it isn't to the likes of me 'the boys' would tell their saycrets."

"Now, Tony, you needn't purtend that to me," remarked the old woman in a wheedling voice. "You know what's going on as well as any one."

A pleased grin broke over the vagrant's hideous face, but at this moment his attention was diverted by the entrance of a good-looking young man.

"Here is Brian himself!" he exclaimed joyfully. "You're just in time, man alive! I'm waiting for you."

"What's up now?" asked Brian half sullenly.

"They're wanting ye, avick! but may be you haven't heard the news."

"I heard nothing strange; what have you to tell?"

"He's come, begorra!"

"Who is come?"

"The counshellor from Dublin! who else?"

Brian started.

"He was not expected till to-morrow," he remarked moodily.

"Thrue for ye, but he's come any how."

There was a gloomy silence for a few moments. It was broken by Brian's inquiring in a husky voice what was wanted with him.

"Meself doesn't know," was the evasive answer.

"I must break me long fast first," said Brian, with an angry scowl at the omadhawn, who was grinning provokingly, enjoying the pain his unwelcome summons gave him.

Aileen now placed the evening meal on a small deal table covered with a coarse white cloth. Black Anthony was not invited to sit down at the humble board, but was handed some food which he ate ravenously. While the widow and her grand-children were silently and sadly eating their simple supper of oat cakes and milk, the little party was increased by the entrance of a tall muscular peasant, in whose dark eyes gleamed the savage light of fiendish passion. Through a chink in the boarded partition, which separated Aileen's little room from the kitchen—as the larger apartment was called— Dalton could see and hear all that was passing, and a shudder passed through his frame as his eye fell on the fierce countenance of the new comer. With a muttered imprecation he demanded what was keeping Brian.

"Isn't there enough widout me for this business?" asked Brian sullenly.

"But ye're wanted to sind up to the Lodge to see if the counshellor is there," retorted the man sharply.

"There's Tony! send him instead of me," pleaded Brian.

"I darn't go, Brian!" broke in Tony hastily. "Mister Meredith forbid me the house, and threatened to set the dogs on me."

"Why do ye think he has got to the house," inquired Brian.

"Because we cant find him no where, and we have been pathrolling the road to Mr. Meredith's ever since nightfall."

"And if he has got safe there, shurely ye don't mane to attack the house, Dan Connor?" demanded Aileen, indignantly.

"Of course not! We have nothing agin Misther Meredith. A good landlord he is, no doubt; but if we come across Counshellor Dalton this blessed night we'll batther the life out of *him*, anyhow."

"It's a cruel business, and I don't like it at all," said Brian, moodily.

"Then have nothing to do wid it, Brian, asthore," observed his sister, boldly. "I tell you, Dan Connor," she continued, vehemently, as she looked defiantly at the man, "it is a base act ye intend to do. To think of so many seeking the life of one. It is a cowardly deed, and no good will come of it."

"It is very well for a pretty colleen like yerself to talk so bowldly, Aileen," said Dan, looking admiringly at the girl's handsome face flushed with indignant excitement, "but such bitther words from yer brother or any other mortial man, would soon lay him stretched on the flure. But I'm losing time here. Brian Hanlon," he added, menacingly, "will ye come or will ye not?"

With a deprecating look at his sister, Brian rose without another word and followed Dan Connor and Tony out of the cabin.

"It's a pity I didn't offer to go meself to the Lodge," remarked Aileen as she was left alone with her grandmother.

"Arrah, what for, avourneen?"

"To tell Misther Meredith that he is here. Shure he would send the peelers to convey him to the Lodge. Faix," added the girl with sudden decision, "I'll run up to the House, anyhow, and let them know."

The old woman looked up startled.

"Have you lost yer seven sinses, girl, to think of turning informer. Shure if they even knew we harboured him they would burn the roof over our heads."

The bed-room door now gently opened, and Dalton advanced a few steps into the kitchen.

"Do not, I beg of you, run any risk on my account," he said, with a grateful look at Aileen.

"I'ts bekase I'm afeard black Anthony suspects that you are here," she said thoughtfully. "I saw him more nor once watching that chink in the partition betune us and the room you were in."

"If you think so, I will go away out into the darkness —any where—trusting in Providence, rather than you should incur the ill-will of those malignant men."

"Don't think of it, sir. It would be just going to sartain death to lave this house where your enemies is prowling about."

A faint cry from Mrs. Hanlon now startled Dalton and her grand-daughter.

"Blessed Mary! if there isn't that vagabone's ugly face close up agin the windy looking in at us," exclaimed the old woman in accents of consternation. "You were right enough, Aileen, he suspects something, and is come back for no good!"

Dalton hastily retreated, taking the precautions to bolt the bed-room door against sudden intrusion. With an anxious eye he watched through the chink in the partition for the entrance of Tony. He did not wait long.

"Hooroo! I've found him out!" the vagrant exclaimed, flourishing his shelalah and dashing wildly into the kitchen.

"Be off wid ye, ye omadhawn! what foolery are ye at now?" exclaimed Aileen boldly confronting him.

"It's cute Tony they ought to call me, for I'm the wisest man of them all," he said exultingly, making a rush towards the bed-room door.

Aileen placed herself before it.

"Lave the house this minute!" she exclaimed with passionate indignation. "What did ye come back for, frightening lone women at this hour of the night?"

"Shure he's in there! didn't I see him wid me own eyes. Clear the road and let me at him!" and he pushed the girl savagely aside.

Dalton drew a revolver, determined to defend his life, yet fearful that the report of fire-arms would be heard without and attract more of his enemies to the cabin. In this moment of peril woman's wit interfered in his behalf and saved him from the threatened danger.

"Whisper, Tony, avick," said Mrs. Hanlon in a wheedling voice, laying her hand on the savage creature's arm and pulling him gently back.

He turned on her an angry look, yet stopped to hear what she had to say.

"Are ye mad to go in there alone?" the widow continued, speaking low and confidentially. "Shure he is armed and will shoot ye down like a dog. Wait till Brian comes back."

The mention of fire-arms startled Tony, and he retreated in alarm.

"Thrue for ye, Granny! but I'll go for the boys. They have guns and can shoot too. Hooroo for the fun! I've found him! I've thracked him out! Bedad the great counshellor is caught like a fox in a thrap!" and with an exultant laugh he was about to rush from the cabin when the old woman arrested him.

"Ye needn't be in sich a hurry, man alive! Stop and take a glass afore ye go. The air is sharp out in the mountains, and a dhrop of poteen will keep the cowld out."

The widow Hanlon knew Tony's weak point. The offer of a glass of whiskey was an irresistible temptation.

"Is it the rale stuff," he asked, smacking his lips, his eyes gleaming with brutal satisfaction.

"Faix, it's nothing else. Stop and rest yerself till Brian comes back and smoke a pipe wid me, and tell us all the news that's going."

"Maybe Tony would like the punch betther?" said Aileen, in conciliating tones. She understood her grandmother's motive in offering him intoxicating drink. It was their only hope of preventing his disclosing Dalton's place of concealment.

"If ye have the hot wather and the shugar convanient I'd like it well, colleen," he answered, the savage expression of his face somewhat softened by the unexpected kindness.

The ingredients for making punch were quickly produced by Aileen, and black Anthony was seated in the chimney corner smoking a dudeen—a short pipe—with a noggin of strong punch before him, for the moment forgetting the presence of Dalton in the adjoining room, oblivious of every thing but his own gratification.

An hour passed away in extreme enjoyment such as seldom fell to the lot of Tony *dhu*. Gradually the intoxicating beverage took effect, the heat of the fire and the soothing influence of the weed he was inhaling contributing their aid to steep his senses in forgetfulness. Before another half hour had elapsed he lay stretched upon the floor in the heavy sleep of intoxication.

"He'll throuble us no more to-night!" exclaimed the widow Hanlon, with a feeling of relief, as she gazed upon the prostrate beggar; "but, marcy on us, what a power of poteen it took to lay him stretched! Shure it would be more than enough to kill any dacent man."

"Isn't it well ye thought of offering him the glass, granny? Shure only for it he'd have the boys here in no time, and then nothing could save the counshellor."

Then, opening the bed-room door, Aileen spoke encouragingly to Dalton, telling him with the help of God she hoped he would still escape his cruel enemies.

"If I do I shall owe my life to your kindness," was his grateful answer, "and believe me I shall never forget the obligation."

It was now about ten o'clock. Brian had not yet returned. Notwithstanding the lateness of the hour none of the anxious inmates of the cabin felt inclined to sleep. Dalton alone in the darkness of his hiding place sat nervously listening to every sound without, occasionally conversing with his friends who whiled away the time knitting. Never did the wheels of time seem to drag so heavily, never was the welcome dawn more eagerly longed for than on this eventful night.

It was half an hour after midnight when the stillness of that mountain glen was broken by the measured tramp of many feet. Dalton started from his seat in sudden alarm. Was there a large body of Fenians approaching the cabin, or could it be a military force sent to apprehend them. What a sudden joy thrilled his heart as this thought flashed through his mind. Stealthily he approached the little window of the bed-room and looked out. By the faint star-light a dark mass was seen moving towards the dwelling, but seen so indistinctly that Dalton could not discern whether they were friends or foes. Before long, however, his trembling hopes of a rescue were confirmed as the firelight from the kitchen streaming into the darkness without flashed upon the uniform of the men, revealing an armed body of police.

"Holy Biddy be praised! your honour is saved! now here's the gauger and his men!" exclaimed Aileen, joyfully flinging open the bed-room door.

It was even so. A party of revenue police were still hunting in the mountains, and, attracted by the light in the lonely cabin, had approached to reconnoitre, thus arriving opportunely to take Dalton under their protection.

With many expressions of gratitude he bade adieu to his humble friends, placing in the hands of the widow a roll of bank notes as a marriage portion for the pretty Aileen. Instead of proceeding to Mr. Meredith's he returned to the railway station, arriving just in time for the early train, and when the morning dawned he was several miles from the scene of his night's adventure. At the request of Dalton the police were ordered by their officer not to reveal the secret of his hiding-place, lest the Hanlon family might suffer for their kindness to him by incurring the ill-will of his enemies.

The next morning Tony *dhu* awoke with a very confused recollection of what had occurred the preceding night, so that Aileen and her grandmother had no difficulty in persuading him it was all "a dhrame." But what became of "the counsellor" was a matter of surprise to more than Tony *dhu*. Where had he spent the night and how had he escaped "the boys" in their search for him through the mountains? The omadhawn stoutly affirmed that Ould Nick, who takes care of his own, had flown away with him. But the obnoxious lawyer was safe in his chambers in Dublin, thankful for his providential escape, and determined never again to endanger his life by a lonely walk through the Kerry mountains.

❧

Canadian Illustrated News (24 August 1872), 123; (31 August 1872), 139.

Ellen Vavasour Noel (Ellen Vavasour) (1835–?)

THE HOUSE-KEEPER AT LORME HALL (1872)

Little is known of the life of Ellen Vavasour Noel. She was born in Kingston, Ontario, 14 January 1835, the daughter of Ellen Kyle and John Le Vavasseur Noel. As a child Ellen moved with her parents to Savannah, Georgia, returning with them to Kingston, Ontario, about 1857, the family name Le Vavasseur now Anglicized to Vavasour.

Ellen followed in her mother's footsteps (see page 217), writing short fiction and serials, first under her own name, Ellen Vavasour Noel. She published during the same years as her mother and in some of the same periodicals: *Canadian Illustrated News* (Montreal), *Canadian Illustrated News* (Hamilton), and the *Saturday Reader*. Although her mother signed her works Mrs. J. V. Noel, there may have been some confusion between the two, for Ellen later dropped Noel, using simply Ellen Vavasour.

Like her mother, Ellen tended towards the gothic. She also preferred an oblique narrative in which the story is told by someone else to a first-person narrator, who at times interrupts to comment or moralize. "The House-Keeper at Lorme Hall" is an indirect narrative told by a young Irish nursemaid at Lorme Hall who observes the situation involving the housekeeper and the young mistress of the hall.

The Dickensian stepfather who appears suddenly on the scene is reminiscent of *David Copperfield*'s Mr. Murdstone. The two women involved are at first unwilling to step out of their roles of martyr–victims. But, despite the power of husbands over their wives at this time, the victimized wife does finally object to her husband's profligacy when it is about to threaten her children's future. Through the intervention of the housekeeper, the situation is finally resolved, revealing the solution of the housekeeper's mystery at the same time. While the setting is near Cornwall, Ontario, and the characters frequently visit Montreal, there is little distinctive of either place.

The author succeeds in interweaving several plots within a short space, even contriving a happy closure for the young narrator whose role has otherwise been that of observer of events involving others.

∽

Suggested Reading:

Gerson, Carole. "Mrs. J. V. Noel, Novelist." In *Canadian Notes and Queries,* no. 41 (Autumn 1989), 9–11.

Vavasour, Ellen. "Emilie Vernon." In *Saturday Reader* (Montreal) 3 March 1866, 406–408.

———. "Strange Stories Told at Elm Lodge." In *Canadian Illustrated News* (Montreal) 17 February 1877, 103–104.

THE HOUSE-KEEPER AT LORME HALL

Ellen Vavasour Noel (Ellen Vavasour)

O n the rose-clad stoop of a large comfortable farm-house near Cornwall an old woman is sitting. She has been knitting, but her work has dropped from her hand and she is leaning thoughtfully back in her low rocking-chair.

"Aunty, what are you thinking of?"

On being thus addressed she turned towards the speaker, a bright-looking young girl who has just come out of the house, and said:

"Would you like to hear a story, Nora?"

"A story! that I would, Aunty," Nora eagerly replied, as she seated herself beside her. "Is it about something which happened long ago when you were young?"

"Yes, child; it happened many years ago in the family that I lived with, when I first went to service. I was about your age, Nora, when I went to live at Lorme Hall, some miles from Montreal. My mistress was a widow and very wealthy; she had two children, to whom I was engaged as nurse. I had been living with Mrs. Lorme some months, when she decided upon going to Chicago to visit a relative; I, to my great delight, was to go with her to take care of the children; and we were busily engaged getting ready for our journey when I was unfortunately taken seriously ill; so my mistress had to leave me behind and take one of the house-maids in my place as nurse. Mrs. Lorme left orders that I was to be well taken care of and remain at the Hall until her return. She was a kind mistress, Nora, and a fair sweet-looking lady too. Poor thing, it would have been better for her if she had never paid that visit; but we poor mortals can't see ahead; if we could what a world of trouble we might save ourselves sometimes. 'Tis all right, I suppose, yet it is pretty hard to see things happen as they do often, and still to believe that it is best so for us. When I had recovered a little and was able to go about again, I missed the dear pretty children very much. The great house seemed very lonely and silent as I wandered drearily from one grand room to another, listening in vain for the pattering feet and merry voices of the absent little ones.

"Some weeks went by; I was quite strong again, and Mrs. Barton, the house-keeper, finding that I was handy with my needle, kept me busy, for which I was not sorry, as I did not like being idle. And now, Nora, I must tell you about Mrs. Barton. She had lived for a long time in Mrs. Lorme's family, and when her young lady, to whom she was much attached, got married, she went with her to Lorme Hall, where she became house-keeper. She was a little pale, pock-marked woman; her hair was perfectly white, but not from age, for she was not more than forty. It had become so, she said, when she lost her husband years before, when she was a young girl. I can fancy, Nora, that I see her before me now. Her trim little figure, clothed in grey or brown, for she always wore those colours, and her white hair put smoothly back beneath a black lace cap. She was, as I have said, devotedly attached to her mistress, and Mrs. Lorme returned that affection, placing the greatest confidence in her, treating her like an old friend rather than a servant, and Mrs. Barton was worthy of her esteem; there was not one among the numerous domestics of which she had the charge that did not regard her with respect and kindly feelings. Time passed, the day fixed for Mrs. Lorme's return went by, and yet in her letters to Mrs. Barton she did not speak of coming home. Mrs. Barton, I could see, wondered at her mistress' long absence. It was so unusual for her to remain long away from Lorme Hall. It was now the middle of summer; they had been gone three months when a letter arrived, telling Mrs. Barton that she was going to be married the following week to a gentleman she had met in Chicago, and that in a short time afterwards they would return to the Hall, accompanied by a party of friends. The news, as you may suppose, Nora, created no little excitement. With many wishes for her beloved mistress' future happiness Mrs. Barton set us to work to prepare for the reception of the bridal party. Two weeks later they arrived. The children were wild with delight to get home again. My mistress looked extremely well and happy; her husband, Mr. Crossham, the new master of Lorme Hall, was a fine-looking man, about, I should think, forty-five. We were all favourably impressed with his appearance and pleasing manners. Mrs. Barton was suffering from a violent attack of neuralgia, and did not see him until two or three days after his arrival at the Hall. It was one morning as I was following her up the front staircase to attend to some directions she had just given me, when as we reached the top of the stairs Mr. Crossham passed us going down. I looked at Mrs. Barton to tell her who it was, but the words froze on my lips. She was bending over the balustrade watching his retreating form; her face, Nora, was as white as your collar, and wore a wild startled expression. She turned to me, and grasping my arm in her agitation so tightly that it pained me, in a hollow tone she whispered:

"'Who is that, Kate, who is it?'

"I told her it was Mr. Crossham. Dropping her hand from my arm the words 'Oh, my God,' burst from her lips, as, turning from me, she disappeared down one of the passages leading to her room. Her strange emotion puzzled me exceedingly; but as she did not, when she saw me again, allude to what had occurred, and I did not dare ask an explanation, I was obliged to smother my curiosity as best I could.

"For some time the Hall was a scene of continual gayety, and then when autumn came and the guests began to depart Mr. and Mrs. Crossham went with some of the gay party to New York. The children were left behind, very much I saw against my mistress' wishes, but Mr. Crossham thought it best, she told Mrs. Barton. Poor little dears, it was their first separation from their mamma. Miss Ellie, the youngest, was a fair delicate child about five years old, she fretted and pined sadly for her mamma. Do what I could to comfort and cheer her, it was of no use; the call still was for her dear mamma to come back to Ellie. She could not understand why they had been left at home, although I overheard Master Frank, who was two years older, trying to enlighten her on the subject. He had heard some of the servants' gossip and told his sister that it was their new papa's fault that they were left alone, that their mamma wanted to take them, but he did not care about them and would not let their mamma take them with her. 'I don't care one bit for him, Ellie,' he added, clenching his little fist in his anger and indignation. 'I don't care one bit for him, he is not nice, and I'll tell mamma when she comes back that we don't want him to live with us any longer.' And this dislike increased during his mother's absence. He used to say that Mr. Crossham would not let her come back to them, and on their return home, after fondly embracing his mamma, he turned contemptuously away from his step-father's proffered kiss, saying,

"'I don't want to kiss you, for you took mamma away from us.'

"Mr. Crossham's face flushed either with surprise or anger. He gave a low whistle, and walked into the drawing-room. My mistress did not see this, she had passed down the hall to meet Ellie, but Mrs. Barton did and to my astonishment never reproved the boy.

"A month or two went by, Christmas came. Christmas! ah, Nora! what magic there is in that word to the young. It is a season longed for by them and welcomed with smiles and gladness; but as the years go by and they find, alas, too often, the bright dreams of youth unrealised, and see the vacant places of absent dear ones and miss familiar voices that are hushed for ever on earth, that once joyous time becomes a day of sad regrets, silent heart-aches and yearnings perhaps for that Christmas when all earthly things shall be forgotten. I have seen many Christmases since that one, Nora, and happy ones too, but it was, I think, the happiest in all my life. On that day your uncle George arrived unexpectedly from Ireland. Two years before, when I left the old country with my parents, I had promised to be his wife, though I might have to wait for years before he would be able to claim me. His elder brother had died suddenly, and the farm becoming his, he sold it and came out to America. He is old and gray-haired now, Nora, but a taller, finer looking young man could not be seen than he then was. You may imagine my feelings when I went down to the house-keeper's sitting-room where I was told some one wanted to see me and found that it was George. When I went with him that morning to the little church near Lorme Hall, so prettily decorated with evergreens, berries and flowers, and kneeling by his side thanked God for His goodness to us, there was not, Nora, a happier girl in the world than I was that bright Christmas morning.

"Soon after Mrs. Crossham announced her intention of spending the rest of the winter in Montreal,—Mr. Crossham found the Hall so dull. He had always resided in a city, and disliked the country. As they intended to board, she would take, she said, only one servant with her, and asked me to go. I did so, although I was not very willing, as you may suppose, Nora, to leave the Hall, for George had been appointed gardener there, and I was so happy; still, after my mistress' kindness to us, I could not refuse; besides I was fond of the children, who had become much attached to me.

"The night before we left, Mrs. Barton came into the nursery, where I was sitting by the fire, finishing a piece of work. Since my mistress' marriage she had become greatly changed. Her health seemed to be failing, the pleasant cheerfulness of her manner had given place to a gloomy reserve. As she seated herself near me and I looked on her haggard, troubled face, I again wondered, as I had often done before, what had caused the alteration. She spoke of our departure on the morrow. I felt for her, for I knew how lonely she would be during our absence. I told her so and wished she could go with us.

"'Would to Heaven that I were going with you,' she exclaimed, 'then I could see what he—' she stopped—and getting up from her seat came to my side. 'Kate,' she said in an earnest tone, as she looked eagerly into my face, 'Kate, you are a good faithful girl. I can trust you. Promise me if anything should happen when you are away to make you think my dear mistress is not happy you will at once let me know.' This appeal startled me. What was it she feared. I knew she disliked Mr. Crossham, for I had noticed her shrink from going into a room where she knew he was or turn out of her way to avoid meeting him, and she kept a prying curiosity,—very unusual in her with regard to other things—over every action and word of his. I had also seen her, when she thought no one was observing her, intently regarding him with an expression on her pale face I could never fathom.

"On our arrival in Montreal Mr. Crossham procured apartments at the St. Lawrence Hall, and a dreary enough time myself and the children passed for the rest of the winter in that gay crowded house. My mistress, too, seemed to become weary of the continual round of gaiety Mr. Crossham persuaded her to enter upon, and to long for the quiet comforts of her own elegant home. Spring came at last, but Mr. Crossham put off from week to week our return to Lorme Hall, although my mistress was most anxious to return again to the country. I began to dislike Mr. Crossham, as I became convinced of the utter selfishness of his character. His temper, also, was very violent,—and that he had begun to treat his gentle wife with indifference and neglect, was but too apparent. She was often left alone, and I saw sometimes the traces of tears on her fair face. I did not forget my promise to Mrs. Barton, but expecting to see her almost from day to day I did not write; besides, what could Mrs. Barton do, I thought. If my mistress was unhappy she could not help it.

"Little Ellie, always a delicate child, became this spring seriously unwell. The Doctor ordered change of air; her mother becoming much alarmed about her determined to return home immediately. Mr. Crossham did not accompany us; he had two or three engagements which must be attended to, he gave as an excuse, but if the child got worse to let him know. So my mistress, with her sick darling, returned alone to Lorme Hall. Mrs. Barton questioned me closely as to what had occurred during our absence. 'Did my mistress still seem happy?' 'Was Mr. Crossham kind to her and the children?' I could not satisfactorily answer these questions, and Mrs. Barton seemed much distressed and troubled at my replies. On her removal to the country little Ellie began to recover, though slowly, and then Mrs. Barton, who had not left Lorme Hall for about eight years, went for a few days to Montreal; but why she went she did not tell anyone, not even my mistress.

"Mr. Crossham had not been long at Lorme Hall after his return from Montreal, before his harsh tyrannical temper and heartless conduct towards his wife and her children were noticed and talked about among the servants who sincerely pitied their gentle mistress. How bitterly she must have repented that second hasty marriage, in which she had wrecked her happiness and destroyed the peace of her happy home.

"Towards the close of the summer an infant daughter was laid in my mistress's arms, but it was a delicate babe, and lived only a few days. I was regretting its loss—for my mistress grieved sadly after it—to Mrs. Barton one day. Her answer rather astonished me. I did not know what to think of her when she replied:

"'Kate, I have prayed for that child's death, and now on my knees I thank God for granting that prayer. Don't regret it!'

"Mr. Crossham spent most of his time in the city, spending his wife's money, for he had none of his own. It was now too evident it was for that the mean wretch had married my poor mistress.

"One morning after being absent some days in Montreal, Mr. Crossham returned home, accompanied by a Captain Carter, who had been his constant companion the winter before. He seemed to be greatly excited and in a terrible hurry to get back to Montreal, for he ordered the horses to be at the door again immediately after dinner. He then proceeded to his wife's boudoir where Mrs. Woodford, our clergyman's wife, an old and dear friend of my mistress, was sitting with her, for she was spending the day at the Hall. I happened also to be just then in the room, placing fresh flowers in a vase, but my mistress at that moment was in the adjoining apartment. Mr. Crossham, bowing to Mrs. Woodford, enquired where Mrs. Crossham was, and being told he followed her into the next room, closing the door carefully after him.

"We heard him talking to my mistress, his voice becoming louder, the tone more angry as the conversation continued.

"There was a veranda on that side of the house. I went out on it to take some plants that were there, out of the sun. The plants were near my mistress' windows, which also opened on the veranda. I heard Mr. Crossham exclaim passionately,

"'You refuse, madam! it must be signed.'

"'I will not rob my children,' was my mistress' answer in a cold determined tone.

"I left the plants and walked to the end of the gallery, for I would not listen to their conversation. Five minutes later, when I again passed through the boudoir, I saw that my mistress had joined Mrs. Woodford, but her flushed and agitated looks showed that something unpleasant had occurred. I went down to the dining-room. Mrs. Barton was there and Master Frank was playing in the room. Presently, Mr. Crossham with Captain Carter entered the apartment and approached the sideboard on which the decanters of wine stood. As soon as Mr. Crossham saw Master Frank he called to him in angry tones to stop his noise and clear out of the room. The boy delayed an instant to collect his

ELLEN VAVASOUR NOEL (ELLEN VAVASOUR)

playthings, whereupon Mr. Crossham rushed at him, and with one blow struck him to the ground, saying with a muttered curse, 'That will teach you, sir, to obey me!'

"Mrs. Barton sprang to the poor child and lifted him in her arms.

"'Come now, Crossham, upon my word that is too bad,' exclaimed Captain Carter, who seemed ashamed of his friend's conduct. 'I hope, ma'am,' he continued, addressing Mrs. Barton, 'that the boy is not much hurt.'

"She did not answer him, but turning to Mr. Crossham with pale face and flashing eyes, said,

"'Wretch, twenty years have not changed you, then; you broke your father's heart, now you would kill this child, because his mother is not weak enough to let you any longer squander his property.'

"At these strange words of Mrs. Barton's, Mr. Crossham started, a change came over his countenance—a startled look of fear and astonishment—but with an effort he recovered his self-possession, saying to Captain Carter:

"'The woman is either mad or drunk. Pack up your traps instantly,' he exclaimed, turning to Mrs. Barton; 'after such language you shall not remain an hour longer in my house.'

"'*Your* house!' replied Mrs. Barton scornfully: 'your house, indeed! When my mistress tells me to leave her house I will do so, but not before.'

"In his rage I think he would have struck her had not Captain Carter interposed. Casting a look on him of withering contempt and hatred, Mrs. Barton, closely followed by me, left the apartment. Giving Master Frank to me she went up to my mistress' room.

"Early in the afternoon Mr. Crossham and his friend returned to Montreal. The business which made Mr. Crossham pay such a hasty visit to the Hall was not satisfactorily arranged, for he left in a terrible temper, my mistress having shut herself in her room, refusing to see him again as he desired.

"Some days went by—dark rainy days—and within the Hall all seemed as gloomy as the weather without. My mistress, pale, sad and silent, spent most of the time in her own apartment; while Mrs. Barton, restless, excited, and more mysterious than ever, wandered uneasily about the house. Mr. Crossham did not return to the Hall; he wished, I suppose, by staying away to alarm my mistress, to frighten her into giving him the money—a large amount which he required to pay some debts he had contracted—my mistress very justly refusing to deprive her children of so large a sum. I trembled with fear for my mistress on Mrs. Barton's account, as I thought of Mr. Crossham's anger on his return when he would find her still at the Hall, that in this instance, also, his hitherto submissive wife had dared to oppose him.

"One afternoon I was sitting at one of the front windows sewing. Hearing the noise of a carriage approaching the house I looked out and saw Mr. Lorme—a cousin of my mistress—accompanied by a respectable-looking man, driving up to the door.

"'Here is Mr. Lorme!' I exclaimed to Mrs. Barton, who was passing the room; 'Mr. Lorme and some stranger with him.'

"She came quickly to the window and looked out with an eager, inquiring gaze, and then clasping her hands, her face bright with happiness, her frame trembling with emotion, she said:

"''Tis he! Merciful Heaven, I thank Thee!' as she hastily quitted the apartment, leaving me to imagine who the stranger could be whose arrival occasioned her such joy.

"I soon became aware that something unusual had happened, for Mr. Crossham was written to return at once to the Hall, and Mrs. Barton sent for Mr. and Mrs. Woodford, who, with Mr. Lorme and Mrs. Barton, were closeted for a long time with my mistress. All the satisfaction I could get from Mrs. Barton was that the stranger was a relation of hers whom my mistress' cousin had brought to see her.

"That day passed and part of the following before Mr. Crossham made his appearance. Mrs. Barton, who was on the watch for his arrival, called me to come with her, and conducting me to a room near the library, said:

"'You will soon now, Kate, hear a secret, the knowledge of which during the past year has nearly killed me.'

"She was pale with excitement and trembled violently. I made her sit down while I went for a glass of water. In passing through the hall I saw Mr. Woodford, who, with his wife, had been nearly all the morning in the house, go into the library, followed by Mr. Lorme and Mr. Crossham.

"I waited for some minutes in silent wonder by Mrs. Barton, who with her eyes fixed on the opposite door seemed to have forgotten my presence. Sounds of voices followed, the tones waxed louder, I could distinguish Mr. Lorme's and Mr. Crossham's in angry altercation. Some of the servants passing through the hall attracted by the noise stopped in alarm to listen. Presently the library bell rang loudly. Mrs. Barton started up saying, 'Come now, Kate, you must hear all, come with me.' I followed her across the passage to the library door at which she knocked, Mr. Woodford opened it, and as we passed in closed it again.

"Mr. Lorme with flushed brow and flashing eyes stood at the table, near him, with a pale defiant expression on his handsome face, Mr. Crossham was standing.

"'Madame' said Mr. Lorme addressing Mrs. Barton, 'the time has come for you to throw aside the mask which you have so long assumed and to denounce this—pointing to Mr. Crossham—villainous imposter. Who is he?'

"'My husband,' was Mrs. Barton's reply.

"Mr. Crossham laughed scornfully. 'A likely story indeed! Woman! you know it is an infernal lie!' he passionately exclaimed. 'I never saw your ugly face before I saw it in this house as that of one of my servants.'

"'Yes, you have, Robert Carson,' and Mrs. Barton advanced and looked steadily at him. 'Ah! you start at the sound of that name. 'Tis many years since you heard it, no doubt. I can hardly blame you,' she continued in bitter accents, 'for not recognizing me, for I am sadly changed since that night, twenty years ago, when you fled as a thief from your father's house. I was young then, and these white locks, since bleached by sorrow and the disgrace you brought upon your home, you then praised for their dark beauty; disease had not then marred my face. I cannot blame you for not knowing me, but you are little changed. Thoughts of the father whose heart you broke, of the wife you so cruelly and disgracefully deserted, have not troubled you, Robert Carson. Did you never wonder what became of me?'

"To this address Mr. Crossham listened with well-affected surprise and indignation, although I thought at some of her words his countenance changed slightly. To her last words he replied in an insolent sneering tone.

"'Your story, woman, is not well got up. It is rather singular that it is only now after being my servant for more than a year, that you find out I have the honour to be your husband.'

"'It is not only now that I find that out. With horror I recognized you, as this girl can prove,' and she turned to me, 'the first time I saw you after you came here, and for a while I was nearly crazed by the dreadful discovery and the perplexity I was in as to what I should do. At length, I determined to keep my secret. I knew my dear mistress loved you, and I thought that you perhaps had become a better, as well as an older, man, and maybe you believed me dead. It would be no sin, I hoped, to act so, and I kept my secret till I saw time had not changed you one whit, that you were breaking my beloved mistress' heart, squandering her property, and bringing ruin and wretchedness on this house.'

"'Lorme, this farce has lasted long enough. The plot, I confess, is not bad, but you must prove that this woman, not your cousin, is my wife,' said Mr. Crossham in a cool scornful manner.

"'You then deny the truth of her statement?'

"'I do, most assuredly, every word of it, and defy you to prove that it is true,' and Mr. Crossham drew himself up and looked boldly into Mr. Lorme's face.

"A slight smile of triumph gleamed for an instant in Mr. Lorme's eyes. Looking towards Mr. Woodford, he said, 'bring in our witness, Woodford.'

"Mr. Woodford opened the door and ushered in the stranger who had come to the Hall the day before with Mr. Lorme.

"Mr. Crossham started back as if an unseen hand had suddenly struck him, and gazed in a sort of horror and amazement at the stranger who had drawn near and was intently regarding him.

"'Do you know this man?' Mr. Lorme inquired of the new comer.

"'I do; he is Robert Carson, and with deep shame I acknowledge it, my brother,' was the reply.

"'This woman,' pointing to Mrs. Barton, 'claims to be his wife, but he denies it; can you tell whether what she says is true?'

"'Sir, it is true! She is his wife! Robert!' he continued, addressing Mr. Crossham in stern, bitter accents, ''tis useless for you to deny it. She is Susan Copely, whom years ago you lawfully married.'

"''Are you satisfied that I can prove it, infamous scoundrel that you are!' Mr. Lorme passionately exclaimed. 'A felon's doom awaits you; soon the world will know that the dashing Mr. Crossham has turned out a swindling impostor, a consummate villain.'

"Nora, I shall never forget the expression of Mr. Crossham's, or rather, Robert Carson's countenance. It was livid with rage. His eyes actually glared with hate and fury as he confronted Mr. Lorme. He made a rapid dive into one of his pockets, something gleamed in his hands as he drew it forth, and God knows what would have followed had not his brother, who was a large powerful man, rushed quickly upon him and wrenched the pistol from his grasp.

"I screamed with horror, and rushing to the door fled from the room.

"Soon after, our late haughty master in shame and ignominy departed from the Hall never to return. He was allowed, as Mrs. Lorme desired it, to escape unpunished. He immediately left Montreal, and we heard no more of him until about two years afterwards when his brother wrote to tell Mr. Lorme he had been shot in a gambling-saloon in California.

"And now, Nora, I will tell you part of Mrs. Barton's story, which she afterwards told me. Robert Carson was the son of a respectable farmer in England. She was married to him when quite a girl. Not long after their marriage he had stolen a considerable amount of money and escaped to America. His father died heart-broken at his son's conduct, and the rest of the family, taking her with them, immigrated to Canada, and from there to one of the Eastern States; but Mrs. Barton, as she called herself, remained in Montreal with Mrs. Lorme's father's family and afterwards, as I have said, when her young mistress got married became her house-keeper. She had never met or heard of her guilty husband until, to her horror and amazement, he came to Lorme Hall as her mistress' husband. He did not recognize her, and her reasons for not making herself known have been already stated. I told you, if you recollect Nora, that after our return from Montreal Mrs. Barton went there. It was to see Mr. Lorme, to whom she revealed everything, and asked his advice, for he was a lawyer. They wrote to her brother-in-law, with whom she had frequently corresponded, to come to Montreal to bear witness to the truth of her story. Mr. Carson had gone to the far West on urgent business, but on receiving their letters on his return home, he started as soon as possible for Montreal.

"Mrs. Lorme told Mrs. Barton that in Chicago where she had met Mr. Crossham, as I will still call him, he was considered a gentleman and moved in good society, and so Nora, he was very gentlemanly in appearance and fine-looking, too. It was some time before my poor mistress recovered from the shock she received, but at last in her children's love and the peaceful rest of her beautiful home, the remembrance of that dark page in her life's history grew fainter as time passed.

"Mrs. Barton never left her, as a loved and trusted friend she remained at Lorme Hall until her death."

∽

Canadian Illustrated News (Montreal) 18 November 1872, 315–316; 23 November 1872, 331–332.

Isabella Valancy Crawford (1850–1887)

A Rose in His Grace (c.1880)

In her struggle for economic subsistence in the difficult
Canadian literary market of the 1870s and 1880s, Isabella
Valancy Crawford wrote popular short fiction whose
imagery echoes that of her better-known poetry. Like
Susanna Moodie, she turned her hand to both prose and
poetry in the struggle for income from her writing. Ironically Crawford's sole volume of poetry to appear in her lifetime, *Old Spookses' Pass, Malcolm's Katie and Other Poems*
(1884), now a critically esteemed work, had to be published
at her own expense.

   Crawford was born in Dublin, Ireland, probably
on Christmas Day, 1850, the daughter of Sydney Scott and
medical doctor Stephen Dennis Crawford. She was the sixth
of twelve children, of whom only three survived beyond
childhood. Around 1854, the Crawfords appear to have
emigrated to Wisconsin, and by 1858 the family had moved
to the backwoods settlement of Paisley, Bruce County.
There, because of his alcoholism, Dr. Crawford pursued
an unsuccessful medical practice. Crawford's girlhood was
spent close both to nature and to the educated sensibilities
of her parents, who tutored her themselves. By 1864 the
family had relocated to North Douro (Lakefield), thanks
to the help of the Strickland and Traill families, where the
young girl became friendly with both Catharine Parr Traill
(see page 39) and her daughter Katie. In 1869, the Crawfords
moved to Peterborough. Dr. Crawford's death in July 1875
left the family impoverished. By 1876, Crawford's invalid
sister Emma Naomi had died, her brother Stephen, who was
now working in Algoma, could offer little financial help, and
Crawford was the main support of her mother.

   In 1883, the poet and her mother, always her
greatest encourager and confidante, moved to Toronto,
where they lived in a succession of downtown rooming

houses. Crawford probably sought to be closer to some of the newspapers and periodicals that published her work. But, as a single woman, her social and professional contacts were more limited than those of her male contemporaries: for example, she never knew the young Charles G. D. Roberts, who edited *The Week* in Toronto in 1883–1884, although he later admired her work.

Crawford died of heart disease on 12 February 1887. The body of work she left behind has grown in reputation as later critics have appreciated its richness and complexity. The canoe and the rose are recurring motifs: the title of "A Rose in His Grace" bears witness to the latter.

"A Rose in His Grace" is typical of Crawford's prose in that it follows the sentimental pattern of popular magazine fiction of the day. A virtuous and innocent heroine endures poverty and misfortune, two states that Crawford herself knew at first hand. But Posie—Crawford loved floral images—finds the love and prosperity that Crawford herself did not find in life. One wonders, too, if Posie's inspirational power in the reform of an alcoholic did not owe something to the Crawford family's distress and Crawford's wishful thinking over her father's problems. Moreover, the social and familial horrors of alcoholism and the temperance question were fictional and social preoccupations of the day, preoccupations also evident in May Agnes Fleming's life and Mary Eliza Herbert's work (see page 109 and 139, respectively). As with many of Crawford's stories and fairy tales, humour and shrewd description lift these tales above the level of the insipid or the hackneyed, evident in this story in the amusing opening description of Aunt Dulcia's likes and dislikes.

Crawford submitted scores of stories to periodicals: this one does not appear to have been published in her life-time. She felt frustrated by her lack of recognition. In February 1887, she wrote, in a letter now at Queen's Archives, to another writer: "I have contributed to the *Mail* and *Globe*, and won some very kind words from eminent critics, but have been quietly 'sat upon' by the High Priests

of Canadian periodical literature." An annotation at the
end of the story suggests that Crawford may have also
considered the title of "Two Roses and a Ring." However
severe the travails, she proudly identified herself as a
professional writer, for the undated manuscript is signed
"By Isabella Valancy Crawford[,] Author [of] 'Hate.'"

↜

Suggested Reading:

Crawford, Isabella Valancy. *Selected Stories of Isabella Valancy
    Crawford*, ed. Penny Petrone (Ottawa: University of
    Ottawa Press, 1977).

Farmiloe, Dorothy. *Isabella Valancy Crawford: The Life and
    the Legends* (Ottawa: Tecumseh, 1983).

Hale, Katherine. *Isabella Valancy Crawford* (Toronto:
    Ryerson, 1923).

Ross, Catherine Sheldrick. "I. V. Crawford's Prose Fiction."
    In *Canadian Literature* 81 (Summer 1979), 47–58.

Tierney, Frank, ed. *The Crawford Symposium* (Ottawa:
    University of Ottawa Press, 1979).

A Rose in His Grace
Isabella Valancy Crawford

Aunt Dulcia had certain "loves" as well as numerous "likes" and some very strong "dislikes." Her "loves" were babies, beggars, curiosities, invalids, fresh air, her niece Posie, black satin dresses, old paint, and old plate and roses. Her "likes" embraced nearly all the world and its inhabitants; and her "dislikes" were bad cookery, travelling, hypocrites, and her cousin once removed, Squire Peter Silver of Silvercreek Hall, a residence Posie vaguely understood to stand in that indefinite region, "the country."

Aunt Dulcia was a city blossom, and her little villa clung to the edge of Brooklyn, and Posie was certainly a city flower, a pale little lily bell, with great sweet eyes, dainty feet and hands and too slim and airy a figure to satisfy a sculptor, but healthy as an exotic is healthy while it is guarded by crystal walls and saturated by heat and light. Aunt Dulcia was rich though her villa, Rosyglow, was like a gabled toy, and the ponies under her phaeton minute Shelties: and Posie was her heiress, the last little blossom left on her stately family tree, except Squire Peter Silver, who was a cranky old skeleton, Posie understood, and anything but a blossom, more of a prickly pear or a thistle, indeed, according to Miss Dulcia.

Editorial note: Proper names that were inconsistent in the manuscript have been regularized and are indicated in the text by square brackets.

ISABELLA VALANCY CRAWFORD

"It isn't my nature to hate anyone," she would say, indignantly shaking her pretty old head, "but I do detest that man—God forgive him, he's a flint-hearted disgrace to our name. He turned his only son out of doors for marrying a girl a little below him, both of them died, poor things! and he took home their only child, a little boy, only to thrust him out for some boy's trick when the lad was about fifteen. I was in Italy then or I should have adopted Peter myself, and I often tried to find the friendless lad but never could. Isn't it strange, Posie, how people vanish in this great, big world."

While Posie was a child she would nestle her lovely head in Aunt Dulcia's satin lap, jealously, and "I am glad Peter is lost," was her only comment on this family legend. But as she grew up, sweet, womanly, and tender, Peter the unlucky became a reproachful ghost throwing a little shade into her sunshine and it was at her suggestion a "Personal" was put in the city papers beseeching Peter Silver if still alive to communicate with Miss Dulcia Silver of Rosyglow Villa Brooklyn.

"I would like to help the poor boy," said Aunt Dulcia tenderly, "but you are my heiress, Posie—nothing can alter that." Nothing came of the Personal, and Peter faded out of Posie's mind which began to be occupied with a pair of melting black eyes, a faultless mustache, and a silver tenor voice which chimed in deliciously with her, just as the handsome feet belonging to the owner of said tenor kept such enchanting time with her wee white satin boots of which articles of dress she wore out an inconceivable number being as fond of dancing as the "sun upon an Easter day."

René Acton was well born, well bred, well off and really amiable, so Aunt Dulcia was prepared to say "yes" when he should ask for Posie—and Posie—well her heart was faintly stirring with soft winds and gentle motions, and she thought, innocent, pure child, that it was love which gave the new joy to her life when it was but the wonder and delight her enlarging mind and soul drank from every source.

"Posie!" cried Miss Dulcia. "Here's another tramp in the kitchen. Susan says he's been drinking. Come and look at him and tell me whether he ought to get anything."

This was a daily scene, and Posie jumped up and tripped out to inspect the tramp and pronounce on his worthiness or the reverse. She was going to the Park to skate with René and was a most charming, dainty creature in her dark blue velvet and sea otter, as she ran lightly into the pretty kitchen, a rose in her hand, half blown and delicious, which she intended for René's buttonhole.

The tramp cowering over the glowing range lifted stupid eyes and stared at her. A dismal picture of broken down young manhood, sodden with drink, tempest beaten, want-tortured, with something in his face which ought to have been pride but was only sullenness, as Miss Dulcia, delicate, dimpled and fair in her black satin and laces inspected him on one side, while Susan, the pink of all old cooks, grimly eyed him as she basted the turkey for dinner.

Posie with clear, grey eyes of infinite compassion and innocence, the budding rose in her hand, went up to him slowly—he was very dirty, and alas! smelled awfully of bad whiskey. "I'm afraid you *have* been drinking, poor man," said the girl, "but Auntie, this once, darling, it's such a bitter, awful day! do give him something."

So it was, with a sun like a diamond, a sky like a blue stone, and a wind like a scimitar—a cruel day. "Posie, I can't hear of it," said Miss Dulcia firmly and setting wide the kitchen door, "Go out, you wicked creature—if you can buy whiskey you can buy food—I never help drunkards." He rose, stared at her dazed for a moment, and turned to go, staggering slightly as he went. A tall, gaunt wretch, with a bandaged head, an arm in a sling, and fluttering rags smelling of tar.

"You *know* you are got up," said Miss Dulcia with all the rebuking sternness she could manage to throw into her pretty old face. "You wicked man, pretending to be one of God's affected. You will bring a judgement on yourself. Posie, Posie, I really can't, my darling, now don't ask me."

For Posie was pleading silently with great sweet eyes and coaxing hands. The tramp turned as he reached the door and looked at her, holding to the handle with one dirty, shaking hand to steady himself.

"All right, old lady," he said in a husky voice, "I'm off. I guess you're partly right and partly wrong—it's mostly so with folks—yes, I'm off—it's no place for me; I know that very well."

Posie ran to him, catching his great, grimy, hairy hand in hers which looked and felt like flower petals on his hot brown skin.

"Oh!" she cried, "if you would only *not* do it—drink, you know."

He looked curiously down into those divinely pure young eyes, and suddenly burst out laughing.

"I'll give it up, by Gracious, I will, if you'll give me that rose and a kiss. If I'm worth saving you'll do that, and I'll take any oath you like and prove I can keep it too."

Posie turned lily-white, then burning, ruby red. Miss Dulcia gave a scream of horror. Susan seized the poker, fell vengeance in her eye. Posie tore her hand from his, horror and outraged pride in every feature.

"How *dare* you!" she gasped. "Oh, how *could* you?"

He laughed loudly.

"I knew you wouldn't—Good Lord! I know I'm a brute, and it's too late to be anything else now. Well! I'm off."

He was gone and the door shut, but before they could stop her, Posie rushed out after him sobbing excitedly into the bright, bitter day: bareheaded, for the fur *toque* still lay on the couch in the drawing-room.

The tramp was plodding down the garden path, his head hanging, his feet dragging, a shambling, degraded, repulsive spectacle under the cruel glare of the ruthless sun, the keen wind lashing him as it sported with his thin rags and frowsy hair—but no longer reeling. Something had sobered him very effectually.

"Oh, please, stop!" gasped Posie at his side—he paused and stared.

She was white as a little spirit of the snow and tears large and bright rolled down the delicate cheeks and sparkled like jewels on the velvet and fur from which her dainty head rose like a flower. She was not absolutely beautiful but you always saw more of Posie's soul than herself, and *that* was almost divine.

"Put down your face," she said, breathless in the icy wind, and she only reached a little above his sharp elbow, stooped and shambling as he was. "I have come to kiss you —and give you the rose." Some spark of manliness was certainly left in this dirty and repulsive wretch—his pinched face became more wan—poor Posie's truthful eyes proclaimed so clearly what a brave sacrifice she was making— she who had never even let René kiss a curl of her hair! René, the beautiful, the beloved, the clean!

"By gracious, I believe you'd do it!" he exclaimed, in amazement.

"Yes. I would do almost anything to make you better," she answered, quivering under his eyes which she suddenly discovered might be exceedingly bright, handsome eyes under changed conditions.

"Well, do it then!" he said, seeing her repugnance and terror. "And I'll take the oath and—*keep* it."

Poor Posie trembled like a leaf as he bent his face towards her; that begrimed, bristly, haggard face set off by the dirty white bandage, and smelling as to breath so vilely of whiskey, but she held up her quivering lips heroically— and shut her eyes as she did when surf bathing at Long Branch: it would be over in a moment—that was a comfort: but it was not: no kiss fell on her lips, brow or cheek, but a broken groan made her open her eyes swiftly.

"I couldn't do it," he muttered hoarsely. "I was only trying you—such kisses are for angels not devils—but you have saved me all the same. I'll swear whatever you tell me to swear. They exchanged long looks, hers exceedingly grateful at this respite, his humble and mournful—and then in sudden torture he cried out:

"It's too late—it's too late!"

Then as suddenly he fell on his knees in the snow and catching her hand rested his forehead on it—over René's ring, and made a fearful and binding oath to which Posie listened trembling and awed. And then he rose, straightening his shoulders, and lifting his head. "Don't think worse of me than I deserve," he said very brokenly. "These," touching the bandages on arm and head, "are not frauds. I had a bad accident and I am only two days out of hospital. Will you believe me?"

"I do, quite," said Posie cordially, "and so will Auntie —do come back and see her—she will help you now."

"No! I could not: the rose—will you give—"

His voice died away for it was already in his fingers, and in another moment Posie glided into the drawing room and laid her cold cheek on Miss Dulcia's satin shoulder.

"Why, where did you run, child darling? I thought you had gone to shut the gate after that poor wicked creature."

Posie made instant confession, and shewed a little bare finger where ten minutes before a pretty pearl hoop had coiled.

"I gave it to him, Auntie; I had no money in my pocket, and he would not let me come in for any. Are you angry?"

"I'm never angry with you, Posie," said Miss Dulcia very tenderly. "Here comes René with his skates; how handsome he looks."

⁓

Three years later, Miss Dulcia is in Heaven; Posie is crying in loneliness on old Susan's spare shoulder, in a grim and dismal lodging and Squire [Silver] is in full possession of Rosyglow; for no will of Aunt Dulcia's was forthcoming and he was heir at law, by an old will of Miss Dulcia's father which the daughter had been at liberty to set aside in favor of Posie, and which every one thought she had done. René is a married man these two years having run away with a dashing actress, fortunately leaving Posie perfectly heart whole.

Posie is reading disdainfully a formal letter from Squire [Silver's] lawyer offering in five lines to provide for her future which she has just received and deeply scorns.

"I don't care, Susan; I can get music pupils or go into a store, or something, but Aunt Dulcia, oh dear darling Auntie! hated the Squire and I *won't* receive anything from him—I couldn't Susan."

"He might leave ye his heir, my lamb," says Susan, cautiously.

"Or turn me out as he did Cousin Dulcia and poor, poor little Peter. No, I'll stay with you, Susan. 'I had rather be a thorn in a hedge than a rose in his grace,' the dreadful old tyrant!"

But the winter is on them like a tiger, Susan gets sick and helpless, and brave Posie finding no situation and her little store dwindling, begins to droop in the chill winds. Her pretty head falls like a lily bell, her eyes grow starry indeed. She is frightened at the turmoil of the roaring city as a child is frightened at a crossing in a crowded street; for the city she has known had been one of lovely homes, operas, balls, satin raiment, and charities which have not brought her actually in contact with the cruel breakers on the ocean of life, and when a second formally urgent letter arrives from the Squire's lawyer, again offering her a home at Silvercreek, she accepts ruefully. Susan finds a home with a niece until brighter days dawn; and one bright, crisp December night poor Posie finds herself shivering in a ghostly parlor all shrouded in linen from carpet to chandelier, one lamp burning dimly on a far table, and the brine and rawness of the winter sea nipping her cruelly, for there seems to be no fire in room or hall. She shudders as she hears the voice of the sea roaring almost into the windows and doors and the clattering of the "iron branches" of the great trees bending and groaning in the blast, and weeps silently under her thick veil as she recalls darling Aunt Dulcia and pretty, cosy, Rosyglow. Presently she is to face the terrible Squire, a sombre servant has gone to inform him that she has arrived, and her heart is beating as it too often

ISABELLA VALANCY CRAWFORD

does of late like a wounded bird. He is such an awful old man; what will become of her in this awful house with its famine amidst plenty air and her entertainer an old wretch who perhaps has inveigled her here for the express purpose of turning her out again some wild beast of a night if she displeases him. She is sobbing quite too audibly when a man's foot comes along the hall, quickly, into the room and up to her, with outstretched hand.

"Miss [Silver], I'm glad to welcome you to Silvercreek. Come in, it is cold here, but the library is warm. I always sit there myself, so if you don't mind, we'll dine there. You've had a tiring journey, I'm afraid."

Posie assents feebly behind her veil.

"If the Squire won't be vexed," she says in a tearful whisper, "I had rather go to my room; I'm very tired."

Who *is* this tall young man, with the stern face and resolute eyes, who is staring down at her curiously, his hands in his pockets, and the end of his mustache between his strong big teeth. Not a cultivated person, Posie finds time to decide as he continues to stare, rather bewildered.

"Oh, *I* won't object," he says simply, "You must do as you like here, that's the idea, and try and be happy if you can, though it's a gloomy spot, just now, Heaven knows."

He won't object! Posie stares through her veil and her tears and becomes dignified. He is her cousin, the Squire's guest, this frowning young man who is not a [Silver].

"Very well," she says with dignity, "please tell my cousin I am very tired. Good night, Sir." And she glides away after the sombre servantmaid who comes with a light to shew her to her room; he follows into the dim hall.

"You have dropped your glove," he calls after her with a grim smile; she turns and he hands it up to her through the great oak bannisters, her fragile, little hand touching his for a second as she takes it. Her veil is up now, and for the first time he sees her face. A great riot of wind blows round the house and drowns the hoarse exclamation which bursts from his lips, and she goes up and away unconscious of it.

The next morning a little note lies on her pillow: "Dear Cousin Dulcia. I was surprised last night to learn that you were not aware that my grandfather has been dead a year, and that *I* am the Peter [Silver] who succeeded as his heir to your Aunt's property: very unjustly. I am aware my grandfather advertised for me. I answered it—came to Silvercreek and we were reconciled before he died. I am going to Europe, and shall leave before you are up. Consider Silvercreek as your home until other arrangements can be made. Very faithfully, your cousin, Peter [Silver]."

Posie blushes like a little rosy star on her white pillow as she reads this astounding note—it is very well the new Squire has gone to Europe or she never could stay of course. It would not be proper, she is aware of that, and yet when she trips down the echoing stairs, things *do* look queerly grim and lonesome and most so in the library which is bright with a great wood fire and where a dainty breakfast is set out for her in solitary state—such solitary state that she cries into her coffee cup, and chokes over her buckwheat cakes, as the solemn sea stares greyly in at her through the gaunt windows, and snow begins to tap at the blank panes. Posie is a sociable little soul, and it is all so lonely from her black dress to that dim sail away on the bleak edge of the horizon. It is so unutterably silent in the huge house that she is glad to cry herself to sleep in Squire Peter's deserted leather easy chair round which clings a dreamy perfume of Latakia,[1] and forget her troubles in a tender sweet dream of Miss Dulcia and Rosyglow. She wakens up suddenly—surely someone has called her! Oh, there it is again, "Posie, come to me." She laughs as she wakens thoroughly, the dream voice dying away as she rubs her eyes, and finding that the wind is down she steals out to the chill beaches to marvel at the solitariness and sullen majesty of the scene. She wanders a long way without meeting a soul, [Silvercreek] Hall is a very lonely spot, and

---

1. Latakia: Syrian port city on the Mediterranean opposite Cyprus, famous for its tobacco exports.

rather likes the awfulness of being the only human entity visible under that great dome of granite grey, hers the only ears listening to the shrieking gulls and tossing sea—it is novel, and the air is bracing, and with brave little feet she toils on round a distant jut of rocks and comes face to face with—Squire Peter—standing like a statue, and as white as a ghost, apparently watching the incoming tide which is dashing about two yards from him.

"Dear me!" cries Posie. "I thought you had gone to Europe."

"I have only got so far, however," he answers, in a strangely repressed voice; but his eyes flash and a great flush rises over his face. "Posie, I know you can be brave if need be: look! my foot is caught in the link of this heavy chain—I can't—get—it—out—the tide is rising—"

Posie's hands went up to her heart—she understands him. He is standing there helplessly waiting to be drowned. She falters dizzily and he catches her in his arms, up against his breast.

"Let me go!" shrieks the poor child. "I will go for help, you shan't be drowned. I will run like the wind."

"You shall in a moment," he says, though he knows perfectly well that before aid can come the sea will have beaten him down, and beaten his life out. "In a moment. I was calling you an hour ago and you have come. I almost thought you would. Have you forgiven me, little cousin, for robbing you unintentionally?"

"Don't keep me!" cries Posie, struggling in his arms. "Let me go." He still holds her closely.

"You will know soon that I was contemplating restitution. My lawyers are drawing out a deed of gift to you of all your Aunt's property," he says eagerly, "and I never knew till last night that my cousin Dulcia and Posie were one and the same person."

Posie bursts from him, but he catches her again.

"Before you go," he cries, "look at me, don't you know me?" His voice arrests her headlong flight. She pauses, gazes, trembles. No, his handsome, pallid face, his bright, stern eyes awaken no memories—she thinks his mind wanders.

"Yes, you are my cousin Peter," she says quietly. "Oh, *don't* keep me!"

"Before you leave me, Posie," he says, "kiss me, my good angel."

She knows him now; as his face bends to hers, she knows him and with all the old terror and horror bursts from him. "I know you *now*," she gasps. "Oh, *why* did you let me?" Then she flies like the wind in search of that aid he knows cannot come in time, and he folds his arms and watches the sea rushing at him, calmly—he has ceased to struggle, his imprisoned foot is too swollen to be released, and he meets his doom like a man.

"I knew how she would feel," he says to himself, sadly. "She should never have known only for *this*! What horror of me was in her dear eyes, and oh, surely, surely I love her."

Posie found help at hand, two or three laborers returning to work, and guided by her they came. Before ten minutes Squire Peter, freed, but with a sadly wrenched and injured foot is lying high and dry out of danger, and the men have gone to [Silvercreek] for a carriage to bring him back to the hall. Posie stands apart, watching him, her heart bleeding over that dreadful foot and the tortured look on the man's face, but which indeed comes altogether from his mind—his foot—he does not feel. He looks at her and she comes to him timidly.

"You will go back to Rosyglow by this evening's train," he says with a groan. "You see I cannot leave [Silvercreek] for some time. Rosyglow—I have never been there but once, is ready for you and the papers will follow you up. Never forget Posie that you have twice saved me."

Posie is back at Rosyglow with Susan. Rosyglow, her very own, and she is again an heiress—she hears nothing of Squire Peter, except one formal note in which he tells her he is recovered and going away for a time and so the winter slips away and June and its roses come graciously and royally, but Posie is not the Posie of old. She is as sweet tempered as before but far more pensive, and if possible more

ISABELLA VALANCY CRAWFORD

daintily fragile and flowerlike—far too much so. Susan thinks with a heart pang as she watches her moving amongst the quaint flower beds in the side garden with the evening light softly on her. Posie has a rose in her hand, and is in white and her soft silken hair waves round her delicate head like the Clytie's lovely locks, her cheeks are purely pale but her lips are red and her eyes are glorious, a touch of the purple pansy in their grey. A shadow falls at her feet and she looks up with a little cry. Squire Peter stands before her his hat in his hand, and his bright eyes devouring her: he is absolutely handsome for the moment, but agitated as well he may be when he remembers the last time he knelt in that garden in the snow and took an oath he has nobly kept. He looks into her eyes long and steadily.

"Can it be true, Posie?" he whispers, "that you are glad to see *me*." Glad! the rose in her hand is pallid beside her—she looks down at it, smiles, and lays it in his large, strong hand with a look so shy and sweet that he is answered.

"I tried heartily to keep from you," he says, "but what could I do? You drew me with invisible chains—and I am here."

He will not give, even to her, the little pearl ring she gave him that day three years and a half ago, he shews it to her on a chain over his heart, and later, the withered rose with the faint, delicious scent clinging to its ashes.

"God only knows," he says reverentially, "how many fearful hours of temptation and despair *these* and the memory of your face tided me over: but oh, my pure darling, it will always push me back from you, the memory of our first meeting!"

However, in two long years of further waiting which he dooms himself to, he finds that he is at fault in that fear; and she finds that every day he becomes more worthy of her love, and every hour dearer.

Posie no longer cares for the City. Squire Peter [Silver] is essentially a country gentleman, and [Silvercreek] is so beautiful that she seldom cares to leave it—her husband

and her children are there and with them abide her Sun and Moon and Stars.

～

"A Rose in His Grace," holograph manuscript, Isabella Valancy Crawford Papers. Queen's University Archives, Queen's University, Kingston, Ontario.

The Canadian Short Story Library, Series 2

The revitalized Canadian Short Story Library undertakes to publish fiction of importance to a fuller appreciation of Canadian literary history and the developing Canadian tradition. Work by major writers that has fallen into obscurity will be restored to canonical significance, and short stories by writers of lapsed renown will be gathered in collections or appropriate anthologies.

John Moss
General Editor

New Women: Short Stories by Canadian Women, 1900–1920
Edited by Sandra Campbell and Lorraine McMullen

Voyages: Short Narratives of Susanna Moodie
Edited by John Thurston

Aspiring Women: Short Stories by Canadian Women, 1880–1900
Lorraine McMullen and Sandra Campbell

Pioneering Women: Short Stories by Canadian Women, Beginnings to 1880
Lorraine McMullen and Sandra Campbell

The paper used in this publication meets the minimum requirements
of American National Standard for Information Sciences -
Permanence of Paper for Printed Library Materials, ANSI Z39.48-1992.

Printed by
Ateliers Graphiques Marc Veilleux Inc.
Cap-Saint-Ignace (Québec)
in November 1993